The Unknown Pope

The Unknown Pope

Benedict XV (1914–1922) and the Pursuit of Peace

JOHN F. POLLARD

GEOFFREY
CHAPMAN

Geoffrey Chapman
A Cassell imprint
Wellington House, 125 Strand, London WC2R 0BB
370 Lexington Avenue, New York, NY 10017–6550
www.cassell.co.uk

First published 1999

British Library Cataloguing-in-Publication Data
A catalogue record for this book is available from the British Library.

ISBN 0-225-66844-0

Typeset by Ensystems, Saffron Walden, Essex
Printed and bound in Great Britain by Biddles Ltd, Guildford and King's Lynn

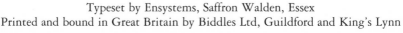

Contents

List of Illustrations

Acknowledgements

I owe a particular debt of gratitude to Reggie Norton, without whose inspiration and moral and material support this book would quite simply not have seen the light of day. Anglia Polytechnic University Inter-Schools' Research Committee gave me leave of absence and helped to finance various research trips as well as giving me a reduced timetable to complete writing. I am also grateful to Michael Walsh for persuading me to write it, and for reading drafts of chapters. Stewart Stehlin, Peter Kent and Noel Currer Briggs also helped by reading drafts and making comments, and Noel has once again made the index. Theo Schulte and Alexander Baer gave me much help with knotty questions relating to the First World War and Germany's role in it. Piers Brendon and John Cornwell gave pearls of wisdom about writing biographies. For any errors of fact, and for all opinions and interpretations, the responsibility is of course mine alone. Joe Cremona kindly put me in touch with the Della Chiesa family in Rome, and I am deeply grateful to members of that family for their hospitality and for all the help they gave me, especially access to their family archive. I also wish to thank the staff of the Secret Vatican Archives, especially Mgr Charles Burns (now retired), Fr Chappin SJ of the Archive of the Congregation for Public Affairs of the Church Archives, the Archiepiscopal Archives in Bologna, the library of the Istituto Luigi Sturzo, the Biblioteca Nazionale and the library of the Istituto di Storia Moderna e Contemporanea in Rome. I am greatly in the debt of James Walston for taking most of the photographs, and to him and Nora Walston for their friendship, help and hospitality in Rome over many years. I must also pay tribute to Brian Williams, who did excellent research work on my behalf during the last stages of writing the book. I wish to thank Ruth McCurry and Diana Smallshaw for guiding me through the stages of production. Last, but by no means least, I must acknowledge the moral support of Pompey.

Sutton-in-the Isle,
June 1998

To the memory of Peter Hebblethwaite,
vaticanista straordinario

Introduction

On 3 September 1914, Cardinal Giacomo Della Chiesa, Archbishop of Bologna, was elected Pope. When the American Cardinal Gibbons, Archbishop of Baltimore, arrived at the Vatican and was told the news he is reported to have said of Della Chiesa 'Who's he?'[1] His ignorance can be excused, as can that of the Romans, who were equally puzzled at the announcement of the name of Della Chiesa. Giacomo Della Chiesa was not a very well-known figure outside of his Bolognese exile, and had been a cardinal for only four months. He became a world figure during his pontificate, 1914 to 1922, when he attracted hostility from both sides as a result of his efforts to bring the First World War to an end, and gratitude from some of the many people, military and civilian, who were helped by his humanitarian activities.

His reputation was to suffer further misfortunes after his death. Indeed he faded into almost complete obscurity, perhaps on account of the shortness of his reign – only seven years and five months in all. Peter Hebblethwaite describes him as '. . . the most invisible and unappreciated pope this century'.[2] Fernand Hayward wrote a biography of him entitled *Un Pape méconnu: Benoît XV*, 'The Unknown Pope: Benedict XV'. By the Second World War he had become largely forgotten. In dictionaries and encyclopedias which deal with religious and ecclesiastical matters, he has attracted scant attention – *The Oxford Dictionary of the Christian Church*, for example, devotes only twenty lines to him[3] and the *New Catholic Encyclopedia* less than two pages: Popes Pius X, Pius XI and Pius XII all get more coverage.[4] Curiously, he is immortalized in the pages of a novel – Anthony Burgess's *Earthly Powers*.[5] In Italian, there is only one serious, full-length biography of Benedict, written by Vistalli, and that was published in 1929; admittedly, since then, some useful biographical essays have been published.[6] He has fared better in English: in 1959 Fr Walter Peters wrote *The Life of Benedict XV*. This is a very serious and scholarly study which should be read by anyone interested in the story of Giacomo Della Chiesa. But it suffers from a major defect, the author's limited knowledge of the contexts in which Benedict operated, in particular the Italian political one. It has also, inevitably, become outdated with the passage of time and the opening up of various private and public archives. Those of the Vatican are now open to the end of Benedict's reign and it has also been possible to consult the Della Chiesa family archives and the archives of the archiepiscopal curia in Bologna. In addition, biographers now have available to them both the letters of Benedict to his friend Valfré di Bonzo and to his vicar-general in Bologna, Ersilio Menzani. Most important and most precious of all are the diaries of Baron Carlo Monti, life-long friend and the intermediary between Benedict and the Italian government for the whole of his reign.

In this book I have tried to go beyond the limitations of Peters, setting Giacomo Della Chiesa firmly in the appropriate historical contexts. I have used both the primary source material now available and the many books which have been based on it: the works on his peace diplomacy are especially numerous, as the Bibliography shows. One of the strengths of Peters' account of Benedict is the wealth of personal detail and anecdotage that he manages to weave into it: I have chosen not to reproduce most of that in order to preserve space for other matters. It is for the reader to judge the merits of my approach.

Just about the only thing for which Benedict XV is remembered is his 'Peace Note' of August 1917 in which he offered the warring powers proposals to bring about the cessation of hostilities. The Peace Note was, in fact, only one, albeit the most important and dramatic, of many, many initiatives which Benedict and his Secretary of State, Cardinal Gasparri, took either to stop the conflagration from spreading or to bring the First World War to an end. In a broader sense, Benedict's whole pontificate was dedicated to the pursuit of peace as he saw it: peace among the nations of Europe; peace in human society torn by class conflict and ideological clashes, and peace in the Church after the excesses of the anti-Modernist campaigns of his predecessor, Pius X. He had only limited success in his efforts, but he deserves to be remembered in history for the noble project to which he committed himself and his pontificate.

Notes and references

1. Moynihan, p. 329.
2. Hebblethwaite, p. 105.
3. Cross (ed.), *Oxford Dictionary of the Christian Church*, p. 156.
4. *New Catholic Encylopedia*, vol. II, BAA–CAM, pp. 279–80.
5. Burgess, p. 199: 'Pope Benedict XV, that great pacifist prelate to whom neither the Germans nor the Allies would listen, Giacomo Della Chiesa, James of the Church, lawyer and diplomat, hopeless with money, his prodigality of aid to the needy having put the Vatican in debt, he had died and been succeeded by Pius XI . . .'
6. For instance, G. De Rosa in *Dizionario degli Italiani (Bellucci–Beregand)* and Monticone in Guerriero and Zambarbieri (eds), *Storia della Chiesa*, vol. XXII, I: in French there is Jankowiak's entry for Benedict in P. Levillain (ed.), *Dictionaire de la Papauté* and in English the essay on Benedict in Carlo Falconi, *The Popes in the Twentieth Century*.

1

From Genoa to Rome

Benedict XV, Giacomo Della Chiesa, is one of the odd men out among twentieth-century Popes. Unlike five of the seven Italian Popes this century – Pius X, Pius XI, John XXIII, Paul VI and John Paul I – Benedict XV was not born and brought up in the classic Catholic milieu, that is among the rural middle/lower middle class or peasantry of north-eastern Italy, Lombardy and Venetia. Rather, like Pius XII, he came from an urban, and in his case, aristocratic, family. And the particular urban milieu into which he was born, Genoa, was not an especially Catholic city, unlike the Lombard towns of Brescia and Bergamo or the Venetian cities, Padua and Treviso. A great port city, with a proud past as an independent republic until 1799, Genoa was a radical, tumultuous place and was most notable as the home of the explorer Christopher Columbus and the birthplace of Giuseppe Mazzini, the ideologue and leader of the Italian democratic nationalist movement.

Giacomo Giambattista Della Chiesa, to give him his full name, was born prematurely on 21 November 1854, the sixth child of his parents (two of his siblings died in infancy), the Marchesi Giuseppe and Giovanna Della Chiesa. The family formed part of the Genoese patriciate; its name and coat of arms were inscribed in the Golden Book of the former Republic, and it had achieved particular prominence in public life in the sixteenth century. His mother's family, the Migliorati of Naples, was also aristocratic, and had already provided a Pope – Innocent VII – whose reign was, however, brief and undistinguished (1404–06). By the 1850s, the Della Chiesa family was no longer as wealthy as they had once been, forcing them to live in what one of his earliest biographers, Vistalli, has described as 'a modest, bourgeois house' in Genoa,[1] though retaining the family property in Pegli, a village which is now a suburb of Genoa itself. Moreover, as Giacomo was to acknowledge when he became Pope, he would not have been able to continue his education without the support of relatives. According to Count Carlo Sforza, a contemporary Italian politician who knew him well:

> The Della Chiesas were relatively poor, while Durazzo Pallavicini was the wealthiest patrician of Genoa. When after the University, young Giacomo wanted to enter the Accademia dei Nobili Ecclesiastici ... his rich cousin Durazzo assumed the quite considerable expense involved. Thus when Durazzo led a delegation of Genoese to greet the new Pope, and addressed Benedict with the words 'Your Holiness . . .', The Pope answered: 'You call me Holiness! Why, we are old cousins and we always were.' And addressing the kneeling deputation, he said: 'Gentlemen, if I am Pope you have among you the one who made it possible; it is my cousin who paid for my studies.'[2]

It was a loving family atmosphere in which Giacomo was raised, even if his father appears to have been a little cold and distant in his relations with his children. On the other hand, Giacomo was close to his mother, his sister Giulia and his brothers Giovanni Antonio and Giambattista ('Baccino') and remained so throughout his life.

The smallness and physical frailty consequent upon Giacomo's premature birth, which also left him with a limp, meant that much of his early education was at home. In 1866 he entered the Istituto Danovaro e Giusso, one of the best academies that the Ligurian city could provide. Here he met and made friends with Pietro Ansaldo, a scion of the noted Genoese steel manufacturing firm, and Carlo Monti. Giacomo seems to have maintained these and other friendships, like the one with Teodoro Valfré di Bonzo, throughout his life: another friend from his adolescence was Giuseppe Migone, whose son Giuseppe would eventually become Giacomo's chaplain and secretary as Archbishop of Bologna. Yet in his childhood and teens Giacomo was not notably garrulous – he actually spent much time reading – nor did his physique encourage sporting activity. And into his adult life, Giacomo retained a certain reticence of manner. Francis MacNutt, a rich American convert and a high-ranking lay member of the papal court in the reigns of Leo XIII and Pius X, wrote of Giacomo thus: 'He was never confidential with me and I did not feel that I knew him after twenty years much better than I did after one.'[3] Giacomo was clearly a successful, though not especially exceptional, pupil. His exercise books, preserved in the Della Chiesa family archive, demonstrate interest, diligence and competence in a diverse range of subjects – from ecclesiastical history to mathematics, French composition to German grammar.[4] What also emerges from these sources, and from the accounts which he kept meticulously from the age of nineteen, is a neat, ordered and tidy mind and the development of his characteristically neat, consistent handwriting.[5]

If Giacomo's studiousness emerged at an early age, so too did his vocation to the priesthood: his interest in the Mass and 'preaching' are described in picturesque detail by Walter Peters.[6] His piety, which was founded on his devotion to the Blessed Sacrament and the Sacred Heart of Jesus, not to mention to the Madonna della Guardia, the form under which Our Lady was locally honoured in Genoa and district, emerged early. Very quickly, Giacomo decided he wanted to be a priest and he came under the influence of the writings of Cardinal Alimonda, Archbishop of Genoa, and that of his own uncle, who became his chief spiritual guide.[7] His was an obviously Catholic home[8] and it must have felt a serious conflict of loyalties on the question of Church–State relations. On the one hand, his father had the natural loyalty of a Genoese aristocrat who had been in the service of the Savoyard royal family which, in the person of Victor Emmanuel II, came to the throne of the united Italian kingdom in 1861; on the other, there was the problem that this same monarch progessively 'despoiled' the Papacy of its temporal power, that is to say its territorial sovereignty over the Papal States of Central Italy, as the process of Italian unification proceeded between 1859 and 1870. This Church–State conflict, the 'Roman Question' as it is called, was one of the dominant factors in Italian politics until 1929. How that conflict resolved itself for the elders of the Della Chiesa family is not clear, but all of Giacomo's earlier biographers stress his passionate commitment to the papal cause from an early age.[9]

Graduation from high school precipitated a family crisis: Giacomo wanted to proceed immediately to the diocesan seminary to train as a priest. His father resolutely opposed this on the grounds that he might not yet know his own mind and that everyone, including a priest, should have a university degree in the new secular society in which they were living. Only when he had successfully completed his university studies, the Marchese argued, should he dedicate himself to priestly training. This was a sensible strategy given the modesty of the family means (the family possessed little in the way of landed property at that time) and the number of siblings to be provided for. Both his brothers, Giovanni Antonio and Baccino, took up a secular profession – the navy. Giacomo accepted reluctantly, but by way of compromise was allowed to study scholastic philosophy and apologetics as a lay student at the diocesan seminary while also studying at university.

University was a challenge for Giacomo, not because of the intellectual demands it made on him, rather because of its strongly anti-clerical atmosphere. When he entered the Royal University of Genoa in 1872, like the other academic institutions in the kingdom, it had already been strongly secularized. Italy's Liberal–Conservative ruling class, aided and abetted by more radical parliamentary elements, having confiscated much church property, and reduced the powers and privileges of the Church and its influence in politics, now sought to eliminate its influences from the educational system as well. A year after Giacomo's admission, they finally abolished the faculties of theology in state universities.[10] Giacomo quickly showed where his loyalties lay by entering the 'Society for the Promotion of Catholic Interests' and eventually becoming its secretary. In this he was swimming against the tide: most of his fellow students, all from aristocratic or upper middle-class families, adopted a secularist, sceptical and sometimes strongly anti-clerical attitude. When Giacomo graduated from the University of Genoa in 1875 with a doctorate of laws (*dottore di giurisprudenza*), his father agreed to his pursuit of an ecclesiastical career. But the Marchese's ambitions for his son would not countenance sending him to the diocesan seminary: Giacomo had to go to Rome, to the Collegio Capranica and the Gregorian University, which the Marchese believed would permit a more rapid career development than staying at home. Time proved his judgement to be sound.

Rome

When Giacomo arrived in 1875, Rome was a difficult place for an aspiring cleric to live in. Five years after the occupation of Rome by Italian forces, following the capture of the city by Italian troops in September 1870, and its proclamation as the capital of Italy, the Eternal City was undergoing massive changes. The Quirinale Palace, formerly the Pope's chief residence, was now the official seat of the Italian monarchy and Pius IX had retreated to the Vatican, whose 'prisoner' he declared himself to be. Other ecclesiastical properties had been secularized too, including the Jesuits' Collegio Romano which had become the National Library. An array of new, monumental edifices were going up to accommodate the state bureaucracy and demonstrate its authority to the world, and whole new residential quarters were being built to house the bureaucrats. In 1871, the Italian Parliament had passed the Law of Papal Guarantees as a means of regularizing relations between Italy and the Holy See on a unilateral basis, because Pius IX was not prepared to negotiate. The Law of Guarantees was not a bad law; it established the immunities and privileges of the Pope as a sovereign, and gave extra-territorial status to the Vatican and the papal villa at Castelgandolfo.[11] But Pius IX refused to accept the Law, and tension remained between the Vatican and the 'usurping' government in Rome, sometimes flaring up into serious anticlerical outbursts, like the brawl which accompanied the transportation of Pius IX's body to the Basilica of San Lorenzo in July 1881. That Giacomo was strongly affected by this atmosphere is demonstrated by the prayer card at his ordination:

O Peter, Prince of the Apostles, whom we venerate on the throne of Rome, and who illuminates the peoples with the light of truth, give me the strength to maintain your rights sacred and inviolable, and to repel with an indomitable heart the unhappy assaults of the enemies of the Papacy.[12]

Giacomo's early career in Rome was unremarkable: he was a diligent student, who attended lectures assiduously, especially those of Fr J. Franzelini (official theologian to the First Council of the Vatican), Fr Antonio Ballerini, the famous moralist, and Fr Camillo Mazella. His education, like that of several generations of clergy trained in the centre of Catholicism, was in '. . . the narrow orthodoxy of the Roman schools'.[13] Giacomo's first pastoral experience was as catechist to the children of the parish church of S. Maria in Aquiro near the Pantheon and he was ordained on 21 December 1878, in the presence of his family, by Cardinal Monaco La Valletta, the Pope's vicar for the Rome diocese in St John Lateran (the cathedral of Rome). He celebrated his first Mass, not at the tomb of the Prince of the Apostles as he had planned, and as most newly ordained priests in Rome aspired to do, but prophetically at the altar of the Cathedra in the apse of St Peter's.

We have a remarkable piece of evidence of his early preaching style as a priest, and implicitly of his conventional, paternalistic attitudes to the 'social question', in the sermon he gave on the Eighth Sunday after Pentecost in the village church of his own, beloved Pegli. No doubt the parish priest was both relieved to be excused the task of a Sunday sermon and pleased to have the bright young Rome-trained cleric to take his place. No doubt also, Giacomo's parents and family listened with immense pride to his efforts. What is, therefore, fascinating is the honesty and directness with which he approached his task. He divided his hearers into three classes of people – *agricoltori* (peasants), *commercianti* (shop-keepers and tradespeople) and what he described as *agiati* (the 'well to do') – and proceeded to address his sermon to each one separately, but without a hint of condescension. To the peasants he recommended prayerfulness at work and the avoidance of blasphemy; he warned the tradespeople to store up spiritual goods against that day when '. . . not only will all trade and commerce cease, but when all need of earthly goods will come to an end', and he finished by reminding the well-off of their good fortune and, therefore, of their supreme duty to set a good, Christian example to everyone else.[14]

The Marchese's optimism about his son's career prospects in Rome were rewarded when Giacomo eventually graduated doctor of theology *cum laude* in 1879. In 1880 he also received a doctorate in canon law. Given these considerable academic accomplishments, it is surprising that Sforza says: 'Della Chiesa himself admitted he knew nothing about theological questions. He had not had a seminary education, as he did not become a priest until he was twenty-six.'[15] He was wrong on all three counts. Giacomo may not have been either an intellectual or even a natural academic, but he was educated at the Capranica College which was a seminary; he was ordained at twenty-four, the normal age, and he had a theology degree, which most priests did not have. In all probability, in his scrupulously honest way, Giacomo put it about that he was not an expert in theological questions, which he undoubtedly was not. In the meantime, he had entered the Academy of Noble Ecclesiastics, the school for high-flying clergy and the training ground of Vatican diplomats. The prestige and importance of the Academy is attested by the fact that Cardinal Consalvi, who had successfully negotiated the restoration of the Papal States at the Vienna Congress of 1815, Pope Leo XIII (1878–1903), the great Cardinal Rampolla del Tindaro, Secretary of State to Leo XIII, Cardinal Merry Del Val, Secretary of State to Pius X between 1903 and 1914, Pope Pius XII (1939–58) and Pope Paul VI were all alumni and Pope Pius XII taught there. Giacomo very quickly shone in this élite atmosphere, and of all the academic institutions he frequented, he regarded it as his true Alma Mater. It was at the Academy that there occurred in 1881 an event which was to shape Giacomo's life for the next twenty-seven years: he met Monsignor (as he then was) Rampolla when he was giving the traditional address each student was obliged to make each year. Mariano Rampolla del Tindaro was a formidable but saintly Sicilian aristocrat, who was to have a brilliant career in the Holy Roman Church, only failing to reach the papal throne because of Austrian intervention in 1903 (see p. 18). Rampolla quickly took a liking to Giacomo. Impressed by his intelligence and industry, he had him appointed Professor of Diplomatic Style at the Academy and *apprendista* (apprentice) in the Congregation of Extraordinary Ecclesiastical Affairs, that part of the Secretariat of State which dealt with relations with states and of which Rampolla was secretary.

Madrid

Within a very short time, Giacomo's career took a further turn. In 1883 Rampolla was appointed to the Madrid nunciature, the second most important posting in the Vatican diplomatic corps after Vienna, and decided to take his new apprentice with him as secretary to the nunciature. Thus began not only Giacomo's first-hand experience of Vatican diplomacy in action, but also his close relationship with the great Sicilian cardinal who was to become both his mentor and his friend. Rampolla was to remain as nuncio in Madrid for another four years. Having served in the Madrid nunciature in the 1870s, he was not surprised to find a difficult situation there a few years later. The Spanish Church was riven by deep tensions, most of them generated by the problem of living under the restored, Liberal monarchy, which, to the traditionalist Carlists, like the Bishop of Osima, was anathema. Rampolla was initially hampered in his work by the need of his two young subordinates, Giacomo and a colleague, to learn Spanish. Nevertheless, he testified to their commitment and intelligence in a letter to Jacobini, Cardinal Secretary of State.[16] An incident which occurred during Giacomo's service in the Madrid nunciature illustrates how quickly his extraordinary sense of professional devotion developed, and is revealed in a letter to a friend whom he had made at the Academy, Valfré di Bonzo, like him from the Piedmontese aristocracy. Because of the posting to Madrid, Giacomo had not been able to be present at the latter's consecration as Bishop of Cuneo in 1885. A year later, Giacomo paid a brief visit to Italy, but as he explained in a letter to his friend, he was again unable to visit him because, 'the Pope added that he would give me some papers for the Nuncio, and I, naturally, did not dream of saying that it was not my intention to return immediately to Madrid. It would have been a gross dereliction of the first order I had received personally from the Pope.'[17] This strict sense of duty and service was to remain with Giacomo for the rest of his life.

Spain was an important 'learning experience' for Giacomo in other ways; in a letter to Valfré di Bonzo in 1883 he wrote: 'Madrid . . . is literally a school of contemporary life.'[18] On the surface, Spanish politics presented many similarities with those of his native country: a Liberal, parliamentary monarchy made to function largely by *caciquismo*, an Iberian version of the electoral clientelism and corruption which pervaded the politics of Liberal Italy.[19] But below the surface, the subversive activities of the republicans and the continued tendency towards *pronunciamientos* – military *coups d'état* – rendered Spanish politics potentially much more unstable. The death of King Alfonso XII in 1885 and the long minority of his posthumous heir – Alfonso XIII – did not help. The shrewd grasp of the complexities of Spanish politics which Giacomo quickly gained is revealed in other letters to his friend. In 1883, following a failed *pronunciamiento* he warned of the dangers of a revolution[20] and following a very serious republican uprising in Madrid in 1886 he wrote: 'The condition of this country is not a happy one. We are on the morrow of a military insurrection and perhaps on the eve of yet another. The government has lost a lot of prestige, the army is corrupt and much of the officer class desires a republic. It seems unlikely that the regency of Maria Christina can last for another fifteen years.'[21] Only in respect of this last prediction was he to be proved wrong.

Though he made many friends in Spain, and was the beneficiary of a great deal of Spanish hospitality, he missed Rome and his work there. In a letter of 24 March 1883 to Valfré di Bonzo he wrote: 'I am so grateful for your apostolic efforts in providing the spiritual exercises for the pupils of The Carissimi . . . how much I envy you, now that I am not able to be involved in that holy work!'[22] Acquisition of Spanish would soon make it possible for him to hear confessions and to preach, but it was a poor substitute for the pastoral work, albeit limited, that he had carried out in Rome. His letters also mention the 1884 earthquake and 1885 cholera epidemic but, typical of his modesty, they fail to reveal the humanitarian work which he and the nuncio carried out during both disasters.[23] Nor do they give any intimation of the close relations which he developed with the Spanish Court, which would ensure strong Spanish support for his proposed appointment as nuncio to Spain in 1907 (see p. 25).

Back to Rome

In June 1887, Monsignor Rampolla was appointed Secretary of State to Pope Leo XIII and cardinal, and Giacomo returned with him to Rome. The city to which they returned had changed much during their years in Madrid. Its political life, and therefore the politics of Italy, was now increasingly dominated by Francesco Crispi, formerly one of the radical democrat Garibaldi's 'Redshirts' and now an almost reactionary upholder of the monarchical principle. But Italy's relations with the Vatican under his rule were more influenced by his intransigent, irredeemable anti-clericalism, than by his opportunism. Pope Leo XIII was, accordingly, no more reconciled to Italy than his predecessor, Pius IX, whom he had succeeded in 1878. Leo continued to seek some resolution of the 'Roman Question' by diplomatic means. Having tried, unsuccessfully, to play off Germany against Italy following the end of the Bismarckian *Kulturkampf* (the campaign against the church), the Pope and his new Secretary of State now turned to wooing France, the 'Elder Daughter of the Church'.[24]

If anything, by 1887, the Vatican's international situation in relation to Italy had got worse. In that year, Italy renewed its Triple Alliance with Germany and Austria-Hungary on better terms, though thanks to the Emperor Franz Josef, the latter still refused to guarantee the Italian possession of Rome.[25] That was little consolation for Leo XIII who was to threaten to leave the city on at least three occasions during his reign.[26] Nor was he convinced by the Austrians' repeated attempts to persuade him that the stability of the Italian monarchy, which the Triple Alliance was meant to ensure, was of benefit to the Vatican.[27] Thus the policy of Rampolla was to seek by all means possible closer relations with France. In 1890 Leo XIII launched the *Ralliement*, an attempt to persuade French Catholics, bishops, clergy and laity, to accept the democratic republic and seek to render it Catholic and conservative. But by the turn of the century, this policy was in ruins. The majority of French Catholics did not heed Leo's pleadings, and the Dreyfus Affair, when French Catholics lined up with Nationalists and anti-Semites against the democratic French Republic in the row over a spy trial, demonstrated that they were even more estranged from their government than ever.[28]

Inevitably, Giacomo was increasingly drawn into the implementation of these policies, as the Secretary of State's most loyal and favourite subordinate. As *minutante*, his job was to prepare detailed briefings for his boss on the various questions submitted to him — a true apprenticeship indeed for later high office. Leo's wide-ranging diplomacy, including the missions he sent to both Canada and the USA in the 1890s would have increased enormously the young *minutante*'s knowledge of the complexities of the world-wide Church. In particular, he would have seen the detailed report of special legate Mgr Germano Straniero, on the strength and problems of the American Church. As Anthony Rhodes says, 'Leo XIII was the first pope to appreciate the potential importance of the United States to the Catholic cause.'[29] On the other hand, until his appointment as Sostituto of Ordinary Ecclesiastical Affairs in 1901, Giacomo rarely left Rome. Thus he had little experience of either Paris or Vienna, the other two major diplomatic postings after Madrid, and none of London or Berlin. Only in 1888 and 1889 did he go to Vienna on confidential business for the Cardinal, to sort out the troubled affairs of the Austrian Christian Socialist party whose leader, Karl Lueger, had embarked on a particularly virulent anti-Semitic campaign.[30] It is likely that the second visit had more to do with the recent suicide of Crown Prince Rudolf and the death of his lover Mary Vetsera at Mayerling. If the latter was the case, then Giacomo was richly rewarded with orders and decorations by the Emperor Franz Josef. In 1887, he was also involved in the controversial visit of the German Emperor William II to the Vatican. The behaviour of both the Emperor's suite and of his wife, who refused to wear the customary black mantilla, caused immense offence in the Vatican.[31] Giacomo was heavily involved in William II's second visit, in 1902, and was honoured with the Great Cross of the Order of the Prussian Crown.[32]

The years between Rampolla's appointment as Secretary of State and Leo XIII's death in 1903 were momentous ones for both Italy and the Vatican. Giacomo's attitude to all the major events of this period appears to have been exclusively determined by his hostility towards the Italian 'Liberal' State, which was typical of Italian clergy of his day. It was not simply a question of the injustices which it had imposed upon the Papacy; it was its founding ideology – ninteenth-century Liberalism, with its strong secularizing tendencies – that he abhorred. The extreme distrust of Leo and Rampolla towards the Italian State must also have been a factor in determining his attitudes on political matters. In 1893, he wrote to Valfré di Bonzo, without a hint of irony: 'There is little or nothing new in Rome, at least in our camp; as for the adversary, there is a great to do over the golden wedding anniversary of the King and Queen.'[33] For Giacomo, as for most of the Italian clergy, the State and its ruling class were the 'adversary', the enemy. Of his reactions to the 'End of Century Crisis', that is the series of economic difficulties which resulted in social distress and disorder, and the ensuing political conflict which assailed Italy in the 1890s, we know almost nothing, but when the crisis reached its climax in the assassination of King Humbert II by an anarchist at Monza in 1900, he commented, 'what terrible food for thought', and then immediately went on to advise Valfré di Bonzo how to handle requests from the civil authorities for requiem Masses, etc., observing the formalities which the continuing conflict with the Italian State imposed.[34] He had always been sceptical of the attempts by some of the higher clergy, most notably Bonomelli of Cremona, but also his friend Valfré di Bonzo, now Bishop of Como, to encourage efforts at a reconciliation between Church and State. He was not even sympathetic to the inevitable desire of many Catholics to learn from the horrors of the 'End of Century Crisis', and unite with Liberal-Conservatives against the Marxian-orientated Socialist party and trade unions which had emerged during the course of it. In particular, he disapproved of Pius X's willingness to permit a relaxation of the *non expedit*, the Vatican decree of 1864 which forbade Italian Catholics from participating in national elections, as a means of meeting the Socialist challenge.[35]

On the other hand, Giacomo clearly approved of *Rerum Novarum*, Leo XIII's great social encyclical. In 1897, six years after the publication of the encyclical, he wrote to Valfré di Bonzo as follows: 'The Holy See wishes to see the bosses and the rich taken down a peg or two, and does not disapprove of the talk about the rights of the workers; at the same time, however, it is necessary not to forget to remind them of their duties.'[36] He almost certainly shared the feeling, general among Italian clergy at that time, that industrial capitalism, which was making its first major appearance in Italy in the 1880s and 1890s, was the 'evil child' of philosophical and political liberalism, seeing in the latter's emphasis on self-centred materialism the root cause of many social problems. *Rerum Novarum*, while condemning Socialist solutions to the problems which industrial capitalism had thrown up, also criticized the excesses and injustices of that system, and urged Catholics to involve themselves actively in remedying them, including the setting up of trade unions. Benedict XV's openness on the 'social question' would be in stark contrast to that of Pius X, who came very close to condemning trade unionism altogether.

Giacomo very quickly developed a mastery of the Vatican and its peculiar ways. This is amply demonstrated in his correspondence with Valfré di Bonzo, in which he gave him sound, practical tips on how to solicit financial support from the Vatican for his pet venture, *L'Ordine*, the diocesan newspaper of Como,[37] and then explained how to deal with visiting *personaggi*, i.e. members of the Italian Royal Family and Government ministers, in the still strained atmosphere between Church and State: 'What is absolutely to be avoided is meeting them at the station and taking part in banquets or receptions. At the most, a courtesy visit should be paid to the King, accompanied by your secretary and the vicar-general of the Diocese . . . but in normal clerical day wear NOT full canonicals,' he explained to his friend.[38] He even dared to advise Valfré di Bonzo about his relations with his fellow bishops. In November 1896, he warned him of the dangers of too close a relationship with Mgr Geremia Bonomelli, Bishop of Cremona: 'I trust that he will not take you too much under his protection because here in Rome a man is judged by the company he keeps.'[39] This was very sound advice: Bonomelli was a very controversial figure in the Italian Church because of his 'softness' on the Roman Question. He had repeatedly advocated reconciliation with the Italian State, which was emphatically not the policy preference of the Vatican at that time.[40]

Giacomo quickly became known as *il piccoletto* ('the little one'), because of his stature and gait. These passages help to explain why so many people in the Vatican bureaucracy deferred to *il piccoletto* when a difficult decision had to be made. Peters actually cites him as acknowledging this: 'Once as Pope, he was recounting an incident about a well-meaning group whose members had blundered into a very difficult situation. Over his otherwise so fastidious lips the following remark slipped out: "They would have been in a fine mess, if *il piccoletto* had not stepped in and pulled them out." '[41] And this story suggests that the claim that Giacomo even saved Rampolla himself from several hasty decisions was not far from the truth.[42]

Meanwhile, Giacomo's personal life assumed a pleasant routine. Having installed himself in an apartment in the Palazzo Brazzà, in the Piazza S. Eustachio, he found in the local parish church an outlet for his pastoral gifts. Here he celebrated Mass, helped recite the daily offices, preached and heard confessions, earning after his death the erection of a monument in his memory from its parishioners. His spiritual life did not finish there: in addition to his duties in the Secretariat of State and his part-time work in the parish, he contributed to the spiritual life of two priestly confraternities.[43] In 1892, after his father's death, he invited his mother to come to live with him, just like any other Italian parish priest. He was very genuinely fond of his mother and enjoyed the domestic happiness which her presence provided. MacNutt has left this picture of the Della Chiesa Roman household:

My relations with him [Giacomo] were unbrokenly good. His mother, a charming, dignified old lady, the Marchesa Della Chiesa, had, during my student days, an apartment near the Piazza in Aquiro, where I was invited and met his sister. To be thus received in the family circle of that particular class of Italians, people of good ancestry and title, but not of the fashionable world, signified more than some of my readers may realise.[44]

But like other over-solicitous parents, the Marchesa could prove an embarrassment to her son on occasion. The story goes that at a social function, having been presented by her son to the Cardinal Secretary of State, the Marchesa took the opportunity to venture her opinion that Giacomo's talents were not sufficiently recognized. Rampolla is alleged to have replied: 'Signora, your son will take only a few steps, but they will be gigantic ones.'[45] Whatever the truth of the story, in reality, by comparison with some of his contemporaries, Giacomo's career had hitherto been unspectacular. Already his friend Valfré di Bonzo, only one year older, had been a bishop since 1885 and was to be promoted Archbishop of Vercelli in 1905. The career of another colleague, Mgr Rafaele Merry Del Val, who was ten years younger, was in even more striking contrast with that of Della Chiesa. According to Roberto Perin, 'Leo XIII entrusted him [Merry Del Val] with special missions to London, Berlin and Vienna. He was held in such esteem that at the young age of twenty-seven he entered the pope's household as secret papal chamberlain.'[46] In 1897 he sat on the papal commission that declared Anglican orders of bishop, priest and deacon to be 'null and void' on the grounds that the Church of England had lost the Apostolic Succession at the Reformation. Merry Del Val strongly supported that judgement[47] and in the same year he was sent to Ottawa as special apostolic delegate, the fourth in a series of five Roman prelates appointed to investigate the troubled affairs of the Canadian Church. By 1903 he was President (principal) of the Academy of Noble Ecclesiastics and a titular archbishop. On the other hand, it was not until 1901, when Giacomo was already in his late forties, that this close confidante and collaborator of the

Cardinal Secretary of State was raised to high office in the Vatican. On 15 April, he was appointed Sostituto, that is papal Under-Secretary of State with the title of 'Right Reverend'.

The simple explanation for Giacomo's slow career progression may have been Rampolla's desire to keep him by his side. As late as 1902, when Leo XIII had considered Giacomo as a possible archbishop of his native city, Rampolla had dissuaded the Pope from this appointment in order to keep him in the Vatican.[48] But there were almost certainly other reasons. Unlike Merry Del Val, or even Valfré di Bonzo, Della Chiesa lacked the appearance, demeanour or perhaps even the personality of a high-flying ecclesiastic. A contemporary, Cardinal O'Connell of Boston, was struck by his physical unattractiveness: 'He might pass unnoticed for any impressiveness of appearance, for his figure was rather angular and he walked with something of a limp. His complexion was sallow and his head, generally tilted to one side, gave no indication of the very fertile brain within it.'[49] Confirmation of this impression of Giacomo comes from another source, Francis MacNutt, who was in regular contact with Giacomo and wrote this about him:

> In person he was undersized, of a sallow, bilious complexion; he had an impenetrable mat of black hair, prominent teeth, and everything about him was crooked: nose, mouth, eyes and shoulders – all were out of drawing. Despite these blemishes, his bearing was dignified, his manners courtly though a trifle stiff, and he could never be mistaken for other than he was – a gentleman.[50]

The picture of him at his consecration as bishop (see Plate 8) gives graphic reality to this description.

Contemporaries were divided in their judgement of Giacomo's role in the Vatican. MacNutt, for example, was a little dismissive:

> He was usually esteemed a great diplomat. Frankly, I must say that he impressed me as a meticulous, accomplished bureaucrat; a conscientious, painstaking understudy of Cardinal Rampolla . . . He possessed a vast store of carefully sorted information upon which to draw; he was accurate and very precise,

acquainted with all the rules and traditions of his chancellery and not ignorant of those of other governments. In matters of protocol – etiquette, precedence, etc. – he was as infallible as a man could possibly be. Of brilliancy or originality, I never perceived a trace, but since an exhibition of such traits was not required during his years of subordinate service, it was proof of the greatest wisdom and tact on his part to dissemble any such he may have possessed. What he became as Pope, others more competent than me must judge.[51]

On the other hand, at the time of Della Chiesa's appointment as *minutante* in 1887, Mgr (later Cardinal) Agliardi wrote to a friend, 'this young man is regarded as being a new Consalvi'.[52] Agliardi changed his tune in 1914 (see p. 62).

While Giacomo's equally well-known timidity, his avoidance of the spotlight, would also have contributed to his relative obscurity in the Vatican, there is no denying his power and influence there after his promotion in 1901. Along with the Secretary for Extraordinary Ecclesiastical Affairs, Mgr Pietro Gasparri, who was appointed at the same time, the Sostituto was the most important person in the Vatican after the Secretary of State himself. Their offices were the 'clearing houses' of all essential matters in the government of the Roman Catholic Church. To them came many other Vatican officials and bishops from all over the world, giving them a remarkable knowledge of the world-wide Church. Frequently, in the absence of the Secretary of State, the Sostituto dealt directly with the Pope himself. It is clear that by 1901, his lack of physical and social grace notwithstanding, Giacomo had established for himself a unique reputation as a cautious, discreet and diplomatic powerbroker. An indication of his powerful position in the Vatican is given by this incident, which took place shortly after the death of Leo XIII in July 1903, related by Francis MacNutt:

On July 28th there was a venomous attack in *L'Italia* on the Accademia [of Noble Ecclesiastics, in which MacNutt had also studied] and its alumni. Bishops Merry Del Val, Misciateli, della Chiesa and myself were mentioned by name and described as forming a close *camarilla* of ambitious spirits, bent on controlling the Vatican. The hope was expressed that the new Pope, whoever he might be, would have the strength and courage to suppress us. We were even denounced as a threat to the spread of the Catholic religion! This from an anti-Catholic paper![53]

One suspects that the story was 'planted' by a Vatican malcontent, and even allowing for MacNutt's mistake in describing Giacomo (and Misciateli) as a bishop, when he did not receive that rank until four years later, the essence of the story is correct – by 1903 both Merry Del Val and Della Chiesa were powerful people.

The election of Pius X

Neither Giacomo's power nor his peace was to last for long. Less than two years after his appointment as Sostituto his world was turned upside down by the death of Leo XIII. Because of the sudden and unexpected death of Mgr Volpini shortly afterwards, the cardinals were obliged to appoint another secretary to the impending conclave, the official who was responsible for making all the practical and legal arrangements. Cardinal Camerlengo nominated Merry Del Val and Gasparri. Then Della Chiesa was nominated in the latter's place. Finally, Merry Del Val was elected. Peters argues:

> This apparently insignificant election was a decisive event that did much to change the history of the papacy in modern times and set in motion a remarkable chain of circumstances. In that very hour Giacomo's star began to wane, and for almost a decade· its light as an influence on world affairs would be totally extinguished.[54]

All this requires explanation. In the first place, of crucial importance to Giacomo's future was the failure of Rampolla to get elected Pope. The strongest candidate until the fifth ballot, Rampolla was effectively knocked out of the contest by the intervention of Cardinal Puszyna, Archbishop of Cracow (then in the Austrian Empire), who pronounced a 'veto' on behalf of Franz Josef. Thereafter, despite Rampolla's very dignified reaction, his vote declined and Cardinal Giuseppe Sarto, Patriarch of Venice, was elected in his stead, taking the name Pius X. It seems fair to assume that, but for this incident, Rampolla would have been elected, even allowing for the opposition to him in the Sacred College. If that is the case, then Giacomo would also have stood some chance of being appointed Secretary of State.

With the election of Sarto as Pope, therefore, changes were bound to occur in Della Chiesa's life. By tradition, a new Pope meant a new Secretary of State – the tradition was not to be broken until 1922, when Pius XI insisted on keeping his predecessor's Secretary of State, Pietro Gasparri. Rampolla was accordingly retired – given the insignificant post of Archpriest of St Peter's and made Prefect of the congregation which supervised its fabric. But the choice of his successor was unexpected, and was to have unfortunate consequences for Della Chiesa in his position as Sostituto. The obvious candidate, in fact, was Cardinal Ferrata, but it was precisely his great experience and standing – he had served as nuncio to France and in the Secretariat of State – that ensured that he would be passed over. Pius X, like his predecessor of the same name, was a man of strong will. To have appointed Ferrata would have meant accepting as collaborator a man who was at least his equal. With Ferrata out of the running, the two under-secretaries, Della Chiesa and Gasparri, were both eligible (Gasparri more so than Giacomo, since he had been an apostolic delegate in South America) yet they too were passed over. The man whom the Pope did choose, Mgr Merry Del Val, was young, very young – only thirty-eight – and inexperienced, thus he would be a true executor of the Pope's wishes in a way that neither Ferrata, Gasparri or perhaps even Della Chiesa could have been.

Son of Spanish aristocrats, but with British connections and education, Merry Del Val was a protégé of Leo XIII, who had forced him to abandon plans to enter the Scottish College in Rome and had him sent to the Academy of Noble Ecclesiastics instead.[55] It was a little unusual to enrol someone there who was not already ordained (though MacNutt had been), and for Merry Del Val it was a personal tragedy because it effectively precluded the career in pastoral ministry he so desired. Following his ordination, he very quickly rose up the Vatican ladder as we have seen; indeed, shortly before the conclave of 1903 he had actually been on the *terna* of candidates proposed by the canons of Westminster for election as ordinary of that archiepiscopal see.[56] Yet despite his meteoric rise, according to Perin he was less than popular with the French Canadian bishops, and in the Vatican his youth earned him the soubriquet *il ragazzino* ('the little boy') and his fastidiousness that of *la ragazzina* ('the little girl'), and more importantly, his analysis of the situation in Quebec was denounced by Archbishop (later Cardinal) Begin as seriously flawed.[57] Not a good start for a future head of Vatican diplomacy.

Having been appointed Secretary to the Conclave, in preference to both Della Chiesa and Gasparri, his superiors in the Vatican hierarchy, Merry Del Val thus came into contact with Cardinal Giuseppe Sarto, Patriarch of Venice, and according to Cenci, Del Val's biographer, it was he who persuaded the reluctant *papabile* to accept the tiara.[58] Sarto was very deeply impressed by Merry Del Val, and continued him in service as personal secretary until he had made a decision about the Secretariat of State. Merry Del Val was to become Pius X's most faithful servant, indeed their relationship was an extraordinarily close one by any standards, more like that of father and son. There is not a little analogy beween this relationship and that between Rampolla and Della Chiesa. Merry Del Val was devastated by the Pope's death in 1914: Della Chiesa had been equally distressed by the death of his mentor and friend the previous year. While Pius X undoubtedly laid down the main lines of the Vatican's diplomatic policy, the suave, brilliant aristocrat with an easy command of six languages would undoubtedly have exercised a strong influence upon it. Count Giuseppe Dalla Torre, who was one of the most influential Italian Catholic laymen in the first of half of the twentieth century claimed that Merry Del Val, 'enjoyed the complete and absolute confidence of the Pope'.[59] While Merry Del Val was not the 'evil genius' of the Vatican during Pius X's pontificate, he certainly had a powerful influence upon its policies which did not please either Della Chiesa or Gasparri, his two immediate subordinates.

The first major bone of contention was France. In the wake of the Dreyfus Affair, relations between the Third Republic and the Vatican were severely strained, but at least they continued to exist on a diplomatic level. All this changed shortly after Pius X's election. The visit of President Loubet of France to the Italian King in the Quirinale Palace in April 1904 provoked a rupture. Whereas non-Catholic sovereigns, princes and heads of state were permitted to visit the King of Italy, provided that they visited the Vatican first and followed Vatican protocol to the letter, Catholic heads of state were effectively debarred from setting foot in Rome. The papal protest to other powers about the visit leaked out and, splashed all over the French press, was taken as a deliberate insult in the Elysée and Quai d'Orsay.[60] France then withdrew its envoy to the Vatican, claiming that Vatican was only keeping a nuncio in Paris in order to influence the elections.[61]

Loubet's visit to the Quirinale was almost certainly a deliberate provocation on the part of a militantly anti-clerical French government. The subsequent attitude of the Vatican was high-minded but counterproductive. When the French Law on the Separation of Church and State was passed in 1905, and the *associations cultuelles* were set up to provide a legal framework for the holding of all Church property, and therefore effectively the continued practice of the Catholic faith, Pius X forbade French bishops and priests to have anything to do with them, even though the bishops had decided by a clear majority to the contrary.[62] Relations progressively deteriorated thereafter. They were not helped by the Pope's refusal to allow the writings of the extreme right-wing, anti-Semitic politician and author Charles Maurras to be placed on the Index of Forbidden Books, while the ideas of Marc Sagnier and Le Sillon (both of a Christian Democratic tendency) were. According to Cobban, 'Action Française [of which Maurras was the leader] was treated as an ally by Pius X'; given that this was an extreme right-wing, Nationalistic and anti-Republican organisation, it could only have inflamed French anti-clerical feeling.[63]

One wonders what Leo XIII and Rampolla would have done in the circumstances: it is hard to see how they could have avoided the rupture with France given the anti-clerical mood in that country. But Larkin is undoubtedly right when he says that, 'Certainly, the consequences of the Separation in France would have been less crippling if Rampolla had been materially in charge.'[64] Unfortunately, Rampolla was not in charge any more and did not approve of the new policies. Della Chiesa was, however, still in office and according to Sforza, he tried to avoid the worst:

> As long as he remained, as Under-Secretary of State, until his exile to Bologna, della [sic] Chiesa tried, respectfully and prudently to prevent the relations of France and the Vatican from degenerating to the point of disastrous rupture, the obvious conclusion according to him, of Pius X's and Merry Del Val's policy. He gained nothing by his efforts except to be no longer received by the Pope.[65]

Sforza's judgement is almost certainly correct, though there is no evidence that the Pope refused to see Della Chiesa any more. On the contrary Papa Sarto seems to have retained his esteem for him. But Della Chiesa's subtle, patient brand of diplomacy was no longer acceptable in the Vatican – it was associated with Rampolla and the policies of the previous pontificate. It was, therefore, even dangerous for Della Chiesa to continue to frequent his former boss and mentor who appears by now to have been effectively ostracized. Indeed, Merry Del Val himself made it clear that under the new regime, it was 'not diplomatic'.[66] Rampolla and Della Chiesa must have been even less happy with the 'needlessly gladiatorial methods' Merry Del Val used in the disputes which developed with Spain in 1909, following the expulsion of some religious orders, and with Portugal after the Liberal revolution of 1910.[67]

It is also doubtful whether Della Chiesa was happy with Pius X's policy towards Italy. Under the pressing fear of the rise of a Marxian Socialist working-class movement, especially following the events of the 'End of Century Crisis' in 1897 and 1898, Pius X moved the Italian Church towards a lessening of the dispute with the Italian State, in common cause against socialism. In particular, after 1904, he repeatedly relaxed the *non expedit* decree, permitting Catholics to vote for Liberal-Conservative candidates who promised to protect the Church's interests and, most importantly, not to support the introduction of a divorce law,[68] even allowing Catholics to be candidates. These so-called 'clerico-moderate' alliances were created in an attempt to stem the Socialist electoral tide at both a local and national level. This was a realistic policy, a further retreat from temporalistic intransigence. Despite the ritual reiteration of the protest over the Italian 'usurpation of Rome', Papa Sarto's attitude towards the Italian royal family was much less inflexible than that of his predecessor. There is evidence, for example, that he received members of that family in the Vatican, and the 'black aristocracy' – the great Roman families who remained loyal to the Pope and eschewed the new occupant of the Quirinale after 1870 – found their social, not to say, financial position more and more difficult in the new pontificate.[69] It is likely that Della Chiesa was exceedingly sceptical about the wisdom of these political manoeuvres, but was forced to conform to the new Vatican line. The report of the Prefect (civil governor) of Rome province, when consulted by the Ministry of Justice on Giacomo's suitability for nomination as Archbishop of Bologna – the State held a veto over such appointments – noted that:

> though Della Chiesa closely associated himself with the temporalistic policy of Cardinal Rampolla, it would appear that since the beginning of the pontificate of Pius X, he has allowed himself to change his attitude sufficiently to bring it into line with the present policy of the Vatican.[70]

The anti-Modernist crusade

Of all his various policies, the pontificate of Pius X will probably be remembered most for his crusade against 'Modernism'. This attack on theologians, biblical scholars and ecclesiastical historians – most of them French, like Loisy – who sought to use modern scientific methods in their work, became an obsession with him. In 1907 he issued two major statements, *Lamentabili* and *Pascendi*, against them and their ideas which he defined as the 'synthesis of all heresies'. Very soon, a purge of seminaries, theological faculties and of the priesthood itself got under way, and a strict anti-Modernist oath was imposed on all clergy. Pius X's chief collaborator in this 'sacred terror' was Mgr Umberto Benigni. It was he who ran the headquarters of the anti-Modernist 'secret police', under the innocuous title of the Sodalitium Pianum (alias La Sapinière) organization: operating from the Secretariat of State where he was himself an official, Benigni's agents and informants spread throughout Italy, France and other parts of Catholic Europe.[71] No one, not even bishops, cardinals and high-ranking prelates, was spared the denunciations of Benigni's agents or the suspicions of Pius X. Cardinal Ferrari, Archbishop of Milan, Cardinal Maffi, Archbishop of Pisa, Cardinal Amette, Archbishop of Paris, and Cardinal Fischer, Archbishop of Cologne, were all subjected to humiliating harassment for their 'softness' on Modernism.

Hebblethwaite claims that 'One of the first victims of *Pascendi* was Giacomo Della Chiesa',[72] and he implies that this was why he was appointed to Bologna in December 1907. As is clear from his pastoral activities as archbishop of that city, Della Chiesa disliked the excesses of the anti-Modernist crusade and even found himself occasionally a target of them (see pp. 44–5), but he was emphatically not himself a Modernist and it is extremely unlikely that any suspicion of Modernism on his part ever crossed Pius X's mind. Certainly, he would never have considered promoting Della Chiesa to such an important see if he had thought him remotely unsound on that score. On the other hand, others obviously did think he was unsound – it is the only way to explain his remark to the cardinals after his election as Pope in September 1914: 'And We assure you that the Holy Father is not a modernist!'[73]

Like Angelo Roncalli (later Pope John XXIII), Della Chiesa, while sympathizing with some of the ideas of the so-called modernists, was very careful to keep on the right side of the fence. On the other hand, his cautious attitude towards doctrinal controversy, and his penchant for fair play, would undoubtedly have brought him into conflict with the anti-Modernist zealots, the so-called *integristes*, in the Roman Curia – such as Cardinal De Lai, Prefect of the Concistorial Congregation, and the Spanish Capuchin friar Cardinal Vives y Tuto (Vives fa Tutto, 'Vives does everything' as he was known in the Vatican), Secretary to the Holy Office of the Inquisition, who, along with Pius X and Merry Del Val, were the chief supporters of Benigni. According to Bedeschi, these three constituted a triad which effectively controlled the Vatican during the pontificate of Pius X.[74] Ironically, when Vives went mad in 1908 and had to be confined,[75] Rampolla was appointed in his place and remained there until his death in December 1913. But in a letter to Bishop Bonomelli he complained that he only saw the Pope four or five times a year, and had no control over the Index or the bishops.[76]

Internal Vatican politics, then, were the causes of Della Chiesa's removal to Bologna, and Merry Del Val was almost certainly the prime mover, anxious to rid himself of an uncomfortable subordinate. It is significant that it was also in December 1907 that Gasparri left his post in the Secretariat of State, being very conveniently appointed head of the commission for the codification of canon law and cardinal, a useful way of separating the two men. We know that he too was opposed to the anti-Modernist crusade. Of the Sodalitium Pianum Gasparri said that it was 'an occult, espionage organisation above and beyond the control of the hierarchy . . . a kind of Freemasonry unheard of in the history of the Church'.[77] Carlo Falconi argues that the removal of Della Chiesa had the blessing of Pius X, who saw it as an opportunity to remove the friction between his favourite and a powerful subordinate.[78] As Sostituto, Della Chiesa could reasonably have expected his next career step to have been posting to a major nunciature – Madrid, Paris or Vienna. There were rumours of his appointment to Madrid throughout Pius X's pontificate, one such surfacing in the pages of the Roman newspaper, *Il Messaggero*, on the day that Pius X decided to appoint him to Bologna. Not surprisingly, Rampolla encouraged the idea as far as he could, even though, given the deterioration of relations between Church and State in Spain, it would not have been an easy posting. 'As far as I am concerned,' he wrote to Della Chiesa in Bologna, 'if there is any need to help, I will do it gladly, but I count for nothing any more.'[79] There is also evidence that the Spanish Government would have welcomed his appointment.[80]

But sending Della Chiesa to Madrid was not a solution likely to appeal to Merry Del Val; as nuncio, Della Chiesa would still have been in continuous contact with the Secretariat of State. Furthermore, at the completion of his posting, Della Chiesa would have been entitled to the cardinal's hat and a powerful position in the Roman Curia – an even less attractive prospect for Merry Del Val. In a letter to a friend in 1912, following renewed rumours that he was to be sent to Madrid, Della Chiesa remarked: 'But I must not get involved in matters of diplomacy: I was thrown out of it, and I really do not wish to return.'[81] This said, in July 1918, Benedict told his friend Carlo Monti that Merry Del Val did want to send him to Madrid, but that Pius X wanted him to go to Bologna.[82] The only possible explanation for the contradiction in these statements is that by the time he was elected Pope, Giacomo was prepared to forgive and forget, and that for political reasons he was also anxious to play down the rift between himself and Merry Del Val. Certainly, such a rift existed, even though two previous biographers of Della Chiesa denied it. Vistalli argued: 'The claim that there existed a conflict between Mgr Della Chiesa and Cardinal Merry Del Val was an unedifying legend that, for a period of time, enjoyed credence with a certain element of the press',[83] and Peters insists: 'it is quite evident that much of the animosity [between Della Chiesa and Merry Del Val] which writers hint at existed only in the minds of those who craved the sensational'.[84] However, the antagonism between them is clear, and the most damning evidence is provided by the testimonies of two witnessess at the beatification process for Merry Del Val.[85] Merry Del Val did not believe that Della Chiesa was worthy of the cardinalate. This much is proved by the failure to raise him to that rank for seven years after he became Archbishop of Bologna, one of the Italian archiepiscopal sees invariably entitled to the honour.

Thus Della Chiesa's appointment to Bologna was a defeat, and a banishment from the Vatican, and judging by the letter cited above, he clearly saw it in those terms. It was comparable, in fact, as Falconi argues, to the exile of Mgr Giovanni Battista Montini (later Pope Paul VI) to Milan in 1954[86] and the analogy is reinforced by the fact that Montini was refused the red hat while

Pius XII was alive, but like Montini's exile to Milan, his time in Bologna was to provide Della Chiesa with the pastoral experience which made his election to the Papacy in 1914 possible. Bologna was a convenient exile for an uncomfortable subordinate. The accounts of the way in which Pius X conveyed the news to Della Chiesa confirm his and Merry Del Val's involvement,[87] and the pontiff's decision to consecrate his new archbishop himself was merely a consolation prize. Nevertheless, it was a handsome one as consolation prizes go and confirmed the Pope's personal esteem for him. Della Chiesa was consecrated in the Sistine Chapel, with his friend Valfré di Bonzo as a co-consecrator and the Pope was present at his consecration breakfast, an exceptional honour.

By the end of 1907, Giacomo was probably only too glad to leave Rome. Life could not have been easy since the retirement (and effective disgrace) of Rampolla in 1903. The abandonment and humiliation of his great friend by enemies in the Vatican must have been exceedingly painful for him. Equally, like his friend Gasparri, he could not have enjoyed executing policies with which he profoundly disagreed. Moreover, his personal life in Rome had rather lost its edge. In 1902, consequent upon his appointment as Sostituto, he had been forced to leave his mother in Palazzo Brazzà and take up residence 'in a dingy apartment between the Sistine Chapel and St. Peters'.[88] Even worse, in July 1904, his beloved mother had died. Bologna, therefore, offered a new life and a new beginning.

Notes and references

1. Vistalli, p. 13.
2. Sforza, p. 165.
3. MacNutt, p. 312.
4. AFDC, white envelope.
5. AFDC, white envelope.
6. Peters, pp. 5–7.
7. Falconi, p. 96.
8. Ibid., p. 95.
9. Vistalli, p. 20.
10. Binchy, p. 463.

11. For an account of relations between the Papacy and Italy in this period, see Jemolo, ch. III.
12. As quoted in Vistalli, p. 11.
13. Duffy, p. 250.
14. AFDC, Discorsi sui vangeli domenicali.
15. Sforza, p. 164.
16. ASV, Apostoliche Nunziature, Madrid, Rampolla, 16 March 1883.
17. Rumi (1991), letter of 4 November 1886.
18. Ibid., letter of 20 February 1883.
19. Ibid., letter of 14 November 1886.
20. Ibid., letter of 19 August 1883.
21. Ibid., letter of 14 November 1886.
22. Ibid., letter of 24 March 1883.
23. Peters, pp. 19–20.
24. For an analysis of Rampolla's policy, see Rhodes (1983), p. 118 and Seton-Watson, pp. 214–34.
25. Ibid., p. 216.
26. Ibid., p. 215–17 and 222.
27. Ibid., p. 216.
28. See Larkin (1974), p. 134.
29. Rhodes (1983), p. 216.
30. Schmidlin, p. 20.
31. White, p. 205.
32. These are preserved in the AFDC.
33. Rumi (1991), letter of 24 March 1893.
34. Ibid., letter of 12 January 1900.
35. Falconi, p. 98.
36. Rumi (1991), letter of 6 July 1897.
37. Ibid., letter of 27 May 1896.
38. Ibid., letter of 25 August 1896.
39. Ibid., letter of 8 November 1896.
40. Ibid., letter of 9 September 1898.
41. Peters, p. 24.
42. Ibid.
43. Ibid., pp. 22–3.
44. MacNutt, p. 313.
45. Falconi, p. 102.
46. Perin, p. 83.
47. Leslie, ch. V.
48. Falconi, p. 100.
49. O'Connell (1934), p. 340.
50. MacNutt, p. 311.
51. Ibid., p. 312.

52. As quoted in Cappa, p. 12.
53. MacNutt, p. 245; Bedeschi (1968), p. 60, quotes the words of the 'Modernist' priest, Romolo Murri, about the Academy: 'Today it is a seminary of inept people whose vanity is shown in the swish of multi-coloured, silk cassocks.'
54. Peters, pp. 31–2.
55. Cenci, pp. 32–3.
56. Leslie, ch. VI.
57. Perin, pp. 125–6.
58. Cenci, pp. 32–3.
59. As quoted in Bedeschi (1968), p. 52, n. 39.
60. Larkin, p. 53.
61. Ibid.
62. Ibid., p. 60.
63. Cobban, p. 92.
64. Larkin, p. 60.
65. Sforza, p. 165.
66. Migliori, p. 23.
67. Falconi, p. 76.
68. Pollard (1996), pp. 76–7.
69. MacNutt, p. 255.
70. ACS, Ministero dell'Interno, Direzione Generale (henceforth MI, DG), Affari di Culto, Bologna, 18 January 1908.
71. For an analysis of the anti-Modernist crusade see Falconi, pp. 32–71 and Chadwick (1998), pp. 346–59.
72. Hebblethwaite (1984), p. 62.
73. As quoted in Peters, p. 81.
74. Bedeschi (1968), p. 338.
75. Falconi, p. 50.
76. Marcora, p. 234, letter of Rampolla to Bonomelli, 10 November 1910.
77. As quoted in Penco, p. 493.
78. Falconi, p. 101.
79. AFDC, Lettere e Scritti Vari, Rampolla to Della Chiesa, 28 December 1911.
80. Falconi, p. 102.
81. AFDC, Lettere e Scritti Vari, Della Chiesa to Sardi, 11 January 1909.
82. *Diario*, II, pp. 358–9, 25 July 1918.
83. Vistalli, p. 17.
84. Peters, p. 38.
85. Falconi, p. 103.
86. Ibid., p. 108.
87. Peters, pp. 54–5 and Falconi, pp. 104–6.
88. Vistalli, p. 14.

2

Bologna

On 17 February 1908, Giacomo Della Chiesa arrived in Bologna. Six days later he was enthroned in the metropolitan cathedral church of St Peter and took possession of his diocese. Given the great regional and local diversity of Italy at this time, its great dioceses were equally different one from another, Milan from neighbouring Brescia and Bergamo, Padua from Venice, and Bologna from the other great episcopal sees of the Emilian plain – Parma and Modena – each with its own peculiarities. In Bologna's case that includes the fact that until 1918 all children born in the city had to be baptized in the cathedral and that though the episcopal chair of St Petronius was in the cathedral, the latter was outstripped in size and magnificence by St Petronius' own church.

The city, the province and the region

Bologna la grassa ('Bologna the fat'), that is how Della Chiesa's archiepiscopal city has traditionally been known in Italy, and at the time of writing, after fifty years of left-wing rule, like other cities of the Emilian plain, it boasts a standard of living and a quality of life among the highest in Europe. With its excellent, rich cuisine and its beautiful streets, its famous colonnades (*porticati*) and towers, and its integrated transport system, it is undoubtedly one of the better places to live in Europe. The region of which Bologna is the capital, Emilia-Romagna, has also been dubbed 'Sodom and Gomorrah', by one of Della Chiesa's successors, John Paul II, for its unchecked materialism and hedonism.[1] In 1907, there was already as much shade as light in the life of Bologna as there is now, as far as the city's Catholics were concerned.

Until 1859, Bologna had been the second city of the Papal States, with a cardinal legate as governor, and its administrative and legal institutions, its ancient university and its charitable institutions had been firmly under clerical control. But the 'liberal revolution' of the Risorgimento period and in particular the victory of both the pro-Piedmontese forces inside the city, and Victor Emmanuel II's army outside ensured that by the spring of 1860, Bologna had become one of the first provinces of the new, united Italian state. The ruling class of the new state, the agrarian-mercantile block, quickly took possession of Bologna's various institutions and effectively secularized them, according to Renato Zangheri, historian and former Communist mayor of the city.[2] Throughout the 1870s, however, some obstinate Catholic opposition remained, and that this also had a popular base is testified by the grist tax riots of the middle of that decade when there were shouts of 'Long live Pius IX'.[3] But the anti-clerical forces had definitively triumphed, and in 1880 with the defeat of the Right, their influence increased, buttressed by the power of a network of masonic lodges. The University was also strongly anti-clerical in tone, thanks in part to the influence of Italy's greatest living poet Giosuè Carducci, who had written 'a poem in praise and defence of Judas Iscariot, and an adulatory hymn to Satan'[4] and who also had a following among the poor of the city. After the turn of the century, the politics of the city continued to drift Leftwards; the Radicals and Republicans gained a foothold in the city council, thanks partly to the persistence of a kind of 'Garibaldinian social-ism' (i.e. non-Marxian) among the artisan class.[5] Neighbouring Romagna was, after all, the Republican stronghold *par excellence* in Italy, after a long, turbulent history of opposition to papal rule which was chronicled in the Risorgimento moderate Liberal leader Massimo D'Azeglio's pamphlet, *Degli ultimi casi della Romagna.*[6] And republicanism in the Romagna retained a following among both urban and rural poor until the middle of the next century. But conflict between the monarchist Liberal-Conservatives and the Republicans in the city brought no relief to the Catholics for republicanism was as virulent a carrier of anti-clericalism as either mainstream liberalism or socialism.[7]

Owing to the lack of industrialization, Bologna itself remained an essentially agrarian, administrative and university city: Cardoza describes it as the 'acknowledged, if unofficial, agricultural capital of Italy ... a hub of commercial, administrative, and political activity between the regions of northern and central Italy', thanks especially to the rich cultivations – hemp and grains – on the plains of the province.[8] Without industrialization, however, there was as yet no very large industrial, urban proletariat. As a result, the city of Bologna lacked the presence of strong working-class organizations. It would not be until after the First World War, following limited industrialization, that Bologna would emerge as the 'red city', *Bologna la rossa*, the indisputable capital of the 'red belt' of central Italy. Paradoxically, the working-class movement developed most strongly in the countryside of Bologna and neighbouring provinces. The peculiar social structure of this area with large numbers of landless labourers (*braccianti*), and miserably poor sharecroppers (*mezzadri*), proved an ideal breeding ground for agrarian socialism. A similiar pattern was recognizable in the adjacent provinces of Ravenna, Ferrara and Modena.[9] Furthermore, according to Cardoza, 'Rapid growth of socialist labour came partially at the expense of the Catholic professional unions which entered into crisis in 1904 as a result of pressures from the leagues and internal conflict between clerical conservatives and Christian Democrats.'[10] Within Bologna province itself, Budrio and to a lesser extent Imola were the epicentres of bitter agrarian disputes from 1883 onwards, and consequently in the 1920s witnessed the awful violence of the reaction against a triumphant agrarian socialism–agrarian Fascism. As Leo XIII had already recognized, the Marxist-orientated working-class movement with its vigorous agrarian wing would ultimately prove to be the Church's strongest rival for the souls of the Italian people. Not surprisingly, Della Chiesa had his baptism of fire in this regard precisely during his stay in Emilia-Romagna: it was here, according to Veneruso, that 'he learnt to recognise and evaluate the power and nature of socialism'.[11]

The emerging 'red threat' brought about a partial reconciliation between Catholics and Liberal-Conservatives in the late 1880s: under the patronage of Cardinal Archbishop Svampa, clerico-moderate electoral alliances kept the Bologna city council out of the hands of the extremists between 1886 and 1902. Thereafter, it was the Catholics who were isolated from power. It was in this extremely unpropitious situation that Della Chiesa arrived to take up his pastoral ministry in January 1908 and it is not surprising therefore that the Royal Procurator of the city should inform his superiors in Rome in that month that, 'the appointment of Msgr Della Chiesa as Archbishop of Bologna has created a good impression in the clerical camp, while the other section of the citizenry has remained perfectly indifferent'.[12]

The office and duty of a bishop

On 10 February 1908, in advance of his arrival in the diocese, Della Chiesa sent his first pastoral letter, entitled 'What is the office of bishop?', to his flock. In it, he defined the office of a bishop as that of 'superintendant' (a definition, therefore, with which most Anglican and Lutheran authorities at that time would also have agreed), as the good father of a family and as a 'Good Shepherd of his sheep', a fairly traditional, conventional conception of his role. Equally conventional was his conception of the duty of the 'sheep' – to obey.[13] Della Chiesa also stressed the teaching role of bishops, and his subsequent annual pastoral letters dealt with the various aspects of the Christian life: 1910, 'The Spirit of Obedience'; 1911, 'The Spirit of Humility'; 1912, 'The Spirit of Prayer'; 1913, 'The Spirit of Charity' and 1914, 'The Spirit of Mortification'.[14] Thus Della Chiesa's was a ministry dedicated, as he had made clear at the beginning of his first pastoral letter, to the salvation of souls. To this end, he set about re-organizing the diocesan administration. As first vicar-general, he appointed the auxiliary bishop, Vincenzo Bacchi.[15] His second vicar-general was Mgr Ersilio Menzani, archdeacon (dean) of the cathedral, whom he clearly trusted and relied upon. According to Albertazzi, 'Ersilio

Menzani (1872–1961) was Giacomo Della Chiesa's protégé, and Benedict XV wanted him first as director of the diocesan bulletin and then vicar-general'; furthermore, during the long periods that he was away on parochial visitations, he gave Menzani full delegated powers in such matters as appointments.[16] The other major appointment was that of Giuseppe Migone, the son of a friend, as his secretary: the Archbishop of Genoa was persuaded to release him from service at the Genoese church in Rome. Della Chiesa's household was completed by a small 'community' of priests who worked in the diocesan curia (administration) and shared his life in the archiepiscopal palace.

After his arrival in Bologna, he quickly established a demanding daily schedule for himself. He rose at 5 a.m., and after saying his morning prayers, Breviary, Mass, meditation and thanksgiving he would breakfast at 7 a.m. Between breakfast and lunch at 1.30 p.m., he would deal with correspondence and appointments. This would be followed by a visit to the Exposed Sacrament in one of Bologna's churches, and by more Breviary interspersed with further business. Shortly after the recitation of the Rosary and supper at 8.30 p.m., followed by a period of conversation with his household, he retired to his study for yet more reading and more writing: this routine he also followed after being elected Pope.[17] Peters says that Della Chiesa was perfectly capable of working all the way through the night.[18]

Despite the problems created for him as Archbishop by the continuing Roman persecution of Modernists and Christian Democrats, most of Della Chiesa's time was taken up with more routine matters, and most of his problems were mundane. In a letter in 1909 to a friend, Mgr Vincenzo Sardi, Apostolic Delegate at Constantinople, he wrote:

> So far I can honestly say that I have not had very serious difficulties: the majority are caused by the odd priest who finds the vow of celibacy hard to bear. Here it is not really a question of modernists or marxists, largely because the level of ecclesiastical studies is very low, and priestly spirituality is lacking: I find the latter perplexing because the Seminary is run by a good

rector yet as soon as the young priests leave the seminary they forget how to meditate![19]

His first priority, from the beginning of his ministry in Bologna, was the need to carry out a complete pastoral visitation of his diocese. It was by no means unusual for a new diocesan to inaugurate a complete visitation of his parishes, the example having been set by the great Counter-Reformation bishop, St Charles Borromeo of Milan, in the sixteenth century. But Bologna was a big diocese, the fourth largest in Italy, with a population of roughly six hundred and seventy thousand souls, so it was bound to be a very big undertaking and it must therefore have taken up a very large part of his time. It was made physically arduous by the fact that whereas the northern portion of the diocese consisted of plain, the southern portion was composed of the foothills and mountains of the Apennines; thus in a letter of 3 March 1909, Della Chiesa claimed that he had already visited 65 parishes, with 400 to go, 100 of which could only be reached on horseback.[20] Finally, on 13 December 1913, a solemn Te Deum was held in the cathedral to celebrate completion of 392 visitations.[21]

As well as physically inspecting the fabric, fittings, equipment and records, on a visitation the Bishop usually celebrated Mass, gave Benediction of the Blessed Sacrament, and delivered an appropriate homily in the parish being visited. Where appropriate, he also visited hospitals, prisons and religious houses. According to Molinari, 'Benedict XV made his pastoral visits leaving behind a memory of his very limited oratorical skill but also his very warm and friendly approach'.[22] This seems to be a rather harsh judgement. While the file of material on the visitations preserved in the Della Chiesa Family Archive does not suggest that they were terribly exciting spiritually or theologically, it has to be remembered that he was very often speaking to a usually uneducated, and often illiterate, audience and that he must have written hundreds of them.[23] They are, inevitably, very didactic, with a great use of rhetorical question and various biblical texts to exhort his hearers to charity. Apart from a few Latin texts, the language is plain, simple and clear. On a visit to the city parish of St Martin, he recalled the fact that he had been there the year before, during the procession for Our Lady of Carmel, that it was the second city church to be visited and he added a typically personal touch, pointing out that he knew that the parish priest had served for twenty-five years.[24] He expressed himself pleased with the state of the church and especially with the fact that special efforts had been made so that 'the poorer children had been provided with the proper garments for the common feast', and he concluded by saying that the pastoral visit was 'a gift which the Lord made to enrich them spiritually. "If you keep my commandments"'.[25]

The outcome of the Archbishop's visits was not always so satisfactory. The diary of the pastoral visits, compiled by Della Chiesa's chaplain and travelling companion, demonstrates that in several places his superior was not impressed by the way in which the church or other ecclesiastical buildings were maintained, and said so. At Vimignano the chaplain wrote, 'Oh! The visit to the parish certainly did not give the Bishop that satisfaction which he ought to expect – there was a lot of disorder and much neglect'[26] and at Serravalle Della Chiesa was profoundly displeased: 'the Archbishop remarked that the church . . . is in great need of repair and of order. He was astonished by the fact that not even the imminence of a pastoral visit had had the effect of prompting some effort to render the house of the Lord a little more decorous'.[27] According to the diary, Della Chiesa's next step in these cases was to send in the local rural dean who was set to work to bring about improvement, and Della Chiesa did not brook disobedience of his orders.[28]

From his visitations it quickly became clear that one of the major problems facing the Bologna diocese was a lack of religious instruction; indeed, the inadequacy of the religious knowledge of the children of a parish, which Della Chiesa insisted on testing himself, is a recurring theme in the accounts of the visitations. At its root, the problem was essentially political. In Italy in this period, the school became a major battleground between Catholics and Socialists and the prize was the soul of Italian children. In the decades immediately following unification, the battle had been between Catholics and the anti-clerical Liberal ruling élite, supported by Radical and Republican elements, and in 1870 they secured a victory of a kind through the passage of legislation which made the teaching of the catechism optional in primary schools.[29] But since the day-to-day administration of schools was the responsibility of local authorities, the effects of the law were patchy. In the 1880s and 1890s the Socialists waged a powerful campaign to win control of local authorities and a key goal was the abolition of teaching the catechism. At this point, in the face of a threatened Socialist take-over, Catholics and Liberals banded together in clerico-moderate alliances. The defeat of that alliance in Bologna in 1902, therefore, meant the virtual eradication of the catechism from Bologna's schools, and a similar situation was to be found in other parts of the province where the councils had been taken over by the Left. Della Chiesa very quickly set to work to find a remedy to the situation. At the diocesan eucharistic congress in November 1909, he announced the establishment of 'local congregations of Christian doctrine', whose job would be to organize the teaching of the catechism in the various deaneries.[30] In the *Bollettino Diocesano* (the Diocesan newsletter), which he himself founded in the following year, a plan of campaign was mapped out: priests were instructed to ensure that all the children in the parish were brought to catechism and asked to check the lists of those receiving instruction against the registers of the primary schools, the result of which was that out of a total population in the diocese of 670,000, 100,000 children were discovered not to be attending the classes; a stress was made on children's attendance at Sunday mass, regardless of their age; the involvement of fathers and mothers was strongly encouraged and the need to use the most modern aids – including films and slides – was underlined.[31] Della Chiesa did not hesitate to employ the much-criticized Don Ravaglia (see pp. 43–4) to write the official diocesan catechism.[32] Della Chiesa's organizational skills, and above all his eye for detail, are very clearly evident in his plan of campaign for the 'catechetical offensive', and it resulted in the creation of a catechism centre near every state primary school in the diocese.[33]

Another problem of an essentially political origin which faced Della Chiesa when he arrived in Bologna was that of civil marriage.

According to Kertzer, 'The battle over civil and church marriage was still being fought in Bologna in 1907.'[34] The difficulty for Catholics was the secular State's insistence on the precedence of a civil over a religious wedding, which was not acceptable in canon law.[35] As a result of the dogged opposition of many parochial clergy, and also quite simply the shortage of money to pay the fees twice, there was strong resistance to civil marriage in Emilia-Romagna generally; thus as far as the State was concerned many children were illegitimate – 17.5 per cent in the region in this period.[36] Della Chiesa's response to the problem was predictably sensible; in the *Bollettino Diocesano* he enjoined upon the parochial clergy the need to preach about marriage once a year and in doing so to urge upon the faithful the unfortunate necessity of contracting both kinds, civil and religious, for their own benefit, especially in order to preserve their legal rights of inheritance.[37]

As indicated by the quotation from the letter on p. 34, Della Chiesa was blessed with a good, well-run seminary, a luxury as far as many of his fellow bishops were concerned. But over the years the seminary did give him a lot of trouble, which largely stemmed from Pius X's new legislation on the education and training of priests.[38] This was to form the basis of seminary studies until Vatican II. It is undoubtedly true that the Pope's concern about the training of the young Italian clergy was largely motivated by fear of 'Modernism'. Certainly, the seminaries, and the soundness of the teaching in them, were a major target of his apostolic visitors, as we have seen, and injunctions about the need to shelter the young seminarian from heretical and simply secular influences were frequently made: Della Chiesa, for example, carried out his instructions in this matter by banning seminarians from reading newspapers and periodicals.[39] But Pius X was aiming at a broader objective, the improvement of what was very patchy provision for clergy training, especially in the south of Italy.[40] His strategy involved not only a reform of the curriculum, but a concentration of clergy-training in larger seminaries, which had the added benefit of bringing them more directly under Vatican control.[41] The consequence for Della Chiesa was that he was forced, very reluctantly, to agree to Cardinal De Lai's suggestion that a new regional seminary be created to replace the diocesan one.[42] In fact, he would have preferred to concentrate the *convitti* (private hostels for seminarians), into the diocesan seminary, but was forced to amalgamate them and the senior and junior seminary into the regional one.[43] A new seminary required a new building, and therefore new land and more funding. In consequence there were long-drawn-out arguments with the State bureaucracy over the purchase of land vacated by the military[44] and over the investment of monies from the sale of the old seminary,[45] with the result that the new building was not opened until 1915, after Della Chiesa had been elected Pope.

This experience must have brought home even more keenly to Della Chiesa the unsatisfactory nature of Church–State relations in Italy under the Liberal regime. He had given advice to Valfré di Bonzo on how to comport himself with the Italian civil authorities, but he himself had had virtually no dealings with them prior to his appointment to Bologna. Now, suddenly, he came up against them in nearly every aspect of his episcopal ministry. In general terms, the Church in Italy was always under the threat of the introduction of further anti-Church legislation; on the other hand, it remained an 'established' Church in legal terms, thus the local State authorities were able to control many of the financial affairs of the Church,[46] hence the difficulties over the new seminary. Relations with those government departments which dealt with the Church were the bane of any Italian bishop's life. In fact, Della Chiesa had had difficulties with the State authorities in financial matters from the start. The revenues of the diocese (the *mensa*), were in the hands of the Economato Generale, the local office of the Justice Ministry responsible for dealing with Church property and clergy payments. With an eye to the inevitable expense of entering into office, Della Chiesa had asked for an extra five million lire to cover special costs from the outset, and his sharp legal mind saw a justification for this claim in all the money that had gone to the State during the vacancies in the see between 1860 and 1908. But the head of the Economato would not wear this, seeing in Della Chiesa's claim a dangerous precedent for the future which would cause enormous difficulties to his budget. He offered, instead, a loan of three million lire, to be repaid over six years.[47] In his reply, Della Chiesa argued that in any case his *mensa* was not sufficient for the normal running costs of a diocese which was the fourth largest in Italy.[48] Unfortunately, we do not know the final outcome of this battle, but given his training in both civil and as well as canon law, we can be sure that Della Chiesa gave the authorities a run for their money.

Carrying out instructions from Rome was an increasingly essential part of the episcopal routine for the new archbishop. In the *Bollettino Diocesano* of January 1911, he announced the liturgical reforms which Pius X had recently introduced and in particular the most important of them, the exhortation to the laity to take daily Communion issued by the Sacred Congregation of the Consistory.[49] Della Chiesa would undoubtedly have had no difficulty with that decree, but Pius X's strictures on the use of 'secular' music in church, and his demand for the universal re-introduction of Gregorian plainchant must have posed a personal problem for a man who was notoriously tone deaf. Nevertheless, he sought faithfully to implement the Holy See's instructions. This reform was long overdue in the Bologna diocese. The British architectural historian and traveller, T. Francis Bumpus, wrote this of the music played at High Mass in Bologna cathedral on his visit in 1907: 'Between each Kyrie and sentence of the Gloria in Excelsis, Credo etc., the organist played a few bars of trivial music . . . [which] was feeble in the extreme, and quite beneath the dignity of a church which contains the cathedra of a Cardinal Archbishop.'[50] It may well be that, like many another bishop, in this as in other matters, he found that his episcopal authority had limits when cathedral canons were concerned. In a letter to Menzani, his former vicar-general, written in 1915, he complained about the Bologna cathedral clergy, who wanted to change the constitutions of the cathedral and become mitred canons.[51]

Modernists and Christian Democrats

While Della Chiesa immersed himself in the normal work of a diocesan ordinary, he could not avoid the problems which followed him from Rome, in particular, the persecutions of Modernists and Christian Democrats. With his departure, and that of his friend Gasparri, the power of the *integristes* in the Roman Curia had been strengthened and they were extending their campaigns to all the major Italian sees. In this regard, Della Chiesa inherited a very difficult situation when he took over in Bologna. His predecessor, Cardinal Svampa had left behind an uncertain legacy. Svampa was regarded in many circles as pro-Modernist because of his interest in much new biblical and theological scholarship, his hostility to the notorious Scotton brothers, two agents of Benigni operating an *integriste* journal out of Vicenza, and his sympathies with political position of the Christian Democratic leader Don Romolo Murri, who hailed from the Romagna. According to the ecclesiastical historian Penco, Svampa 'nurtured strong sympathies for the most avantgarde element in religious culture and action in Italy, especially in the field of biblical studies'.[52] All this got him into trouble at Rome and according to Lorenzo Bedeschi, Svampa

> emerged from his struggle with Merry Del Val with the certainty that the Secretary of State considered him to be a democrat, and a modernist of a Loisyan stamp. Even worse, he had paid homage to the King [of Italy]. This leads one to suspect that Bologna constituted in these critical years a real preoccupation for the Roman curia . . . But a cardinal is always a cardinal, and as long as Svampa lived an inspection from Rome would have caused a scandal.[53]

On the other hand, apostolic visitations had been made to the Milan diocese without regard to the feelings of its Archbishop, Cardinal Ferrari,[54] and in the interregnum between Svampa's death and the arrival of Della Chiesa, Boggiani, the Vatican's anti-Modernist investigator in central Italy, visited Bologna, albeit unofficially and discreetly, on two occasions. His caution may have been due to the knowledge of Della Chiesa's appointment and a consequent fear of upsetting such a powerful Vatican figure.

There is strong evidence to suggest that in fact it was Della Chiesa who was intended to 'cleanse the augean stables' at Bologna, being sent there precisely for this purpose, even though Merry Del Val may equally well have hoped, and perhaps even expected, that he would fail in this task. The Liberal-Conservative newspaper *Il Giornale d'Italia* believed that Della Chiesa had been sent to clear out the 'nests of heresy'[55] and this was confirmed by Cardinal Pizzardo in his deposition for the beatification of Merry Del Val.[56] Della Chiesa was a papal loyalist, who would never have dreamt of refusing direct orders from the Pope or the Roman Curia, however distasteful. Moreover, he spelt out the need for direct obedience to the Pope in the *Bollettino Diocesano*. He made the subject of his Lenten pastoral for 1910 'The Spirit of Obedience', stressing the need to obey all the Pope's decisions[57] and in December of the same year, he warned that, 'When the faithful hear new doctrines, not in conformity with those approved by the Pope, they should not allow themselves to deceived . . . the Pope has spoken. That is enough.'[58] But in his first pastoral he had also laid down a very sensible, reasonable and predictable approach to the Modernist controversy:

> It is far from my intention to condemn every new form of doctrine, indeed I applaud scientific/scholarly progress wherever it is found . . . but I believe that it is increasingly necessary to test every new theory against 'the sense of the Church', in order to have a secure criterion of acceptability. In the field of the religious sciences there are very often controversies which should not be condemned a priori, because they can lead to a further discovery or to the shedding of greater light on a certain truth. It may happen that the supreme ecclesiastical authority has not yet made a definitive pronouncement on the subject, but even so it may already be obvious that some opinions on that subject are not in conformity with the age-long tradition of the faithful. Vice versa, the Church may not have given a definitive response but does not regard them unfavourably.[59]

This was a remarkably enlightened and progressive viewpoint, and it could not have won him any plaudits in Rome.

The suppression of Modernism clearly was a part of his brief, like that of any other bishop, but the new archbishop was slow and reluctant to execute it, in particular to dismiss people. He told Cardinal De Lai that he was afraid of dividing the clergy into two camps, though this may have been an excuse, a rather bare covering for his continued disagreement with Vatican policy.[60] The first major battle with De Lai was over the diocesan seminary, following the inspection by the apostolic visitor De Lucci, but in the end Della Chiesa was unable to prevent the removal of its rector, Mgr Lodi.[61] And despite the support of Della Chiesa, who had been ordered to keep an eye on the teaching staff, the work of Manaresi, professor of ecclesiastical history, was put on the Index.[62] Another victim of the anti-Modernist purge in Bologna was Don Alessandro Cantono who was strongly influenced by the new ideas of the Germans, the Belgians, the French and the English. In particular, he was 'an open supporter of the application of modern criticism to religious history and of the ideas of Loisy and Lagrange'.[63] A very dangerous man indeed. In another age he might have been burnt at the stake. Not surprisingly, there was little Della Chiesa could do to protect him. Occasionally, Della Chiesa was able to get his own back in his struggles with the *integristes* in the Roman Curia. In September 1911, he wrote to De Lai agreeing to the latter's instructions to ban Duchesne's *History of the Church*, which had fallen under suspicion of 'modernism', but he did not let the opportunity pass without taking a swipe at the inefficient workings of the Curia:

> You will permit me to add the hope that the Sacred Congregation of the Consistory should never again have to prohibit a work that has already received the imprimatur of the Master of the Sacred Palaces, not only in the original text, but also in the Italian version. We poor bishops have to work very hard to persuade our priests and people of the utility of maintaining an institution whose head, not once but several times, has demonstrated himself incapable of guaranteeing the integrity of doctrine . . .[64]

Ironically, Della Chiesa had more success in his efforts to defend the clergy of the neighbouring dioceses of his suffragans from the wrath of Rome. With his knowledge of canon law, and the procedures of the ecclesiastical courts, Della Chiesa was particularly effective in defending Don Ravaglia, whom Boggiani had been instrumental in removing from the seminary at Cesena in 1907. In 1909, Ravaglia was accused of semi-heretical opinions on 'evolution and the human science of Jesus', but Della Chiesa agreed with him that he was being judged on opinions he had expressed before the Church had made a definitive judgement on the matter. According to Bedeschi, 'Della Chiesa absolved him with the greatest of equanimity from the sin of heresy for having expressed those opinions'.[65] And when Ravaglia's bishop, Mgr Cazzani, stood his ground in the campaign being conducted against him, and refused to admit the inspection by another apostolic visitor, Della Chiesa supported him, to the extent that when Ravaglia's opponent, Ghino, took his case against him to Rome, Della Chiesa used powerful friends in the Holy Office, presumably Rampolla, to find out if there was a file on Ravaglia there.[66]

On 19 October 1907, the editor of *La Fiaccola*, a local Catholic weekly, had written of the newly appointed Archbishop: 'His appointment has given rise to the most diverse opinions: some papers have called him a "Modernist-eater" while others have described him as [a] very able and prudent man.'[67] 'The others' were, of course, right. In a letter the next day, Della Chiesa wrote to the editor, thanking him for his 'sincere, reverent and affectionate' welcome, and assuring him that he 'had not come to Bologna as a "Modernist-eater" but with the hope of helping all his future spiritual children to save their souls'.[68] That he sincerely and stubbornly tried to do so is evidenced by the fact that on the eve of the outbreak of the First World War, along with Cardinals Maffi of Pisa, Richelmy of Turin and Ferrari of Milan, he was regarded in Rome as being 'soft' on Modernism.[69] As a result, he came under attack from the *integristes*. According to Peters, after his election, Della Chiesa actually found a denunciation of himself for Modernism in the papers of his deceased predecessor.[70] In their zeal to root out Modernist heresy and protect the faithful from its poison, the *integristes* turned their guns on Italy's growing, lay-controlled Catholic newspapers. In particular, they attacked the Catholic newspapers in Turin, Milan, Genoa and Bologna, and had the audacity to criticize the archbishops of those cities for failing to condemn them. Della Chiesa hit back very hard in a cogent and sensible letter.[71] As the American historian, Webster, points out: 'they [the *integristes*] made the one serious mistake of attacking a cardinal who was eminently *papabile*. When Pius X died suddenly in 1914 Cardinal Giacomo Della Chiesa of Bologna, a constant target of *integriste* enmity, was elected to succeed him as Benedict XV; the *integristes* never recovered.'[72]

The bitter battles over Modernism were not the only problem to follow Della Chiesa from Rome to Bologna. Democratic tendencies were the other great bugbear of the Roman Curia during the pontificate of Pius X and they tended to be seen as going hand in hand with Modernism. In some cases this was actually true, most notably in that of Don Romolo Murri, with the result that the movement he led, Christian Democracy, was regarded as tainted with the Modernist 'heresy' even though other leaders like Don Luigi Sturzo were innocent of such offence. In 1904, Pius X and his collaborators in the Roman Curia decided to kill three birds with one stone. They dissolved the Opera dei Congressi, the umbrella for the various organizations of the Catholic social and political movement in Italy, thus putting an end to the squabbles between the two conflicting wings of the Italian Catholic lay movement – Christian Democracy and the clerico-moderates. They also effectively isolated Murri and the Christian Democrats, and brought the Catholic movement under closer Vatican and episcopal oversight. The problems which this caused for the bishops, especially those in the Romagna, were enormous, for that region was the very stronghold of the Christian Democratic movement.

Della Chiesa's attitude towards the Christian Democrats prior to the outbreak of the First World War is difficult to ascertain. He may well have regarded the social reformism of the movement as too radical, and in a letter to Menzani, regarding a mutual acquaintance in 1920, he wrote: 'As far as the socialists are concerned, I would like to whisper in Don Corinto's ear that there was a time when he was close to the dens of the Christian Democrats, step-brothers of the socialists.'[73] And according to Molinari, Della Chiesa was appointed to Bologna to 'hammer the newly-born Democrazia Cristiana' movement.[74] This is entirely plausible, but other evidence suggests that in fact the new Archbishop was by no means hostile towards the movement and its leader. Gabriele De Rosa, the doyen of historians of the Catholic movement in Italy, for instance, says that Della Chiesa 'had strong sympathies for Murri, the orthodox Murri, that is . . . the points of conflict with the Murriani were their fierce independence [of the ecclesiastical hierarchy], their ardent Interventionism [i.e. support for Italy's intervention in the First World War in 1915, author's note] and the philo-socialism of Murri himself'.[75] Della Chiesa's actual involvement in battles over the Christian Democrats were few in number. One, the classic example of a man condemned twice – once for Modernism and a second time for advanced Christian Democratic ideas – is that of Don Ravaglia, who as well as teaching in the seminary was the parish priest of the cathedral in Cesena and involved in the Christian Democratic journal, *Il Savio*. This was criticized by Rome's apostolic visitor as 'motivated by a socialist spirit as far as economic and social questions are concerned'.[76] Della Chiesa did not agree with the severity of Bishop Cazzani's attitude to *Il Savio* – the latter regarded it as a mortal sin to read the newspaper – or his hostile attitude towards the Christian Democratic organization, the Lega Democratica Nazionale. According to Bedeschi, 'Mgr Della Chiesa, on the other hand, with a typically spirited pun [on the name of the newspaper], in order to avoid having to make a judgement called him [Ravaglia] "poco savio" [not very wise]'.[77]

As Zangheri explains, even though the leading Christian Democratic journal was published in Bologna:

> Christian Democracy never developed very strongly in the capital of Emilia-Romagna. Rather, Bologna, of all the cities of Emilia-Romagna, turned a deaf ear to the movement, despite the fact that a number of priests and young laymen, like Giuseppe Bertini, had conducted a veritable campaign of cultural renewal . . . for the supporters of Murri in 1907 Bologna remained a predominantly conservative city.[78]

That was a major part of the problem that presented itself to Della Chiesa when he arrived in Bologna. The conflict between on the one hand, the Christian Democratic supporters of *La Fiaccola*, which condemned the Liberal-Conservative bourgeoisie (and blamed their government for all the strikes in Italy), and on the other the conservative Catholics represented by the daily newspaper *L'Avvenire d'Italia*, was so bitter and open that it constituted a veritable scandal to the Catholic cause. When the *integristes* turned the screw on Catholic newspapers not entirely in conformity with their high standards of orthodoxy, Della Chiesa even came under pressure to sack the editor of *L'Avvenire*, Rocco D'Adria. D'Adria eventually left, and it is not clear whether he resigned voluntarily or whether he was forced to do so by Della Chiesa. This action, and the passage of the newspaper into the ownership of the Trust, a big newspaper company controlled by the clerico-moderate notable Count Grosoli and his friends in the Catholic Banco di Roma, still did not solve the problem. Writing to De Lai in 1912, Della Chiesa told the Secretary to the Congregation of the Council that he had not been happy with the editorial policy of *L'Avvenire* and had told them so. They promised to change. Everyone in Bologna knew this. But he could not suddenly switch his support to the ultra-conservative, *integriste* mouthpiece *L'Unità Cattolica* of Florence.[79]

Politics, socialism and the 'Social Question'

Leaving aside the problems with Christian Democracy, it was difficult for Italian bishops in the early twentieth century to avoid being involved in some way or another in politics, and Della Chiesa was no exception. Under the dominating personality of Giovanni Giolitti, Italian politics in this period was one of relative stability after the tempests of the previous 'End of Century Crisis'; indeed, 1903 to 1914 was dubbed 'the Giolittian era', thanks to the political skill of the Piedmontese statesman. It was also a period of increasing collaboration between Catholics and the Liberal-Conservative ruling élite of which Giolitti was the leading figure. After 1904, the clerico-moderate alliances which had became so widespread at a local level in various parts of northern Italy, also became a feature of national politics. From the 1904 general

47

elections onwards, Pius X made relaxations of the *non expedit* decree, which allowed increasing numbers of Catholics not only to vote in parliamentary elections but also to stand as candidates. The process was carefully controlled through the Church-sponsored Unione Elettorale, and in 1913 not only were thirty Catholics elected to Parliament but following the introduction of universal adult male suffrage, and thanks to the so-called 'pact' between Giolitti and the leader of the Unione, Count Gentiloni, hundreds of thousands of Catholic votes saved the Liberal-Conservative majority from an upsurge in support for the Socialists.[80]

Despite his intransigent misgivings, Della Chiesa was obliged to condone the increasing closeness between local Catholic politicians and their Liberal-Conservative counterparts: according to Zangheri, 'From the political point of view, the clerico-moderate strategy of Della Chiesa was unequivocal.'[81] In fact, he had very little choice in the matter: both the Vatican and his own laity pushed him in that direction. On the other hand, he did not always accept the Liberal candidates endorsed by the Unione Elettorale. In 1913, for example, he refused to give his support to Alberto Bergamini, the editor of the *Giornale d'Italia*, with the result that the revolutionary socialist Enrico Ferri was elected in the suburban San Giovanni in Persiceto constituency.[82] Again according to Zangheri, under the leadership of the Catholic newspaper *L'Avvenire*, now owned by Grosoli's Trust, 'opposition to Socialism became the chief, if not the exclusive, orientation of the Catholic laity of Bologna'.[83]

But the concern about Socialism was also genuinely Della Chiesa's concern and that of his clergy. In the period leading to the outbreak of the First World War, the Marxist-orientated Italian Socialist Party, and the allied network of trade unions, peasant leagues and co-operatives, was extending its influence in Emilia-Romagna as elsewhere in Italy; and as it did so, it sought to build a comprehensive counter-culture to that of the Church, using the *case del popolo* and the *circoli operai* (social centres for workers and their families), to provide a whole range of facilities, including theatrical and musical associations, crèches and cheap restaurants, to serve the worker and his family in competition with the Catholic parish.[84] In its definitive form, this culture was characterized by all manner of secular events and heroes to contest the public demonstrations of Catholic piety and loyalty, particularly the celebration of local saints.[85]

As bishops and local clergy in different parts of Italy pointed out at this time, these practical expressions of militant anticlericalism were a crucial factor in the decline in religious observance and loyalty to the Church.[86] Closer to home, at the Bologna diocesan Catechetical Congress, Don Armando Nascetti denounced the work of the Socialists:

> Is it not clear what this widespread anti-clerical campaign is aiming at? Its chief aim is to draw away children, parents and the people from Christian Teaching. Dear brothers, you know better than me that the recent violent agitations [of the Socialists] is a perfect example. You know only too well that at Parma [a notorious Socialist stronghold] a few weeks ago the national congress of Socialist Youth agreed to undertake an incessant anti-clerical and anti-religious propaganda campaign, establishing reading rooms, and distributing newspapers and books in order to rob God, the Church and the priest of young people, and with their revolutionary spirit, also to destroy the social order.[87]

In fact, the Socialist penetration of Emilia-Romagna had already borne its bitter fruits for the Church: according to Albertazzi, in 1906, 'Mgr Trebbioli was appointed bishop of Imola to halt the abandonment of traditional religion'.[88] Agrarian socialism was widespread and well-organized in Imola (part of Bologna province).

There were also serious problems in Della Chiesa's own diocese. According to Sauro Onofri: 'The agricultural area of the plains was almost completely "red". The success (of the Socialists) in the hill area was modest, while in the high Appenines, the Bolognese "Vendee", Socialism was almost unknown.'[89] The record of the pastoral visitations conducted by Della Chiesa confirms the accuracy of this picture. In the diary entries for the parishes of the plain, we repeatedly find such reports as 'a small number of faithful present, few communicants',[90] 'lots of women, few men'[91] and 'only a few WOMEN were present in church'.[92] This classic pattern of 'dechristianization' was, however, largely confined to the parishes of the plain, where agrarian socialism had taken strongest root. Typical of the situation which he encountered here was this entry in the diary for the visit to the parish of San Giorgio in Panigale: 'Returned to Bologna . . . with a painful impression of the religious conditions in this populous village, which has demonstrated itself not so much hostile to the Archbishop, as indifferent.'[93] Only very rarely was the chaplain able to record the following: 'One hundred and forty-two faithful communicated, a large number considering that in this place, as unfortunately in others, Socialist theories have dechristianized so many families.'[94] Working people were not only deserting regular Mass and Communion, they sometimes abandoned the 'rites of passage' too. In the Romagna, as in France, there was a veritable cult of the 'secular funeral'. As a result, tensions between the working-class movement and the Church could very easily surface at funerals. In Bologna, in 1905, the police reported the case of a young member of the bricklayers' union, killed in a accident, who was given a religious funeral: when the priest arrived at the funeral parlour the man's Socialist comrades abandoned the procession and one of them delivered an oration outside the church in which he declared that 'the presence of the priests and members of the Catholic associations had defiled the body of the worker'.[95]

Della Chiesa and his clergy refused to be intimidated: in a letter to his vicar-general in 1913, he referred to 'the great number of socialists in the parish of Zappoluni, whose parish priest set to work with clenched teeth'.[96] Della Chiesa also used the *Bollettino Diocesano* to condemn the concept and practice of class struggle, a coded way of attacking Socialism, but perhaps also the more militant Christian Democrats.[97] On the 'social question', he continued to take a fairly conventional, traditional stand. Thus in his Lenten pastoral letter of 1909, he addressed himself to 'servants': 'You servants must recognise in your masters over and beyond the human qualities which they have in common with you, the providence of God. Thus, you must accept willingly the decrees of Divine providence which has established distinctions between masters and servants, rich and poor, nobles and plebians.'[98] This paternalistic attitude was common to even the most 'social' of Italian bishops at the time, including Cardinal Ferrari of Milan.[99] Taking this stand, however, did not mean that he was necessarily out of sympathy with the demands of the lower classes. In his 1913 pastoral letter, for example, he laid much stress upon the equal origins of rich and poor.[100] And during his first year in office, that is 1908, he joined with his fellow bishops in a 'collective letter' specifically addressed to the problem of the agrarian struggles that had erupted in Emilia-Romagna at that time. In this letter, the bishops declared themselves to be above and beyond 'the struggles between the various classes by nature of their ministry', but they omitted the usual, indiscriminate condemnation of socialism and recognized the legitimacy of the right of class organization, a courageous stand in view of the threatened denunciation of all, even Catholic trade unions, by the Vatican under Pius X.[101]

During 'Red Week' in June 1914, there was spontaneous and widespread rioting, with churches and landowners' houses attacked, in Emilia-Romagna and neighbouring regions following a so-called 'proletarian massacre' (i.e. a police shooting of working-class demonstrators), which was a clear sign of Giolitti's failure to reconcile the working-class movement with the Italian State. The situation in Bologna was especially tense. Following earlier trade union demonstrations, attended by some violence, supporters of the working-class movement were eventually hounded through the streets and beaten: even *L'Avvenire* protested at this 'white' reaction.[102] It was to this still unsettled situation that Della Chiesa returned after his investiture as a Cardinal in Rome. In his sermon in the welcoming ceremony at the cathedral on 14 June, only a couple of days after the worst incidents, the new Cardinal prayed that, 'the Lord will never again allow in our Bologna the anxieties and the sorrows of recent days . . .'[103]

Cardinal

Along with seven other Italian archbishoprics – Turin, Florence, Rome (the Pope's vicar), Palermo, Naples, Venice and Milan –

Bologna was traditionally a 'cardinalatial' see, that is its head was almost invariably awarded the red hat. But it was almost seven years before Della Chiesa received his. While it is true that Archbishop Mistrangelo of Florence had to wait even longer,[104] the failure to promote Della Chiesa is inexplicable except in terms of a powerful blocking lobby in the Roman Curia. The same reasons which had motivated the desire of Merry Del Val, De Lai and others to remove Della Chiesa from the Vatican almost certainly also played a part in the delay in awarding the title of cardinal. An added worry for his enemies in the Vatican might have been the fear that, following his entry into the Sacred College of Cardinals, Della Chiesa would have 'ganged' up with Rampolla and constituted the core of an influential bloc working against the policies of the *integristes*. Even Peters admits: 'That Merry Del Val and Della Chiesa disagreed sharply on integralism, was no secret to their contemporaries.'[105]

MacNutt suggests that the issue had become a public scandal by 1914, with Bolognese citizens making their views heard in no uncertain way in Rome.[106] Finally, Della Chiesa's vicar-general took the matter into his hands: 'On 8 November 1913 Menzani was received in audience by Pope Pius X and explained with insistent frankness the widely felt aspiration of the Bolognesi that their Archbishop should be honoured with the cardinalatial purple. Pius X is alleged to have commented, "This Vicar General is truly terrible!".'[107] In the Consistory of May Pius X announced the name of Della Chiesa among a list of new cardinals, though Shane Leslie insists that even at this late stage the Pope had been obliged to insert the Archbishop of Bologna's name in pencil, such was the opposition of his Cardinal Secretary of State.[108]

Just how general the feeling was that Della Chiesa had for too long, and unjustly, been deprived of the red hat is demonstrated in this letter of congratulation which Cardinal Gasparri sent to his friend upon his elevation to the Sacred College:

Monsignore, dear friend,
A million congratulations. I am so happy to have you *finally* [his italics] as a colleague. I already knew after the last Consistory, but

the Holy Father swore me to secrecy, a difficult secret to keep because I would have been so happy to assure our friends who were awaiting the event with impatience. How delighted poor Cardinal Rampolla, who loved you so much, would have been!

Affectionate greetings and I hope to embrace you soon in Rome,

Pietro Card. Gasparri.[109]

Merry Del Val, despite his persistent opposition to Della Chiesa's elevation, in the official announcement which he sent as Secretary of State on behalf of the Pope wrote this to Della Chiesa in his own, exquisite hand: 'To this very happy announcement, which I communicate to you on behalf of His Holiness, I add my own satisfaction and my warmest congratulations and wishes, with which I greet your imminent entry into the Sacred College.'[110] Whatever feelings this letter aroused in Della Chiesa, on 28 May he was clothed with the insignia of his new status and two days later he was installed as the titular of the ancient church of i Santi Quattro Coronati. To all this joy must have been added some sadness: his friend and benefactor, Cardinal Rampolla, had died six months before. He had not had the satisfaction of seeing his protégé receive his long-overdue reward.

By the time Della Chiesa left Bologna to attend the conclave, his ministry there had been characterized by two major traits, charity and firmness. According to Mgr Comastri, *parroco* of the city parish of S. Isaia: 'Oh, the heart-felt generosity of that man! It is impossible to calculate the help which he gave to the poor, to needy families and to charitable institutions.'[111] The generosity towards 'his' Bolognesi, lay and clerical, was to continue during his pontificate, even when he was faced by much larger, more global calls on his purse.[112] His firm government was equally well known. According to Veneruso: 'His lack of previous pastoral experience did not prevent him from presiding over the complex world of Emilia-Romagna with tact and firmess.'[113] But perhaps the most impressive tribute to Della Chiesa's achievements at Bologna comes from an unexpected source, the Liberal-Conservative *La Stampa* newspaper of Turin:

He was neither a political intriguer, nor a small or great elector. He was not only respectful of the political authorities but also of the House of Savoy, with whom he occasionally came into contact, but he was also devoted, like any other citizen, to the civil authorities, even those who were contrary to his opinions. Della Chiesa showed energy, firmness, infinite charity and passion in doing good, opportune changes of policy, courage in healing evil. In University circles, where the Jacobin flame of Giosuè Carducci still glowed, and in a city which rises not very far from the revolutionary and anti-papal Romagna, Della Chiesa enjoyed the respect of all and love of many . . .'[114]

Bologna was another formative experience for Della Chiesa. It was his first experience of sole authority and, accordingly, sole responsibility. The place and the job made the man. In particular, it gave him an unparalleled opportunity to manage men, in large numbers. Also, his notorious modesty and shyness began to fade. He acquired, indeed he was obliged to acquire, real confidence and assurance, especially in crowds. The pastoral visitations must have seen to that. The photographs of him just before and after his elevation to cardinal still do not do him justice; the one which *L'Avvenire* printed of him after his election as Pope was probably the worst. But by 1914 he was a very different man from the one who had entered Bologna less than seven years earlier.

Notes and references

1. *The European*, 22–24 March 1991.
2. Zangheri, p. 66.
3. Rhodes (1983), p. 12; Zangheri, p. 76.
4. Rhodes (1983), p. 75.
5. Zangheri, p. 91.
6. D'Azeglio.
7. Pollard (1997), p. 165.
8. Cardoza, p. 12.
9. Ibid., p. 97.
10. Ibid.
11. Veneruso (1982), p. 33.

12. ACS, MI, DG Affari di Culto, 'Placet et Exequatur', Bologna, Procura del Re, 4 January 1908.
13. AFDC, Lettere e Scritti Vari, pastorale del 10 January 1908.
14. AFDC, Lettere e Scritti Vari, pastorali.
15. Peters, p. 59.
16. Albertazzi, p. 984.
17. Peters, p. 59; this is confirmed by Monti, in *Diario*, II, 3 July 1918, p. 348.
18. Peters, ibid.
19. AFDC, Lettere e Scritti Vari, letter to Mgr Vincenzo Sardi, 11 January 1909.
20. Peters, p. 61.
21. Molinari, p. 412.
22. Ibid.
23. AFDC, Discorsi per le visite pastorali.
24. Ibid., discorso per la visita alla parocchia di S. Martino (no date).
25. Ibid.
26. Archivio Arcivescovile di Bologna (henceforth AAB), 'Diario delle Visite Pastorali di S.E.R. Mons. Giacomo Della Chiesa, Arcivescovo' (henceforth diary), p. 186.
27. Ibid., p. 98.
28. Ibid., p. 186.
29. Pollard (1997), p. 167.
30. AFDC, Lettere e Scritti Vari, 'Atti del Congresso Eucharistico Diocesano', 16–18 November 1909, p. 30.
31. *Bollettino Diocesano* (henceforth *BD*), Anno 1, no. 3, December 1910.
32. Ravaglia.
33. Vistalli, p. 124, where he quotes Mgr Comastri, incumbent of the Bologna parish of S. Isaia.
34. Kertzer, p. 186.
35. Binchy, pp. 389–92.
36. Ibid., p. 186.
37. *BD*, Anno 1, no. 3, December 1910, p. 97.
38. The decrees *Pieni L'animo* of 1906, the *Programma generale di studi* of 1907, and the *Norme per l'ordinamento educativo e disciplinare* of 1908; Falconi, p. 24.
39. *BD*, Anno 1, no. 3, December 1910, pp. 97–8.
40. Pollard (1997), p. 164.
41. Guasco, p. 689.
42. Bedeschi (1967), p. 222.
43. For an account of this episode, see ibid., pp. 337–42.
44. ACS, MI, DG Affari di Culto, 'Placet et Exequatur', letter to the Procura del Re, 17 October 1911.

45. Ibid., letter of 27 March 1914 and also Pollard (1997), pp. 160 & 162.
46. ACS, DG Affari di Culto, 'Placet et Exequatur', Bologna, 24 February 1908.
47. Ibid., letter of 29 March 1908.
48. *BD*, Anno 2, no. 4, January 1911.
49. Peters, p. 61.
50. Bumpus, p. 202.
51. Molinari, letter of 3 May 1915.
52. Penco, p. 493.
53. Bedeschi (1967), p. 214.
54. Falconi, p. 105.
55. *La Stampa*, 7 October 1907.
56. Falconi, p. 40, where he cites page 344 of the papers.
57. *BD*, Anno 1, no. 3, December 1910, p. 109.
58. AFDC, Lettere e Scritti Vari, pastorale per la quaresima, 1910.
59. Ibid., 10 February 1908.
60. Bedeschi (1966), pp. 337–42.
61. Ibid., p. 216.
62. Ibid., p. 221.
63. Ibid., p. 224.
64. Bedeschi (1968), p. 371.
65. Bedeschi (1967), pp. 206–7. After his election to the papal throne, Della Chiesa had Cazzani translated to Cremona, a much bigger diocese than Cesena.
66. Ibid., p. 174.
67. AFDC, Lettere e Scritti Vari, memorandum of 19 October 1907.
68. Ibid.
69. Molinari, p. 135.
70. Peters, p. 25.
71. Ibid., p. 50.
72. Webster, p. 21.
73. Molinari, p. 433.
74. Ibid.
75. De Rosa (1977), p. 475.
76. Bedeschi (1967), p. 77.
77. Ibid., p. 182.
78. Zangheri, p. 85.
79. Bedeschi (1967), p. 104.
80. Clark, pp. 157–8.
81. Zangheri, p. 98: Sauro Onofri, p. 131, says that the Mayor of Bologna, Zanardi, refused to commemorate the election of Della Chiesa as Pope in 1914 because, 'the new Pope was one of the chief founders of the anti-Socialist campaign'.

82. *Diario*, II, pp. 192–3, n. 277.
83. Zangheri, p. 98.
84. Pollard (1997), p. 167.
85. Howard Bell, p. 47.
86. Pollard (1997), p. 165, where the cases of Milan and Turin are cited.
87. *BD*, Anno 1, no. 3, 1910, pp. 64–5.
88. Albertazzi, p. 890.
89. Sauro Onofri, p. 131.
90. AAB, diary, p. 483, Buda and p. 560, Bagno di Piano.
91. Ibid., p. 582, Vedrara.
92. Ibid., p. 34, Molinella.
93. Ibid., p. 345, San Giorgio in Panigale.
94. Ibid., p. 295, Calderara di Reno.
95. ACS, MI, DG Pubblica Sicurezza, fasc. 11, Bologna, report of 30 September 1905.
96. Molinari, letter of 13 August 1913.
97. *BD*, Anno 1, no. 3, 1910, p. 109.
98. AFDC, Lettere e Scritti Vari, pastorale, 'Spirito di Fede', quaresima, 1909.
99. Pollard (1997), p. 169.
100. AFDC, Lettere e Scritti Vari, pastorale, 'Spirito di Carità', quaresima, 1913.
101. As quoted in Albertazzi, p. 158.
102. Sauro Onofri, p. 33.
103. *BD*, IV, 1 July 1914, 7, p. 397.
104. Scattigno (1977), p. 213.
105. Peters, p. 67; MacNutt, p. 313.
106. MacNutt, p. 313.
107. Molinari, p. 413.
108. Leslie, p. 94.
109. AFDC, Lettere inviate a S.E. Cardinale Giacomo Della Chiesa (no date).
110. Ibid. This file also contains a letter of congratulations from Emperor Franz Josef.
111. As quoted in Vistalli, p. 19.
112. Molinari, pp. 421–2.
113. Veneruso (1982), p. 33. See also Falconi, p. 110, for an evaluation of Della Chiesa's ministry in Bologna.
114. *La Stampa*, 4 September 1914.

3

Pope

Pius X died on 21 August 1914. Though advanced in years, and plagued by gout, he had not suffered from conspicuously bad health in recent times. The medical diagnosis was pneumonia, a common enough cause of death among old people in those days. But pious contemporaries, and some historians and biographers, have claimed that it was a broken heart, broken by the outbreak of the terrible war which he had repeatedly predicted – *il guerrone*.[1] Others have claimed that he and his Secretary of State, Cardinal Merry Del Val, helped precipitate the war by badly advising Franz Josef that Austria was in the right and should humble Serbia.[2] A little later, Merry Del Val rebutted these claims:

> It is true that after the atrocious crime of Sarajevo I told Count Palffy [Secretary to the Austrian Legation to the Holy See] that Austria should stand firm, that she had every right to substantial reparations, and the right to safeguard her existence, but I never expressed the hope or opinion that Austria should have recourse to arms. I never said anything else.[3]

While this certainly proves that he had not encouraged Austrian bellicosity, it does not suggest either that he realized the full gravity of the situation or that he tried very hard to prevent the outbreak of a war. If one is to attribute any blame at all to the Holy See for the outbreak of war then it would be for its lack of information about the international situation and its inadequate efforts to ameliorate it.[4] In fact, Pius X and Merry Del Val had little in the way of diplomatic leverage with which to play a peace-making role in the summer of 1914. Not only did Pius X's death leave the Church leaderless at a very difficult time and in a condition of internal division as a result of the struggles over 'Modernism', it also left it in a situation of external isolation as well. Following the rupture with France, the Holy See enjoyed relations with only three major powers – Austria, Prussia and Russia – two or three minor Catholic powers in Europe – Spain, Belgium and Bavaria – and a clutch of South American republics. Not since the death of Pius IX in 1878 had the Catholic Church possessed so little influence on the international scene as in August 1914.[5]

The conclave

This was the situation in which the Vatican found itself when the college of cardinals met in conclave to elect Pius X's successor in September 1914. Furthermore, as Alberto Monticone has pointed out, the First World War was a battle between two 'opposing cultures, economies, politico-social models on the basis of which the decisive armed confrontation had been prepared for years'.[6] As became clear in the conclave, these conflicts in the secular world could not be prevented from affecting the Church as well. A leading Catholic journalist of the time, Ernesto Vercesi, described in his memoirs the meeting in the Vatican of the Belgian Cardinal Mercier of Malines and the German Cardinal Hartmann of Cologne: 'I hope,' said Hartmann, 'that we shall not speak of war.' 'And I hope that we shall not speak of peace,' came back the sharp reply.[7] More serious than this anecdotal evidence is the fact that as the conclave opened, German Catholics, inspired no doubt by their government, presented a declaration to the cardinal electors (ironically written in French), justifying their government's decision to go to war.[8] Inevitably, French-Belgian Catholics felt obliged to send a counter-message.[9] Whatever the merits of each of these apologias, they represented in the starkest form the profound divisions which the war had created in Catholic Europe. And as the conclave progressed, the war inevitably weighed heavily upon the minds of individual participants: the French cardinal Louis

Billot learnt of the deaths of two nephews while immured in the conclave.[10] Cardinal Piffl, Archbishop of Vienna, recorded the progress of the terrible battle of Lemberg between the Austro-Hungarian and Russian armies in his diary of the conclave which, written in strict violation of Pius X's new rules about secrecy, provides us with a very accurate and precise description of events in the Vatican in September 1914.[11]

The international situation thus had a profound bearing upon the progress of the conclave. It made the election of a non-Italian Pope, not a strong possibility in any case, even less likely because eighteen out of the 31 non-Italian cardinals belonged to one or other of the two opposing sides in the war.[12] Of the remainder, the three United States cardinals, the Canadian and Brazilian cardinals had only the slimmest of chances of being elected because of their lack of contacts in Rome, not to mention their inability to reach the Vatican before the conclave opened. Begin of Quebec, O'Connell of Boston and Gibbons of Baltimore just arrived in time to hear the announcement of the result (Farley of New York happened to be in Switzerland and was therefore able to reach Rome in time for the conclave). Only the five Spaniards had any serious chance of providing the first non-Italian Pope for nearly four hundred years; the last had been the Dutchman, Hadrian VI (1522–3). The fact that Italy had remained neutral in the conflagration which broke out in August 1914 obviously strengthened the chances that the centuries-old pattern would not be broken and that one of the majority Italian contingent – 34 out of a total of 65 – would be elected. Even then, those Italians who had served in the capitals of one or other of the belligerent powers, like Ferrata (Paris) and Agliardi (Munich and Vienna) were also effectively disqualified on those grounds. Not surprisingly, there are some signs of attempts by foreign governments to affect the outcome of the conclave. According to Cardinal Piffl's diary, Cardinal Hartmann of Cologne tried to dissuade the other cardinals of the Central Powers (Germany and Austro-Hungary) from supporting Della Chiesa on the grounds that not only would his election be an insult to the memory of Pius X but that he was 'of a violent character' and above all was a supporter of Rampolla's policies which, of course, had been anti-German.[13] There is no evidence of French government attempts to influence the voting of the French cardinals: given the Church–State tensions in France, they would not have cut much ice any way. The Austrian foreign minister did warn the cardinals of the Habsburg Monarchy not to vote for either Della Chiesa because he was Rampollite or for Ferrata because he was pro-French, but to support instead Serafini who was a pious man who would continue the late Pope's policies.[14] On the other hand, there was no danger that the Austrian 'veto' of 1903 would be repeated in the conclave of 1914. That was ruled out by Pius X's apostolic constitution of 1904, according to which the traditional right of veto of the Austrian, French and Spanish rulers was permanently abolished.

But it would be wrong to believe that the international situation was the sole or even major factor influencing the outcome of the 1914 conclave; the internal condition of the Church itself, and in particular the bitter, painful question of the anti-Modernist crusade hung over the deliberations of the cardinals. Thus, as well as an international divide, a deep fissure over the issue of Modernism ran through the conclave. The major defenders of the policy of the former pontificate were to be found, predictably, in the powerful phalanx of curial cardinals, Billot, De Lai, Merry Del Val, etc., while the opposition was chiefly formed by the cardinal archbishops of Italian residential sees, like Della Chiesa, Maffi and Richelmy: for obvious reasons, the resident, curial cardinals tended to have a powerful influence on any conclave. It has been claimed that in the late nineteenth and early twentieth centuries, each pontificate represented a profound reversal of its predecessor – the conciliatorist Leo XIII followed the intransigent Pius IX and the integralist Pius X followed the liberal Leo XIII.[15] Would the pattern be repeated in the outcome of the 1914 conclave, or would a candidate be found to carry on the anti-Modernist crusade and Pius X's policies towards France?

The bewilderment expressed by Cardinal Gibbons when he heard the news of the election of Della Chiesa is symptomatic of the lack of public knowledge of the cardinal from Bologna.[16] It helps explain why, in most studies of the 1914 conclave, Giacomo Della

Chiesa's election has been interpreted as the result of a late or even last-minute compromise following the failure of more 'serious', well-known candidates to defeat one another.[17] Most of the these same sources present quite conflicting accounts of the way the voting went, and get it wrong. Seldes, for example, wrote, 'Benedict was elected on the sixteenth ballot . . . with the formidable vote of fifty out of the fifty-seven participants.'[18] It is now clear, however, that Della Chiesa was a front-runner from the start, and moreover that he was the only candidate who consistently increased his vote in every ballot, except for a hiccough in the fifth round (see the voting table). Apart from Maffi, the only other serious candidates were Pompilj, the Vicar of Rome, who was probably regarded as a moderate *integriste*, and Merry Del Val who was the preferred candidate of the curial, Pius X faction. Serafini, a Benedictine, was only really taken up by the curialists as a sort of stop-gap 'frontman', when it became clear that neither Merry Del Val nor Pompilj could defeat Della Chiesa.[19] If anyone was intended as a compromise candidate then it was Serafini and not Della Chiesa, for the latter's candidacy was viewed as a break with the policies of the previous pontificate in respect to both Modernism and France, and a return to those of Rampolla and Leo XIII.

Indeed, the conclave was characterized from the start by attempts to head off victory for the cardinal of Bologna. As we have seen, Hartmann campaigned against him from the outset, as did the Austrian government. We know that an attempt was also made by the curial cardinal Agliardi, supporter of Archbishop Maffi of Pisa, to deny votes to Della Chiesa. He sought to convince the Austro-Hungarian cardinals that Della Chiesa was *mediocris homo* ('a mediocrity'), 'a mere bureaucrat', whereas, he claimed, Maffi was, by contrast, a man of conspicuous intelligence and ability.[20] On the last ballot, which gave Della Chiesa the requisite two-thirds majority, it was the turn of the supporters of the curial candidates, Merry Del Val and Serafini, to fight dirty: Cardinal De Lai, the curial 'popemaker' demanded that the Pope-elect's ballot paper be checked to ensure that he had not voted for himself (as was laid down in the rules of the conclave). It may be that De Lai genuinely thought that Della Chiesa had voted for himself, in which case this would have invalidated his election, but it seems more likely that De Lai, in grudging acceptance of the inevitable, wished both to humiliate Della Chiesa and to fire a warning shot across the Pope-elect's bows to demonstrate the continuing power of the Roman Curia. It could well have been humiliating for Della Chiesa – it may have brought back memories of being *il piccoletto* and of his marginalization after 1903. But he endured it stoically and was not, as we shall see, intimidated. As one of the scrutineers, Della Chiesa himself read all the ballot papers, checking each one of them for the Latin tag which identified who had cast it.[21] When he had finished, and thus established incontrovertibly that he had not voted for himself, he returned to his seat and awaited the call to accept election. What a moral victory, what a comeback for the Leonines and Rampollites!

Voting Results of the 1914 Conclave

(N.B. There were usually four ballots per day.)

	1 September				2 September				3 September	
Maffi	12	16	16	15	13	7	2	–		
Della Chiesa	12	16	18	21	20	27	31	32	34	38
Pompilj	9	10	9	9	6	2	–	–		
Merry Del Val	7	7	7	6	2	–	–	–		
Serafini	4	2	2	2	10	17	21	21	22	18
Ferrata	2	2	1	1						
Bacilieri	–	–	2	1	1	–	–	–		
Gasparri	1	–	–	–						
Falconio	1	–	–	–						
Agliardi	1	–	–	–						
Ferrari	1	–	–	–						
Gotti	1	–	–	–						
De Lai	1	–	–	–						
Richelmy	–	1	2	1	1	1	1	1	1	1
Francia Nava	1	–	–	–	1	1	1	1	1	1
Van Rossum	1	–	–	–						

(*Source*: C. Zizola, *Il Conclave: Storia e segreto* (Roma, 1993), p. 194, based on Piffl's diary.)

The election of Della Chiesa in 1914 can be attributed to a number of factors, but the most important of them was the fact that of all the serious candidates – Maffi, Pompilj, Merry Del Val, Serafini and himself – he had easily the best mix of the curial, diplomatic and pastoral experience required of a Pope facing the horrors of general European war, and the difficulties and uncertainties which it presented for the Church. Maffi's career had been almost wholly pastoral, as had that of Pompilj, whereas Merry Del Val had had no pastoral experience at all, and only very limited diplomatic experience: he was almost entirely a curialist. Serafini's career profile ran a close second to that of Della Chiesa. He had had a successful career in his order, a twelve-year stint as Bishop of Spoleto, and then a brilliant curial career: his very brief diplomatic experience as Apostolic Delegate to Mexico was his weakest point.[22] Again, like the other serious candidates, Della Chiesa fitted the description of the 'ideal' Pope given by the Secretary of Latin Briefs in his traditional oration to the cardinals before the commencement of the voting. According to Mgr Aurelio Galli, the next Pope needed to be 'of superior intelligence, holiness of life and Christian charity'.[23] Della Chiesa, despite his exile to Bologna and his very recent and long-delayed elevation to the rank of cardinal, was eminently *papabile*, hence his strong showing from the start.

There were other reasons for his election. His major rival, Maffi, was seen to be too young and too 'modern' for many of the Italian cardinals, and too 'Italian' for many of the non-Italians. And whereas, like Maffi, Della Chiesa was obviously an 'opposition' candidate to the curial Pius X party, he was seen to be more moderate in his anti-integralism than the Cardinal of Pisa. In international affairs, he was also obviously the 'Rampolla' candidate, his heir in fact, but, again, he was not notably anti-Austrian: Piffl's diary makes it clear that the five Austro-Hungarian cardinals present consistently voted for him, despite their government's objections.[24] We do not know how the French voted, but it is unlikely that they voted in a unitary fashion because Billot, a member of the Curia, was militantly anti-Modernist and was therefore likely to put this issue before any other considerations.

But none of the others would have been prejudiced against Della Chiesa, given his work with Rampolla and his efforts to moderate the policies of Pius X and Merry Del Val. And though Della Chiesa was not as demonstrably pro-Italian as Maffi, there was equally no reason for the Italian government to have had any reservations about his election (see p. 23). This was important; the Italian cardinals in conclave were anxious to preserve good relations with their government which, in its turn, had gone to great lengths to apply scrupulously the Law of Guarantees at the outset of the conclave and to ensure that it was seen to be doing so.[25]

The aftermath

There is some evidence that Della Chiesa did not welcome the prospect of his election. According to Cardinal Gasparri, later his close collaborator, Della Chiesa came to his cell asking for his opinion: he wanted to read a letter declining election. Gasparri said to him: 'If at the beginning of the next session the split in the votes remains, but shows signs of coming to an end, I will make to Your Eminence a negative sign which will mean that Your Eminence should not read Your appeal.'[26] And this is what he says he did, so he could claim in some way to have helped 'make' Della Chiesa Pope. But by the time he was elected Della Chiesa seems to have come to terms with his fate and his calm acceptance of office, so different from the tremulous, tearful reluctance of his predecessor, was very much in character. Traditionally, the Pope-elect is expected to show great reluctance, out of a sense of unworthiness to accept the great office, rather akin to the way in which a newly elected Speaker of the British House of Commons has to be 'dragged' to his or her chair. Della Chiesa's composure can be explained quite simply by his faith. Referring to the papal office which he had now assumed, he wrote in the letter he sent to his brother immediately after his election: 'This is a heavy burden, but the Lord will give Us the strength to carry it.'[27]

Della Chiesa's choice of name came as a surprise. It was not a surprise that he did not choose the name Pius, because he was determined, for obvious reasons, to keep his distance from the previous pontificate and its policies. But many expected him to take Leo as his name, out of respect to the Pope under whom he had risen to prominence in the Church. Instead he chose Benedict, and he later claimed that he was influenced by the example of the founder of the great monastic order and his search for peace.[28] To some extent his choice of name must also have been influenced by the fact that the last Archbishop of Bologna to become Pope used that name, Benedict XIV (1740–58): two other Bolognesi had been elected Pope, Innocent IX (1591) and Gregory XV (1321–3). Benedict XIV was a good example to follow, having been a wise diplomatist and a beneficent and enlightened Pope in an age of enlightenment: even secular, Protestant writers of the period are to be found among his admirers.[29] Two recent authors, Carlo Falconi and Giorgio Rumi, have made the rather fanciful suggestion that Benedict was influenced in his choice of name by that of the reforming Pope in Fogazzaro's *Santo*, a Modernist tract if ever there was one.[30] Given Benedict's positively notorious prudence, it seems highly unlikely.

However calm and collected his behaviour in the Sistine Chapel as the conclave came to end, he must have experienced very powerful emotions as the cardinals came forward, one by one, to make their submission to him. This was his moment of triumph. What must he have been thinking as De Lai performed the obesiance or, even more poignantly, as Merry Del Val got down on his knees before him to kiss his toe? Peters quotes a passage from Dalla Torre who claimed that Benedict was 'incapable of rancour, forgetful of every offence', to suggest that there was no bad blood between them.[31] This a very strained explanation: why employ it here, unless Peters *did* believe that Merry Del Val had offended Della Chiesa? According to another contemporary source, Francis MacNutt, Merry Del Val could not conceal his dismay at Della Chiesa's election: 'One of the Cardinals whose seat in the Sixtine [sic] Chapel was next to Merry Del Val's, was reported to have said . . . that when the election of the Cardinal of Bologna was announced, his neighbour said to him, *sotto voce*: "*Ma! Questa è una calamità"*("Oh, this is a calamity"!). To this he replied: *"Per Vostra Eminenza, evidentemente lo è"*! ("For Your Eminence, it clearly is!").'[32]

The accounts of the scenes that followed the declaration demonstrate how Benedict never allowed the grandeur, pomp and solemnity of occasions to obscure his humanity. When the three papal garments, in small, medium and large, were presented to him in the sacristy, and even the smallest proved too large, he turned to the wretched Vatican tailor and said smilingly: 'My dear, had you forgotten me?'[33] And as the bells of Rome announced his election and he set off to give his blessing to the crowds inside St Peter's from the internal loggia of the Hall of Benedictions above the great entrance, he allegedly began quietly to weep.[34] His humanity was revealed even more sharply when he declined a grand coronation in St Peter's and insisted instead on a somewhat reduced ceremony inside the Sistine Chapel – out of respect for the war and the terrible sufferings it was bringing to the peoples of Europe. There was a precedent for this in the coronation of Leo XIII in 1878, which had been prompted by the extremely precarious situation of the Holy See after the capture of Rome in 1870, and was clearly also intended as a kind of protest against it. But even this gesture on Benedict's part, like so many others of his during the course of the conflict, was misunderstood and he had to get a leading Catholic journalist, the Marchese Crispolti, to write an explanatory newspaper article in order to remove misapprehensions.[35] Despite the claim that the coronation was 'hasty and almost unceremonious'[36] all the rituals connected with it were carried out – including the burning of flax three times and calling out to the Pope, 'Holy Father, thus passes the glory of the world!' As Peters says: 'For his short reign and the inexplicable oblivion into which he fell the symbol was cruelly apt.'[37]

The end of a conclave is necessarily attended by some confusion, even chaos.[38] In his typically matter-of-fact, businesslike way, Benedict took command of the Vatican and very quickly restored order: he had, after all, lived and worked there for twenty years. As Vercesi says, some of his first acts demonstrated that the Vatican was under new management.[39] He took the opportunity to put out a hand of friendship to France. Writing to the European heads of

State announcing his election, he did not fail to include President Poincaré among them.

His personnel changes also signified a 'new course' in papal policy. Merry Del Val tendered his resignation as Secretary of State and, like his predecessor, Rampolla, in 1903, was despatched to head the rather insignificant Sacred Congregation for the Fabric of St Peter's. Again, like Rampolla, he was later appointed Secretary of the Holy Office. He was given 48 hours to leave his rooms in the Borgia apartment and consigned to the apartment in the Palazzina of the Archpriest of St Peter's which Rampolla had occupied in his declining years. According to Falconi, the new Pope tried to remove Merry Del Val even further from Rome by offering him the Abbacy of Subiaco.[40] Out with Merry Del Val went his protégé and friend, Mgr (later Cardinal) Nicola Canali, who was removed from his post as Sostituto and demoted to the rather less important one of Secretary of the Sacred Congregation of Ceremonies. Merry Del Val, Canali, along with two papal chamberlains, Mgrs Caccia-Dominioni and Arborio Mella di Sant'Elia, and Mgr Misciateli, the Prefect of the Apostolic Palaces, the ecclesiastical head of the papal household, were to constitute a sort of unofficial 'opposition', the *Vaticanetto* as it was called, during Benedict's pontificate. Cardinal Gasparri, his deputy Mgr Tedeschini, and the more intimate members of the Pope's household, Mgr Giuseppe Migone and Mariano Faggiani, were all concerned about the influence of this clique, and more especially the presence of some of them in Benedict's own entourage, feeling that the Pope was too indulgent towards them, but as his close friend Carlo Monti argued, 'Benedict XV was not the kind of man who would permit anyone seriously to oppose his policies.'[41]

Out from the Secretariat of State also went Benigni, who was sent to be Professor of Diplomatic Style at the Academy of Noble Ecclesiastics, clearly a demotion because this was the very post Della Chiesa had occupied at the beginning of his career in the Vatican. This was the first major blow struck against the anti-Modernist fanatics. The second was Benedict's first encyclical *Ad Beatissimi* which, while containing a very clear reiteration of Pius X's condemnation of Modernism ('That condemnation, venerable brethren, We now renew to the full'), called for 'concord' among Catholics and an end to disputes. Most significantly, Benedict laid down instructions on an issue very close to his own, unpleasant experiences in the previous pontificate: 'In matters about which the Holy See has not given a decision, and in which, without injury to the faith and ecclesiastical discipline, there may be differences of opinion, each may lawfully defend his own. In such disputes there must be no offensive language, for this may lead to grave breaches of charity.'[42] Benedict went on to demand that: 'If others do not accept a writer's view, he must not cast suspicion on their faith or spirit of discipline', and expressed his 'desire that the practice lately come into use, of using distinctive names by which Catholics are marked off from Catholics should cease'.[43] As Peters says, 'The whole section just quoted refers, of course, to the integralists or "integral Catholics". Benedict does not call them by name, but his reference to an adjective which was recently applied to the word Catholic is unequivocal.'[44] But however clear the change of policy from that of the previous pontificate, the *integristes* were not beaten yet. Though *Ad Beatissimi*, and the wartime conditions, put an end to the most public of the anti-Modernist excesses, unknown to Benedict, Benigni's spy service, La Sapinière, continued to flourish until it was closed down in 1919, following the publication of documents from its archives which had been found by the Germans.[45]

Animated, no doubt, by the same spirit of concord expressed in *Ad Beatissimi*, Benedict made few other curial changes: Cardinals De Lai and Billot retained their positions and Agliardi was, if anything, promoted, being made Chancellor of the Holy Roman Church, having previously held no major curial post. To call these changes a 'purge' would, therefore, be an exaggeration, but they were a demonstration of the fact that Benedict was now firmly in charge. Nor did Benedict behave like his successor, the Archbishop of Milan, Cardinal Achille Ratti, who when elected Pope in 1922 brought a host of his fellow Milanese with him.[46] From Bologna, Benedict brought only Mariano Faggiani, his valet, and other servants, Giuseppe Migone, his chaplain, and P. Beccari, *agente della Mensa*, that is treasurer of the diocese, whom he appointed

Master of the Sacred Palaces, and who after 1929 became Secretary General to the Government of the State of the Vatican City.[47]

The appointment of Cardinal Ferrata as Merry Del Val's successor in the Secretariat of State was another very clear signal of a change of policy: Ferrata was pro-French and had been a close collaborator of Leo XIII and Rampolla and it would be his major task to win back French sympathy.[48] But Ferrata died within a month, at which point Benedict turned to another francophile, his old friend and colleague Pietro Gasparri, to take over the Vatican's top job. Ferrata was regarded as having a very powerful, forceful personality. It is difficult, therefore, to imagine how he would have operated with Benedict XV, and also what his attitude to the war would have been. The choice of Gasparri turned out to be a brilliant one[49] and Gasparri was to go on to serve Benedict's successor Pius XI for another seven years, in which time he was to be chiefly instrumental on the Vatican side for negotiating the Lateran Pacts of 1929 which brought to an end the 'Roman Question'.[50] Gasparri and Benedict nicely complemented each other, though there is no doubt that in matters of policy it was the Pope who had the last word. Sir Alec Randall, a British minister to the Holy See, has left a shrewd pen portrait of Benedict's most important collaborator:

> Gasparri came of farmer stock, and was sometimes nicknamed 'Il Contadino'. His dress, in the years when I saw him, showed an unusual indifference to neatness . . . (it) would cause a certain mild surprise or amusement, until you experienced the vigour of his personality. He had humour, geniality and diplomatic adaptability: his scholarship, though in this he was said to be deeply indebted to assistants, was associated with a solid and enduring work, the New Code of Canon Law. Simple though his life was, austere was not the first adjective one would associate with him. Though of marked piety, he could obviously relax, enjoy a joke and also make one.[51]

To complete his team in the Secretariat of State, Benedict brought in Mgr Federico Tedeschini as Sostituto and retained Mgr Eugenio Pacelli (later Pius XII) as Under-Secretary of State for

Extraordinary Affairs, aided by Mgr Bonaventura Cerretti: both were to render Benedict and the Holy See sterling service during his pontificate. But one of the most important 'appointments' which Benedict made in the area of Vatican foreign relations was that of his old friend, Baron Carlo Monti, as his unofficial 'go-between' with the Italian government, when it requested one at the beginning of his reign.[52] Monti was especially well-placed to perform this role, being director-general of the office for the *Affari di Culto* in the Ministry of Justice (later Ministry of the Interior). *Affari di Culto* dealt with virtually all matters touching upon the Church's relationship with the Italian State especially, as we have seen, Church property and finance under State control and the preventive approval of episcopal nominations. In a letter of 28 February 1915 Benedict wrote, 'Baron Carlo Monti has access to Us at all times', and he later described him as his 'minister plenipotentiary' and 'vice-pope', such were the important and delicate matters which he had to negotiate with the Italian government on Benedict's behalf.[53] For their part, Italian government ministers saw him as their 'chargé d'affaires' in the Vatican. In often very difficult circumstances, even sometimes with less than the full backing of either side, Monti was to perform a vitally important service to both Italy and Benedict during the latter's reign.

Benedict XV as ruler

Benedict, as we have seen, had an 'image problem', to use the jargon of the modern public relations industry. By the time of his coronation, his power to impress had clearly not improved. An American journalist wrote of him thus: 'With his unimpressive figure and his expressionless face there is neither spiritual or temporal majesty.'[54] Benedict XV emphatically did not possess the charisma of either of his predecessors, Pius X or Leo XIII, both of whom were, in their different ways, physically handsome. He was further hampered in his role as Sovereign Pontiff by the fact that, as a result of the war's effect on communications, and especially on those across the Atlantic, there were far fewer pilgrimages to Rome during his reign than had previously been the case. Pius X, Leo XIII and even Pius IX had all been beneficiaries of the increasing tendency of Catholics to visit the Eternal City, and thus the 'prisoner of the Vatican' had come to be better known to his followers throughout the world. The pilgrimages had also very effectively challenged the 'secularization' of Rome by the new Italian authorities. The Rome correspondent of *The Tablet* described the effects which the First World War, and especially Italy's entry into it in May 1915, had upon the Vatican:

> the devout crowds of pilgrims entering by the Bronze Gates, the long stream of sightseers on their way to the galleries and museums, the carriages of foreign prelates who drove every morning to be received in audience by the Holy Father, the swarms of itinerant vendors that hung about the colonnade – they have all disappeared.[55]

On the other hand, the war prompted many more people than usual to write to the Pope, either seeking personal favours – especially the release of POWs which they believed he was capable of achieving – or asking for papal approval, blessing or a public stand on a matter connected to the war (see pp. 113–14). But the physical isolation of the Pope and the lack of personal contact with his flock would hamper the development of his moral authority during the war years.

At least one contemporary observer, J. D. Gregory, the secretary to the British Legation from December 1914 until June 1915, was extremely critical of Benedict's style of rule:

> the present pope is a decided mediocrity. He has the mentality of a parochial Italian who has hardly travelled at all and a tortuous method of conducting affairs . . . He is capable of rising neither to great heights nor of efficiently controlling the ordinary routine of his administration . . . he is obstinate and bad-tempered to a degree.[56]

As numerous entries in Monti's diary show, Benedict could indeed be both obstinate and bad-tempered. The accusation of mediocrity was not new and is even understandable at this point in his career, the claim about his lack of foreign experience is fair, though given his role at the centre of affairs in the Secretariat of State, that does not mean that he was lacking in a knowledge and understanding of world affairs. But the suggestion that he was a less than able manager of men is unsustainable in view of his long experience in the Vatican, and the reputation he acquired there, and the clear evidence that in Bologna he ran a very tight ship. It should also be said that when Gregory wrote his memoirs at the end of the 1920s, his view of Benedict XV had mellowed.[57] Gregory's superior, the British Minister, was also critical of Benedict, claiming that he was a bad judge of men and citing the cases of Mgr Sanz de Samper, the Master of the Chamber, whom he alleged was totally incompetent, and Mgr Gerlach, who was charged with spying for the Germans in 1917 (see pp. 103–7).[58] Benedict's appointment of his friend, Mgr Valfré di Bonzo, to the Vienna nunciature did not turn out to be a complete success either; Valfré di Bonzo was unable or unwilling to conceal his ardent Italian patriotism and his indiscretions eventually isolated him from influential circles in Vienna.[59] On the other hand, the choice of Gasparri, Tedeschini, Pacelli, Cerretti, and Ratti (later Pius XI) to work in close collaboration with him, as well as the appointment of Enrico Rosa as editor of the Jesuit journal *La Civiltà Cattolica* and later Giuseppe Dalla Torre as editor of *L'Osservatore Romano*, the Vatican's own newspaper, suggest that the Pope's capacity to pick able men far outweighed the occasional mistake he made.

Like Paul VI at his election in 1963, Benedict already possessed an unparalleled knowledge of the workings of the apparatus of papal government – the Roman Curia – which a seven-year absence from Rome had not impaired. Like Paul, he had served long enough in the system to understand all its peculiar and convoluted ways of operating: in this respect, he had been well-trained by both Rampolla and Leo XIII. But whereas Paul VI carried out a wholesale reform of the Roman Curia in the 1960s,[60] Benedict changed very little. His predecessor, Pius X, had carried out a much more drastic reform of the structures of papal government. This he had been obliged to do because neither of his predecessors,

Leo XIII or Pius IX, had been willing to grasp the nettle of curial reform during their long reigns and abolish those offices rendered unnecessary by the final abolition of papal territorial sovereignty in 1870, eradicate duplication between the congregations of the Roman Curia or the scandal of unemployed priests who gravitated towards Rome.[61] Benedict's reforms were few and seemingly marginal by comparison: the creation of the Congregation of Studies in November 1915, the merging of the congregations of the Index with the Holy Office in 1917, the hiving off of the Oriental Churches from Propaganda in 1918, the creation of a Pontifical Heraldic Commission in 1916 and minor changes to the organization of the Congregation of the Clergy in 1919.

This relative inactivity on Benedict's part could be explained by his innate conservatism, the shortness of his reign and, above all, by the fact that he had to direct his major energies and attention to the war and the diplomatic effort to bring it to an end. Thus his primary concern would have been the efficient working of the various branches of the Secretariat of State, the department with which he was most familiar and the one whose machinery was most important to him in the pursuit of his peace diplomacy. But not all of his changes in the Roman Curia were as marginal as they might seem at first sight. The creation of the Congregation for the Oriental Churches was certainly not: it was, indeed, central to his whole strategy in Eastern Europe and the Near East as will become clear (see Chapter 8). The detachment of control of the seminaries from the Congregation of the Consistory was clearly intended as a measure to clip the wings of its prefect, Cardinal De Lai, and curb his anti-Modernist excesses in the field of priestly education of which Benedict himself had been a victim as Archbishop of Bologna.[62] The changes which Benedict made at the Congregation of the Clergy were prompted by a serious problem which the Vatican faced during Benedict's pontificate, lack of money. According to Corrado Pallenberg: 'The important and technical character of the business dealt with by the Congregation required a specialized staff. In 1919, Benedict XV attached to the finance office a school attended by young priests who took a three-year course.'[63]

In fact, the financial problems which Benedict faced had their

origin in an epoch long before he came to the papal throne or had
otherwise arisen from circumstances beyond his control. The Holy
See had consistently refused as a matter of principle to take any
part of the annual indemnity laid down in the Law of Papal
Guarantees of 1871 for the financial losses which it had suffered as
a result of the incorporation of the Papal States into United Italy.
Having rejected the Law of Guarantees as an unsatisfactory and
unilateral solution of the 'Roman Question', the Vatican could
hardly take the money which the Law offered. The institution of
the collections of 'Peter's Pence' (the *Obolo di San Pietro*) in Catholic
communities throughout the world did, however, offset the Vatican's difficulties in the short term. And Pius X (1903–14), in his
typically shrewd, peasant fashion, had managed to leave a three
million lire reserve at his death in 1914.[64]

The income from Peter's Pence inevitably fell very sharply
during the First World War. According to Cardinal Gasparri, in
1915, 'of the belligerents, only Germany continues to contibute
Peter's Pence'.[65] The drastic fall in the number of pilgrimages
referred to above was one major cause, for frequently those same
pilgrims had been the bearers of Peter's Pence. Another problem
was that in 1917 the Vatican was forced to commit a considerable
part of its earnings from accounts in the Banca di Roma to bailing
out both Catholic banks and the Italian Catholic press.[66] It was
true, however, that Benedict was prodigally generous in his charity,
giving his all to help victims of war, famine and other disasters
(see p. 113). Indeed, it has been estimated that he spent some
eighty-two million lire in his humanitarian efforts, an enormous
sum by the standards of the time.[67] But Seldes talks about the
'management or rather lack of financial management under
Benedict XV'.[68] Nino Lo Bello is even more categorical in his
criticism of Benedict XV: he says, 'the Vatican was bankrupt on
Benedict's death, and the Secretary of State, Cardinal Gasparri, was
forced to obtain a loan from Rothschilds' in order to cover the costs
of the 1922 conclave, the one which elected Pius XI.[69] In 1919
Gasparri provided a breakdown of Vatican finances to Italian Prime
Minister Francesco Nitti in an attempt, successfully as it turned
out, to dissuade the Italian Government from taxing the Vatican's

income. The breakdown obviously does not paint a very glowing picture of the Vatican finances at that time, but it does suggest that the Holy See was keeping its head above water at that stage in Benedict's pontificate.[70]

Despite wartime financial stringency, within the walls of the Vatican, and in particular within the restricted circle of his court, Benedict XV maintained the traditional style and pomp of the Papacy, reviving traditional ceremonies like the 'Mandatum', the washing of the feet on Maundy Thursday. The advent of the new Pope was a return to the Leonine pontificate in more than just policy. Benedict was a stickler for protocol and etiquette and a more remote figure than his predecessor, and Peters makes the point that: 'There is no denying the fact that with the accession of Benedict XV something romantically simple and homespun had left the Vatican.'[71] But the domain within which he exercised his solemn sovereignty was very small indeed. As Cardinal Gasparri explained, in 1917, 'The Vatican, even with its gardens, is merely a palace, not a state.'[72] In fact, it was also somewhat smaller in area than it became after the signing of the Lateran Pacts in 1929. F. Zanetti, writing at the time of the signing of the Lateran Pacts, said that the new Vatican State 'would comprise the present Vatican, plus the land enclosed by the internal confines of the Vatican gardens and the walls of Rome which girdle the Vatican hill . . .'[73] Indeed, prior to 1929, much of the eventual State of the Vatican City was not included in the area deemed to be 'extra-territorial' by the Law of Guarantees of 1871. Right below the walls of many of the apartments near the Sistine Chapel were Italian soldiers guarding their State Mint, so that in order to achieve private access to the Vatican gardens by wheeled transport, it became necessary to construct a tunnel beneath the Apostolic Palace. Thus, while on the one hand Benedict's little 'kingdom' was small and claustrophobic, it was also lacking in privacy as crowds had access to the Basilica, the museums, the gardens and even parts of the Palace as well. Benedict added little in the way of buildings or beautification to his domain, though he did build the Petrine Museum and the Vatican Observatory, and the odd church in the city of Rome,[74] largely because of financial constraints and the war: thus there are very few examples of his heraldry to be found in the Vatican.

Even though 'the palace and garden' were on the edge of the city of Rome, and connected to it by what can only be described as meandering backstreets – the grandiose Via della Conciliazione approach was not to be constructed until the 1930s and 1940s – they were easily accessible from the Borgo neighbourhood. Indeed, the relationship between the Vatican and the Borgo aptly symbolized the relationship between the Holy See and Italy in this period. The police commissariat of the Borgo was responsible for supervising public order around the Vatican – the various papal forces, including the Gendarmerie, performed those functions inside – but also had the task of effectively spying on the Pope, his court and the Roman Curia.[75] As David Alvarez has demonstrated, during the First World War the Vatican possessed virtually no communications security: police informers inside Peter's City carried away secret papers; the security of Vatican mails and even its diplomatic bags was constantly violated by both Italian intelligence and the War Censorship Office, and the Italian High Command broke nearly all Vatican codes and intercepted all of its telegraph traffic.[76] The Vatican was at the mercy of the Italians for all provisions and supplies, including gas, water and electricity. Perhaps the only really valuable asset it possessed was its allegedly excellent information gathering system, through the world-wide network of dioceses and religious orders. In August 1918, the Japanese diplomat, Prince Ito, while visiting the Italian foreign ministry, insisted on an audience in the Vatican on the grounds that it was a world 'observatory', with the most reliable sources of information.[77]

It was under these difficult conditions that the Pope carried on his work, following a routine that had been established back in Bologna, and probably earlier than that – like many modern popes he seems to have needed very little sleep. Whereas at Bologna he had lived in a sort of priestly community, in Rome his only real company were his former chaplain Migone, the Lombard Monsignori Arborio Di Mella and Caccia-Dominioni, and the German priest, Mgr Rudolf Gerlach (for whom he seems to have had a special affection), whom he appointed as papal private chamberlains (effectively private secretaries) immediately after his election. Popes can hardly be said to enjoy a 'private' life, but if such existed for Benedict then it was the few precious moments that he spent eating with the children of his valet, Mariano Faggiani,[78] or the little time he spent with his family.

Benedict and his family

Unlike his predecessor, Pius X, who passed a few hours talking, drinking a little wine and saying the Rosary each week with his unmarried sisters, whom he had brought to live in Rome, Benedict did not initially see his family on a regular basis. Yet they remained close. On the evening of his election, he wrote to his brother Giovanni Antonio: 'Dearest Brother, I address to you all the first letter I have written after my election as Supreme Pontiff.'[79] According to the present members of the Della Chiesa family, Benedict's brother and sister went immediately to Rome when they heard news of his election.[80] Shortly afterwards, Giovanni Antonio, his wife Eugenia and his son Giuseppe (Pino) moved there permanently. But in 1918 Eugenia died. Benedict's letter to his brother on this occasion was typical both of his piety and his brotherly affection:

> Faith teaches you that in Heaven your beloved Eugenia can work on your behalf, and in a more effective way than that she was able to do down here on earth. Only yesterday the poor invalid received the Viaticum: we can therefore hope that now she sees unveiled the God whom yesterday she was only able to see under the veils of the Eucharist; and if human defects and frailty have kept her in the prison of expiation, all of us will multiply our efforts to hasten for her the beatific vision.[81]

Giovanni Antonio's trials were not over yet, for within twenty-four hours of his wife's death he suffered another blow – a cerebral haemorrhage which left him partially paralysed. This prompted Benedict to institute more frequent and regular meetings with his family; three times a week he accompanied his brother's wheelchair around the Vatican gardens. Despite his notorious lack of enthusiasm for the open air,[82] these outings gave him obvious pleasure. In February 1919 he wrote to his brother:

> My Dearest Giovanni,
> I am looking forward so much to seeing you! They tell me that you are better and I am delighted and hope that you can come to see me in the Vatican Gardens soon. What a pleasure, what a pleasure it will be for me. Until then . . .[83]

As Giovanni Antonio's health declined, he came to rely increasingly upon his son to look after him, and Benedict's concern did not abate. In September 1920 he wrote to Pino expressing his doubts about the proposal to take Giovanni Antonio to Poggio Mirteto (now one of the family estates). In particular, he was not convinced that there would be sufficient night nursing and he concluded his letter, 'I fear that he will be even more bored (at Poggio Mirteto) than at Nettuno'.[84] Two months later, on 10 December, Giovanni Antonio died.

Though his sister did not live in Rome, Benedict nevertheless kept in regular contact with her. Giulia, always his favourite sibling, had married Count Persiceto and lived on an estate in the Veneto region of north-eastern Italy. Her letters were an interesting alternative source of information on the area in which she lived, especially after the catastrophic Italian defeat at Caporetto in 1917 which brought the front line to within eight kilometres of her home, and in 1919 Benedict appointed her as president of the association dedicated to the rebuilding of churches in the region.[85] Benedict never lost interest in his family. In December 1919, Giulia's son, Carlo Persiceto, came to work in Rome. Benedict wrote to Pino: 'You will have heard the news that Carlo Persiceto has obtained a post as technical inspector with the Bank of Rome, based in Rome: now the big problem will be that of finding a house.'[86] But when the war began to affect his family, Benedict's sense of duty, and no doubt his concern to avoid bad publicity, triumphed over family loyalty. According to G. Felice, 'when his sister-in-law in her maternal egoism asked him to save her son (Pino) from conscription, he replied firmly "no", calling upon the young heir to the family name to sacrifice himself for the honour of his country, which he did in fact do'.[87] The letter is a reference to Giuseppe, and his mother presumably hoped that Benedict could find him an 'exempt' employment in the Vatican. Perhaps the 'maternal egoism' of which Felice speaks was one of the human weaknesses to which Benedict referred in his letter to Giovanni Antonio after her death. Later on in the war, unknown to Benedict, Carlo Monti sought several times to have Pino withdrawn from the front line.[88]

Benedict's other brother, 'Baccino', was to be a cause of much anxiety and anguish in the first months of his pontificate. Baccino did not marry and a letter from Benedict to Giovanni Antonio suggests that Baccino was the 'black sheep' of the Della Chiesa family, inasmuch as it refers to Baccino's 'morally and financially disordered life'.[89] Another source claims that Baccino 'was unfortunately implicated in a Spanish banking scandal and the note which appeared in *L'Osservatore Romano* – which was completely vague and crude – bore the hallmarks of the Pope's style and character'.[90] Baccino ceased to be a worry to his brother when, after a short illness, he died on 4 April 1915.

It is said that John Paul II resents what he describes as the 'gilded cage' which he finds himself in at the Vatican.[91] His frustration is especially understandable bearing in mind his athletic lifestyle, but he can and does travel outside of the Vatican: he is the most travelled of all popes. Benedict XV, though of more sedentary habits, also found the Vatican to be a 'gilded cage'. Much more so, in fact, than John Paul II. Benedict, like his three predecessors, was still very much the 'prisoner of the Vatican'. He was unable to leave it for political reasons; he was not even able to visit his cathedral, the Basilica of St John Lateran, or for that matter any other part of his diocese, the city of Rome, which was of course the very source of his spiritual authority. Judging by the very limited contact which he had with his family, Benedict seems to have accepted his 'imprisonment' as a sort of penance for himself, viewing it as a sacrifice in the cause of the Church, and in his quest for peace. The Vatican, then, became not so much a cage as a cell wherein he could, as much as possible, live the life of one of the monks of his namesake Benedict, even though he was himself of the secular and not religious clergy. According to Carlo Monti, who visited him regularly and saw his private apartment: 'Benedict XV desired that the Papacy revert to its traditional outward dignity, and rightly so; but his private life is of a modest, positively monastic, simplicity.'[92] In these circumstances, Benedict lived out his life as priest, bureaucrat, diplomat and Pope for seven years and five months.

Notes and references

1. Gregory, p. 88; Falconi, p. 52.
2. See Falconi, p. 86; Duffy, p. 250, says that the concordat which Merry Del Val signed with Serbia in June 1914 helped increase the tension in the Balkans but does not explain why.
3. Archivio Segreto Vaticano, Segreteria di Stato (henceforth ASV, SS), Guerra, 1914–1918, Rubricella 244, Fasc. 29, 'Tanto per la verità' (no date).
4. Gregory, p. 88, claims that at least two attempts were made by the Vatican in the summer of 1914 to stop the war – without, however, providing any evidence to support his claims.
5. Kent and Pollard, pp. 16–17.
6. Monticone, p. 155.
7. Vercesi, p. 65.
8. Liebman, p. 37.
9. Ibid.
10. Zizola, p. 196.
11. Liebman, p. 41.
12. See AP, 1914, pp. 1–15.
13. Liebman, p. 45.
14. Zizola, p. 196.
15. Ibid., p. 192.
16. Moynihan, p. 329.
17. Schmidlin, III, p. 189, notes 15–23; Seldes, pp. 111–12; Sforza, pp. 163–4, 'The candidacy of della Chiesa did not appear until the fifteenth ballot, on the initiative of Cardinal Gasparri who had been his associate in the Secretary of State's office.'
18. According to Seldes, p. 111, Benedict was elected on the sixteenth ballot. His figures are then more or less as described in Piffl's diary, except that he says Benedict was 'elected with the formidable vote of fifty out of the fifty-seven participants'. See also Vistalli, pp. 25–6.

19. Zizola, p. 195.
20. Liebman, p. 45, who also quotes the words of Cardinal Csernoch, Primate of Hungary and Archbishop of Eszertgom to Piffl: 'Serafini is the candidate of De Lai and all the curial cardinals who do not want to lose their positions. The fact that De Lai is manoeuvring on his behalf is extremely significant. De Lai wants a puppet whom he can control at his pleasure.'
21. According to Sforza, p. 164, 'Not until the third turn did he obtain exactly two-thirds of the votes required for his election. It was evening. The adversaries of the Archbishop of Bologna contested the election, asserting that it would not be regular unless it were proved that della Chiesa had not voted for himself . . . As it was late they decided that all the cardinals that had voted for della Chiesa should repeat their votes for him the next morning, if they wished, in the first ballot . . . When Della Chiesa, who had listened impassively to the discussion, retired to his cell he knew that he was already pope, since he had not voted for himself.' It is a lovely story, and Peters, pp. 77–8, repeats it, but it is not true. As can be seen from the voting table on page 63, Della Chiesa's vote reached the necessary two-thirds on the second ballot of 3 September and the verification took place in the afternoon of the same day.
22. Falconi, p. 94.
23. As quoted in Peters, pp. 76–7.
24. Liebman, p. 45.
25. Garzia, p. 10.
26. As quoted in Gasparri, pp. 156–7.
27. AFDC, Lettere al Suo Fratello Giovanni Antonio, 3 September 1914.
28. Peters, p. 80.
29. For a brief account of the reign of Benedict XIV, see Walsh, pp. 178–82.
30. Rumi (1991), p. 4; see also Falconi, p. 114.
31. As quoted in Peters, p. 82.
32. MacNutt, p. 313. (It is interesting to note that this is one of the few passages in MacNutt relating to Della Chiesa which Peters does not quote.)
33. As quoted in Schmidlin, III, p. 198. n. 3.
34. Peters, p. 84.
35. F. Crispolti (1939), p. 19.
36. PRO, FO, 371/3086, Count de Salis to Curzon, 25 October 1922.
37. Peters, p. 88.
38. Vercesi, p. 65.
39. For a description of the scenes at the conclave of 1958, see Hebblethwaite (1984), pp. 287–8.
40. Falconi, pp. 108–9, where he cites passages from Mgr Canali's deposition for the beatification of Merry Del Val.

41. *Diario*, I, p. 450, 9 September 1916 and II, pp. 3–4, 3 January 1917.
42. Carlen (ed.), IV, p. 144.
43. Ibid.
44. Peters, p. 108.
45. Falconi, p. 132.
46. Among the Milanese whom Pius XI brought in were his brother Count Alberto Ratti, who was high in the councils of the Vatican; Giuseppe Colombo, whom he made national head of Catholic Action; Bernardino Nogara, who was responsible for the Vatican's financial success after 1929; Beltrami, the architect, and Giulio Castelli, the constructor, who were responsible for much building work in and around Vatican City in the early 1930s.
47. Felice, p. 166.
48. Pizzuti, p. 126.
49. According to Dalla Torre, p. 409, 'There are those who hold that Gasparri was a diplomat of the genius of Consalvi, and others who defined him as "the Giolitti of the Church".'
50. Pollard (1985), ch. 2.
51. Randall, p. 61.
52. For an account of the circumstances in which Monti came to be chosen see his *Diario*, I, pp. 171–5.
53. Quoted in Felice, p. 169; *Diario*, I, p. 349, 17 February 1916 and II, p. 247, 12 January 1918.
54. O'Hare-McCormick, pp. 14–15.
55. *The Tablet*, 13 January 1917, p. 49.
56. Quoted in Hachey (ed.), p. xx.
57. Gregory, pp. 88–9.
58. PRO, FO, 371/3086, Count de Salis to Lord Curzon, 25 October 1922.
59. *Diario*, II, p. 31, 10 January 1917 and p. 38, 22 January 1918.
60. Hebblethwaite (1993), pp. 344–6.
61. Falconi, p. 25 and pp. 27–8.
62. Bedeschi (1968), p. 139.
63. Pallenberg, p. 98.
64. Lo Bello, p. 63.
65. *Diario*, I, p. 301, 8 December 1915.
66. AAES, Italia, Fasc. 335, memo of Benedict XV of 2 December 1917 and *Diario*, II, p. 80, 3 May 1917.
67. Jankowiak, p. 221: Generous in his charity to others, Benedict was extremely thrifty in his personal habits. As his handwritten memoranda in the Vatican Archives show, as late as 1921 he was still using the headed notepaper he had had printed for himself when he became cardinal in May 1914.
68. Seldes, p. 246.

69. Lo Bello, p. 61.
70. Gasparri, pp. 376–8; see also *Diario*, II, p. 3, 3 January 1917, where Monti says that Benedict told him that the Vatican was more or less balancing its books at that time.
71. Peters, pp. 95–6.
72. As quoted in Gasparri, p. 234.
73. Zanetti, p. 306.
74. Jankowiak, p. 224; I am grateful to Ron Scarfe for bringing to my attention the colourful story in the *National Geographical Magazine*, March 1939, vol. LXXV, no. 3, p. 382, that 'Benedict XV kept two wolves in the Vatican Gardens'. We have not been able to find corroboration of this story: the Della Chiesa family emphatically deny it.
75. Garzia, p. 72; the reports of the Commissario of the Borgo are to be found in ACS, MI, DGPS, 1914–1918, p. 665.
76. Alvarez (1992), pp. 447–54.
77. *Diario*, II, p. 367, 17 August 1918.
78. Zanetti, p. 239.
79. AFDC, Lettere al Suo Fratello Giovanni Antonio, 3 September 1914.
80. Interview with the Marchese Benedetto Della Chiesa, Rome, October, 1996.
81. AFDC, Lettere al Suo Fratello Giovanni Antonio, 9 December 1918.
82. *Diario*, II, p. 22, 30 January 1917.
83. AFDC, ibid., 6 February 1919.
84. Ibid., letter to Pino, 2 October 1919.
85. *La CC*, 70, 1 (1919), p. 248.
86. AFDC, letter to Pino, 4 September 1920.
87. Felice, p. 167.
88. *Diario*, I, p. 308, 17 December 1915, p. 322, 7 January 1916 and II, p. 197, 4 November 1917 and p. 213, 23 November 1917.
89. AFDC, Lettere al Suo Fratello Giovanni Antonio, 13 April 1915.
90. Zanetti, p. 234. Zanetti almost certainly confused Baccino with his brother Giovanni Antonio. According to the *Diario*, II, 166, p. 291, the latter was asked to lend his name to a banking venture in Spain, but was persuaded by Benedict to abandon the idea for fear of scandal.
91. Bernstein and Politi, p. 369.
92. *Diario*, I, p. 296, 1 December 1915.

4

Benedict, the war and Italy

The Vatican during the First World War

Over four out of the seven and a half years of Benedict's pontificate lay under the shadow of the First World War. It is inevitable, therefore, that much of the most recent literature on the pontificate is concerned with Benedict and the war, and with the controversies surrounding his diplomacy during the course of it, in particular the most well known of all his acts, the 'Peace Note' of August 1917. Much of the rest of his reign also lay under the shadow of peacemaking and its unsatisfactory results, at least as far as Benedict was concerned. In order to understand the development of the Pope's peace diplomacy, it is first necessary to understand the broad lines of policy which Benedict and Gasparri followed from the start, and the impact on the Vatican of Italy's entry into the war in May 1915, which had a powerful conditioning influence on decision-making in the Vatican thereafter. Initially, at least, the policy of Benedict and Gasparri did not appear to differ very much from that of Pius X and Merry Del Val. Almost immediately after his election, the new Pope made his first pronouncement on the war. Benedict's public statement of 8 September 1914 repeated his predecessor's call for prayers to end the war, and included an appeal to the powers for peace.[1] Though the statement lacked neither force nor urgency, there was still a feeling in the Vatican, as elsewhere, that the war would be over by Christmas. But by 1 November, when Benedict published his first encyclical, *Ad Beatissimi*, no such illusion could be maintained. The battle of the Marne in early to mid-September brought the stalemate of trench warfare in the west; the Western Front was effectively established by the end of that month and the battle of Ypres a month later confirmed it. And the stalemate would last for another four years. The military situation on the Eastern Front, between Germany and Austria-Hungary on the one hand and Russia on the other, while more fluid was no less undecided. Turkey's junction with the Central Powers and declaration of war on its Slav neighbour at the beginning of October made a victory on the part of the 'Russian steamroller' even less likely thereafter.

In *Ad Beatissimi*, Benedict addressed himself to the causes of the war, as well as to its consequences. According to his analysis, the causes of the international conflict had their origins in the ills afflicting the whole of human society. He castigated the current 'contempt for authority, the injustice in the relations between classes and the attainment of material goods made into the sole object of human activity and the unrestrained striving after independence', which can be interpreted as a broad attack on liberal individualism in general, and took a swipe at the forces of secularization and anticlericalism at work in human society: '[One wonders] whether it is wise and sensible for public authorities and States to divorce themselves from the holy religion of Christ . . . or whether it is a wise policy to ban from the public schools the teaching of the Gospel and of the Church.'[2] In a paragraph with the interesting title of 'The Classes and the Masses', he condemned 'class hatred' and, in particular, frequent strikes, without, however, reiterating Leo XIII's criticisms of the capitalist system against which the strikes were directed.[3] In his analysis of the specific causes of the war, he drew attention to the 'absence in relations between men of mutual love with their fellow men' and declared 'Race hatred has reached its climax.'[4] In Benedict's vocabulary, 'race' was often synonymous with nationalism. Once again condemning the horrors of the war in no uncertain terms, he urged its solution by declaring, 'Surely there are other ways and means whereby violated rights can be rectified?', but as yet, he offered no clear, practical answer to his own rhetorical question.[5] Presumably, he was still hoping that the warring powers, with his encouragement, would be able to resolve their differences on their own.

Ad Beatissimi was to be the first of many attempts on Benedict's part to bring about an end to the war. In allocutions and encyclicals, in other public statements, and above all in careful, patient, secret negotiations, he and Gasparri repeatedly sought first to prevent the war from spreading, as in the months leading up to both the entry of Italy into the conflict in May 1915 and that of the USA in April 1917, and then to bring the two sides to the negotiating table. It is the sheer, dogged persistence of their efforts that is so impressive, as is their work to provide humanitarian aid to both military and civilian victims of the conflict on both sides. As the Vicar of 'the Prince of Peace', Benedict believed it to be his duty to do no less, and in pursuit of those aims, he and Gasparri sought to preserve a stance of impartiality for the Vatican which the latter justified on the grounds of the 'paternal-universal character of the Pope and the supreme interest of the Church'.[6]

While virtually no biographer or historian doubts the underlying benevolence, pacifism and humanitarianism of Benedict's motives, some, like many contemporary observers, have challenged the impartiality of Vatican diplomacy during the course of the conflict, and its disinterestedness. The Serbo-American historian Dragan Zivojinovic, for example, has argued that, 'Although the Vatican pretended to be impartial and neutral, there is now evidence that its sympathies lay with the Central Powers, particularly Austria-Hungary.'[7] These are serious allegations, especially the first, because Benedict always stressed his impartiality towards the belligerent powers: such was his anxiety to appear above the conflict that he even refused to look at a film of the war sent by the British.[8] But we know that from the beginning of the conflict the Vatican was accused of being sympathetic towards the Central Powers, Germany and Austria-Hungary, to the point that Benedict was regularly described as the *Pape boche* in the French press. But this criticism came not only from hostile, anticlerical quarters. Cardinal Aidan Gasquet, Britain's only curial cardinal in 1914, was appalled by the pro-German atmosphere which he found in the Roman Curia, and among Italian Catholic clergy and laity in general. In November 1914, in a letter to British Foreign Secretary Lord Grey about the imminent arrival of a British mission to the Vatican, in whose genesis he himself had played an important part, he wrote:

> The Pope and his Secretary have been quite correct in their attitude, but the mentality of the clergy generally is astounding ... Germany and Austria and Bavaria have been at work for the past two years and more and when the War started they had the ground well-prepared. Prussia does not leave things to chance and had a good deal of wisdom of the serpent.[9]

Even allowing for Gasquet's patriotic passion, his interpretation of the situation is broadly supported by others. Matthias Erzberger, an influential German Catholic politician, confirmed the strength of the German 'lobby' in the Vatican in a report on his visit to Rome in the spring of 1915, when he sought to persuade Italian politicians from going to war against Austria.[10] Alberto Monticone, the Catholic historian of Italy in the First World War, provides a very clear and plausible explanation of the situation which Gasquet so strongly deplored, and which led to repeated accusations of partiality for the Central Powers on the Vatican's behalf. He argues that, on the one hand, there were strong German influences, political and cultural, in the Vatican due to 'the gamut of German research projects, publications and conferences in Rome on theological, ecclesiological and spiritual topics', whereas, 'there was on the other hand a crisis in the relationship with French culture', due, no doubt, to the Modernist leanings of so many French Catholic intellectuals: he also points to the influence of the Germans in the Jesuit headquarters in Rome, especially Ledechowski.[11] And in a certain sense, the predominance of German/Austro-Hungarian influences in the Vatican merely reflected the broader hegemony of those influences in Italy, as a result of that country's thirty-year adherence to the Triple Alliance.

This situation was not helped by the relatively poor relations between the Entente Powers and the Vatican. Whereas the Central Powers had three diplomatic representatives at the papal court, in addition to the Austro-Hungarian ambassador, and Germany was represented by two envoys, one for Prussia and one for Bavaria, the Entente could count on only two, the Russian and Belgian envoys.

The former had little influence due to the tensions in the Holy See's relations with Orthodox Russia, as a result of which no nuncio was permitted in St Petersburg, and the Belgian ambassador had little clout either. Indeed, contemporary commentators were unanimous in describing the lack of sympathy with which the plight of Belgium (and Serbia) was greeted in the conclave of 1914.[12] Even Gasparri had little time for Belgian claims of victimization, declaring that the little kingdom should have given way to the German invasion.[13] In part, the Entente Powers were to blame for this situation: Britain had withdrawn its unofficial representative in Rome four years after the final collapse of the Pope's temporal power in 1870 (the USA had withdrawn its envoy in 1867), and France of course had ruptured relations with the Holy See in 1905.

Dragan Zivojinovic argues that Benedict was partial to the Central Powers because 'he was elected with Austrian influence' and because he was dependent on Erzberger, the German Centre Party leader, on account of his fund-raising activities on the Pope's behalf: 'This relieved the Pope's situation but made him, and the Curia, dependent upon Germany and on occasion ready to voice views that reflected Germany's desires and needs'.[14] Zivojinovic's allegations are based on evidence in the Erzberger papers which claims that the Vatican was almost bankrupt at the death of Pius X, and that his successor could hardly pay his staff,[15] but as has already been demonstrated, Benedict in fact inherited a strong financial position at his election (Chapter 3). In any case, as Piffl's diary demonstrates, Benedict was fortunate to have obtained the support of the Austro-Hungarian cardinals, though it also shows that their government was less than enthusiastic about him, and that Cardinal Hartmann's voting reflected the German government's distinct hostility to his candidature (p. 62). All this is hardly surprising as he was, after all, Rampolla's protégé and committed to his policies towards Austria, Germany and France, but it emphatically does not prove that he was unduly sympathetic to the Central Powers after 1914. The essence of Rampolla's strategy was that Germany, a Prussian, Protestant power, needed to be balanced by Catholic, cosmopolitan Austria. Again, while it is true that the inflow of monies from Peter's Pence was disrupted due to the war, at a time when the Vatican was spending enormous sums on relief work, it is also the case that Benedict received increasingly large sums from the United States,[16] but no one has suggested that he was in any way influenced in his policy towards that country as a result. Perhaps the last word should be left to J. D. Gregory, who on other matters was highly critical of Benedict, but said of him: 'I am convinced that he is not either temperamentally or politically pro-German.'[17]

What is much more convincing about Zivojinovic's interpretation of the general thrust of Vatican policies and sympathies during the First World War is his claim that Benedict and Gasparri were essentially committed to the preservation or restoration of the *status quo*: there is even a lot to be said for Zivojinovic's argument that it was this obsession, in a rapidly changing international situation, which rendered nugatory many of Benedict's peace efforts.[18] Benedict was not a revolutionary Pope like John XXIII or even an innovatory one like Paul VI; most of his instincts were conservative, especially in foreign relations. It was essentially in the interests of the Holy See that the international *status quo* be preserved. They were also especially aware of the threat which the disruptive forces of socialism and anarchism posed to the social and political order. In particular, Benedict and Gasparri could not be indifferent to the fate of Austria-Hungary, the last Catholic great power and a bulwark against Russian Orthodoxy and Pan-slavism.[19] The collapse of the Central Powers was no more desirable than the westward and southward march of a victorious Russia, which might end in the seizure of Istanbul/Constantinople and the erection of Santa Sophia into a sort of Orthodox St Peter's: the commitments which Britain and France had given to Russia on the eventual partition of the Ottoman Empire were a constant source of anxiety in the Vatican. J. D. Gregory claimed that Benedict was obsessed with Russia.[20] Sir Henry Howard explained why in a report to London:

The Vatican is filled with alarm and foreboding by the agreement made between H.M.'s Government and Russia, giving Russia possession of Santa Sophia, with an extraterritorial zone to which the (Russian) Holy Synod may be transferred – the erection of a rival establishment, as it were, to the Vatican on the shores of the Bosphorus. This can later lead, the Vatican believes, to the Orthodox Church extending its sway to the shore of the Adriatic.[21]

Gasparri confirmed these fears in a conversation with Carlo Monti: 'the installation of the Russians in Constantinople would be a grave blow to the interests of Catholicism', and for Monti's benefit he added that it would undermine Italian influence in the East as well.[22]

The Vatican was not entirely neutral in its attitudes towards France and Britain either, because the former, or at least its government, was strongly masonic and anti-clerical, and the latter was Protestant. Though, as Vistalli has argued, the French and Belgians were both fundamentally Catholic peoples and the British Empire contained significant Catholic minorities,[23] the Vatican had something to fear from their victory, but it also had a lot to fear from that of a Protestant, Prussian-dominated Germany dragging the Habsburg Empire in its wake. Even allowing for the unhappy plight of Catholics in Russia, the maintenance of the *status quo ante* suited the Vatican best. Though their views were to change as time passed and circumstances changed, at the beginning of the conflict Benedict and Gasparri sought an alteration of the international *status quo* as they understood it in only one key respect; they obviously desired a revision of what they saw as the very unsatisfactory relationship between the Holy See and Italy. This aim, and the broader one of seeking to restore the Holy See's international influence and prestige, were powerful influences on the Vatican's diplomatic activities between 1914 and 1920. While it is undeniably true that the underlying motive for the Vatican's attempts to mediate between the belligerents was the desire to end what Benedict described in his Peace Note of August 1917 as the 'useless slaughter' of the war as quickly as possible, such efforts, would and did lead to what the Italian historian Italo Garzia describes as 'a greater international presence' for the Holy See.[24] Under Benedict and Gasparri the Vatican was not, therefore, a totally disinterested observer during the First World War.

The outbreak of the First World War inevitably led to a rapid change in the international standing of the Holy See. Governments quickly grasped the potential moral importance of the Pope as a neutral, given the large numbers of Catholics on all sides. President Poincaré of France sent a carefully neutral but cordial reply to Benedict's letter informing him of his election,[25] and both Germany and Austria put aside initial reservations to woo the new pontiff.[26] Even the usually sceptical and suspicious Italian government recognized the potentially enhanced international position of the Holy See by quickly establishing a permanent channel of communication with the newly elected pontiff through his friend Carlo Monti. Within three months of the outbreak of the war, the British Government also recognized the Pope's new position, as well as the pernicious effects of the palpably strong influence of the Central Powers at the papal court, by sending an envoy to the Vatican. The French at first opposed this initiative,[27] and then confirmed its wisdom by stationing an 'unofficial' envoy to the Vatican, M. Loiseau, in Rome.[28] At the end of 1915, the Kingdom of the Netherlands also re-established relations with the Vatican, sending an envoy to the Pope in order to foster its plans for a peace conference to be held in The Hague.[29] In 1915, a special, non-diplomatic papal delegation in Berne, the first since Switzerland had broken off relations in 1873, was established to supervise joint Swiss–Vatican humanitarian efforts. It was also useful in their attempts to bring about peace, since the Swiss capital was to be the scene of various peace initiatives (as well as being a spy centre) throughout the war.[30] The British legation at the Holy See quickly grasped the significance of these developments; it realized that in collaboration with other members of the 'league of neutrals' – the Netherlands, Spain, Switzerland and perhaps even the United States – the Holy See was building the potential for a serious peace effort.[31] The reaction of the Italian government was rather different and offers the strongest evidence that these developments constituted an enormous increase in the international standing of the Holy See, with the potential to upset the balance of power between the Vatican and Rome. Despite her own improved, albeit unofficial, relations with the Pope, Italy sought to dissuade all three powers from establishing relations with him.[32]

Recognition of its importance as a moral authority also had drawbacks for the Vatican; belligerents on both sides sought to appeal to this authority in pursuit of their own 'moral' agendas. The Entente Powers were especially anxious to elicit the moral condemnation of the Pope for the German violation of Belgian neutrality and also German atrocities in Belgium, most notably the sack of Louvain and the burning of its university library. Another major cause of complaint was the enforced labour, or even worse, deportations of civilian populations from northern France. The representatives of the Allied governments at the Vatican, not to mention the press in Britain, France and Belgium, repeatedly demanded that Benedict condemn these and other manifestations of German 'frightfulness'.[33] The Vatican's response to these demands was to point out that it was receiving complaints about the other's behaviour from both sides, not just from the Entente. Thus in 1916, Russia was accused by the Germans of sending 1500 Jewish families into the front line on the Eastern Front, and in 1917 Germany also complained about the mistreatment of civilian populations by black British and French troops.[34] Indeed, by the end of the war, the Vatican archives were bulging with 'white', 'grey', 'green' and 'orange' books produced by belligerents on both sides containing accounts of alleged atrocities perpetrated by the enemy, along with carefully argued and documented ripostes to them.[35]

The Vatican argued, and quite reasonably, that before it could pass judgement it would need to examine all allegations, thus turning itself into a veritable court of justice, a kind of international war crimes commission for which, of course, it was not equipped: in any case, the nature of the conflict would have made it almost always impossible to carry out proper investigations of the facts.[36] Even in the apparently open and shut case of the violation of Belgian neutrality, the Germans produced a weighty tome of evidence in support of their contention that the Belgians had already violated their own neutrality by conversations with the French high command before the outbreak of the war and that

Belgian civilians had repeatedly broken the rules of war by firing on German soldiers.[37] It could also be claimed with some justification that the British and the French, with very flimsy excuses, had violated the neutrality of Greece in the spring of 1917, taking the country over and deposing its king because of his refusal to comply with their wish to drag Greece into a war against Bulgaria: and they used exactly the same excuse as the Germans – *force majeure*.[38] Gasparri's other argument was that condemnations would have impeded the Pope's humanitarian work, of which the Entente countries were the chief beneficiary, but 'the Holy See preferred the good of suffering humanity'.[39] And when the question of responding to demands for the condemnation of atrocities by various powers came up in the Sacred Congregation for Extraordinary Ecclesiastical Affairs, the consultative body of the Secretariat of State, the very pertinent point was made by more than one cardinal member that such condemnations could seriously damage the Holy See's peace efforts.[40]

In the end, the Vatican limited itself to private protests and generic public statements, a condemnation of all atrocities by all sides, as on 22 January 1915, when Benedict declared in a consistorial allocution: 'And We do proclaim it without modification, condemning openly every injustice by whatever side it has been committed.'[41] When it did, very occasionally, single out an individual target, as in the condemnation of the German violation of Belgian neutrality in a note to the Belgian Government in January 1915, it immediately brought down upon itself the fury of the other side. The German press waxed wrathful for several weeks and attacked Benedict as 'Der Französische Papst'.[42] There was another, fairly obvious, reason why Benedict was so unwilling to morally condemn the actions of either side, and one that was in accord with Gasparri's concern for 'the supreme interest of the Church'. War has always been a problem for a universalistic, worldwide religion like Roman Catholicism. War, and especially the First World War which was strongly inspired by national rivalries and hatreds, cuts across the the loyalty and solidarity of Catholics in a damaging way for the Church. To have systematically condemned the atrocities of each side would have risked alienating the loyalty to the Papacy of countless numbers of Catholics. This was exactly the same dilemma which faced Pius XII in the Second World War, albeit, given the Holocaust and other Nazi atrocities, in an even more serious form.

In following his policy of impartiality, however wisely, Benedict was running grave risks. There was a great deal of hostility towards it, even among Catholics, in the countries of the Entente. Benedict's position was in strong contrast with that of the ultra-patriotic stance of Cardinal Mercier, Primate of Belgium, who was constantly getting into serious arguments with the German occupying authorities, which caused much annoyance in the Vatican: Benedict went so far as to say, wearily, that Mercier wanted to be a 'martyr'.[43] Benedict and Gasparri tried to restrain Mercier, and at the same time protect him from the Germans.[44] Inevitably, Mercier's heroic stance was much preferred in the Entente countries, so much so that their press presented the Belgian prelate as a kind of 'anti-pope' to Benedict.[45]

Italian intervention

During the first eight months of the First World War, the diplomatic policy of Benedict and Gasparri was made easier by the fact that the Vatican was the 'guest' of another neutral power, the Kingdom of Italy. All that changed on 24 May 1915, when Italy entered the war on the side of the Entente. Italian intervention in the First World War was to cause the Vatican huge problems, conditioning the whole development of its diplomatic activity. It therefore opposed that intervention quite vigorously and actively until the last moment.

At the outbreak of the First World War in August 1914 the Italian government had decided to remain neutral. In the circumstances, this was really the only course of action open to the Italians. Even though she was the third partner in the Triple Alliance with Germany and Austria-Hungary, Italy had nothing to gain by going to war on the side of her allies. The attempt by the government of Salandra (prime minister) and Sonnino (foreign minister) to persuade Vienna to sacrifice the *terre irredente* (literally 'unredeemed lands'), that is Trieste and Trento, two Italian-speaking territories still under Habsburg control, as the price of Italian military support, or even continuing neutrality, failed. Vienna believed that a cession of territory on the principle of nationality would undermine the whole basis of the empire. The presence of the British and French navies in the Mediterranean was a further disincentive to hostilities with the Entente. In any case, there was little support from Italian public opinion for entering the war on the side of Germany and Austria-Hungary: only the Nationalist extremists were in favour of this option.[46] Eight months later the Italians had abandoned neutrality and in the secret Treaty of London agreed to enter the war on the side of Britain, France and Russia. The primary motivation for intervening in the war was to complete the process of Italian unification by acquiring the 'unredeemed lands' and secure a more defensible north-eastern frontier. This 'sacred egoism' justified Italy's ditching of her allies of thirty-five years' standing. Italy was made some vague promises in relation to future colonial gains in Africa and the Middle East. Another factor influencing Salandra and Sonnino in their decision to go to war was the belief that participation in a successful war would solve Italy's domestic problems, by generating national unity and restoring the authority of the political class, seriously damaged, so they believed, by the compromises made by their arch-enemy, the Italian elder statesman Giovanni Giolitti, with Socialism and political Catholicism in the preceding fourteen years.

As soon as they became aware of the desire on the part of Salandra and Sonnino to abandon Italian neutrality, Benedict and Gasparri opposed it. Their reasons for doing so were numerous and obvious. In the first place, they were extremely anxious to prevent an extension of the war, and therefore of the bloodletting. There was also the fear that an extension of the war, especially the emergence of an Austro-Hungarian/Italian front line, would prolong the conflict. For the Vatican, another powerful consideration was the direct threat which Italian involvement in the war posed to the survival of the Austro-Hungarian Empire: we have already seen how crucial the Vatican believed the survival of that empire was to the preservation of a beneficial *status quo* in Europe from the point of view of its wider geopolitical and spiritual interests. In this regard, in January 1915, Gasparri sent this letter to the papal nuncio in Vienna:

> At this moment, the Holy Father, who has the greatest of concern for the existence of the Austro-Hungarian Monarchy due to a particular affection towards it and its August and Venerable Sovereign, as well as for the highest interest of the Church itself, notably the survival of the only Catholic great power, not to mention peace in Italy, wishes to open his heart to the Emperor, through your good offices, advising him in the strongest possible terms to avoid war with Italy at all costs.[47]

Benedict and Gasparri also had specific concerns about the involvement of Italy in the conflict. After the experience of 'Red Week' in June 1914, they seriously doubted the capacity of the Italian State to survive a major armed conflict; like many other observers, they feared that such an experience, especially if Italy were to be defeated, would precipitate social and political revolution. In this they shared the concern of the Giolitti, who opposed Italian intervention until it became clear to him that the King, Victor Emmanuel III, had committed himself to the project and that for the Italian Parliament to reject the Treaty of London could lead to the monarch's abdication.[48] But of course, another serious worry was how Italian involvement in the conflict would affect the Holy See and its diplomacy. How would the war affect the Law of Guarantees and the arrangements it had made for the Vatican's relations with other powers? There was no provision in the Law for the eventuality that Italy could find herself at war against powers with whom the Holy See continued to have amicable relations. In that case, how would the Vatican be able to preserve its neutrality, maintaining the distinction between its policies and those of a belligerent Italian government? Finally, according to Garzia, Benedict was afraid that if Italy entered the war she would inevitably be present at a peace conference but that the Holy See would not and thus would fail to make any improvement in its position *vis-à-vis* Italy.[49]

The Vatican's efforts up to the last minute before Italian intervention to mediate between Italy and Austro-Hungary and thus avert Italian entry into the war are thoroughly documented in the Vatican archives. The main thrust of those efforts consisted of an attempt to persuade the government in Vienna to make significant territorial concessions to the Italians. In January 1915, for example, Gasparri addressed an appeal to the Emperor Franz Josef through the papal nuncio in Vienna: 'The salvation of the Empire requires the Emperor to make this painful sacrifice and to make it immediately.'[50] The Vatican also acted as a bearer of conciliatory missives between German and Austro-Hungarian governments and Italy in the negotiations over the cession of territory in the 'unredeemed lands', and over a putative German loan to Italy, etc.[51] When it became clear that the Catholic party in Austria, the Christian Socials, were hostile to the idea of territorial concessions to Italy, it tried to use the good offices of Matthias Erzberger to dissuade them from their opposition.[52] It also sought to persuade the Italian government to accept Austrian concessions, which was difficult given the slowness and reluctance of the Emperor and his foreign minister Burian.[53] As late as 18 May, Benedict was still trying to persuade Salandra that the Austrians would make satisfactory concessions.[54]

The serious consequences for the Vatican of Italy's entry into the war very quickly became apparent. Crucial was the position of the embassies of Austria-Hungary and the German states. Unfortunately, the solution adopted in the Second World War of taking the embassies of belligerent powers into the Vatican was not really feasible in the First World War because the Law of Guarantees did not recognize the Vatican as an independent, sovereign State.[55] The most that the Law granted was a degree of 'extraterritoriality': the Holy See was not even the actual legal owner of the Vatican and Lateran palaces, etc., because the Law only said that the Pope 'enjoyed' them.[56] When the Italian Government asked the Vatican to take moral responsibility for the good behaviour of the embassies if they remained on Italian soil, so that they would not constitute a threat to Italian security, Benedict and Gasparri refused, preferring them to withdraw to Switzerland for the duration of hostilities. Taking responsibility for their good behaviour would have involved supervising their telegram traffic with Berlin and Vienna. There is some evidence that the Central Powers rather relished the 'banishment' of their embassies to the Vatican, since it made it possible for their propaganda to paint the intentions of the Italian government in a bad light.[57] With the departure of their embassies, however, the balance swung against the influence of Germans and Austrians in the Vatican. This situation was obviously not satisfactory for the Central Powers. The Germans in particular feared that the obstruction of communication with the Vatican would impede their influence there, which was one reason why they proposed various territorial solutions of the Roman Question.[58] Benedict and Gasparri seriously considered asking the embassies of the Entente Powers to withdraw as well in order to preserve the appearance of Vatican neutrality, but abandoned the idea as unnecessary and counterproductive: it would merely have further intensified the Vatican's difficulties in communicating with other powers.[59]

The seizure of Palazzo Venezia, the former embassy of Austria to the Holy See, by the Italian government in August 1916, following one of the first Austrian air raids with resulting Italian civilian casualties, in this case in Venice (Venezia), caused further alarm in the Vatican and tense relations with Italy.[60] Benedict claimed that the incident once more demonstrated the inadequacies of the Law of Guarantees, fearing that the Vatican itself might suffer the same fate as Palazzo Venezia at the hands of an Italian government of a more strongly anti-clerical colour.[61] His worst fears appeared to have been realized when the Italian government laid claim to the Collegio Teutonico, the German College which lies on the very edge of the Vatican; though the attempt was prevented, it must have made Benedict and Gasparri think very hard about the future.[62] The exigencies of the war also produced practical inconveniences for the Vatican, the call-up of its staff, lay and ecclesiastical, and members of the Papal Court and even high-ranking prelates: thus Monti spent much time seeking exemptions for members of the various 'armed forces' of the Vatican, especially the Noble Guard, and leading ecclesiastics, including Mgrs Pacelli and Tedeschini.[63]

The withdrawal of the Austrian and German embassies to Switzerland caused precisely the problems of communication for the Vatican which had been predicted, but the problem went further than that. Telegram and mail traffic to and from the Vatican was frequently subject to Italian censorship, causing enormous delays, much to Benedict's fury. Through Baron Monti, and other go-betweens, Benedict and Gasparri repeatedly protested against these abuses.[64] The use of Vatican diplomatic bags (or those of other neutral powers) was no real solution either, as Italy and other belligerent powers on both sides were not averse to intercepting them from time to time (see p. 77). Another consequence of Italy's entry into the war was that *L'Osservatore Romano* was censored like any other Italian newspaper, as was the Jesuit journal *La Civiltà Cattolica*. Benedict felt, and not without reason, that the military censors were rather more lenient towards the anti-clerical rather than to the Catholic press, with serious consequences for him during moments of tension between the Vatican and Italy. As he repeatedly complained, his enemies were allowed to slander and insult him at will, but *L'Osservatore Romano* and other Catholic newspapers were frequently muzzled when they tried to defend him, the most notable example being when the anti-clerical journal *Il Travaso* produced a scurrilous poem against the Pope.[65] Though the Italians did not impede the visits of ecclesiastics of enemy powers, like Cardinal Hartmann for example, they subjected them to intolerable surveillance.[66] The Germans even complained that due to Italian pressure, the Vatican was failing to appoint the numbers of German and Austrian cardinals which the size of the Catholic populations of the Central Powers merited.[67] The precariousness of the Pope's position in an Italy at war was revealed in an even more acute way in November 1916 when the Emperor Franz Josef died. Before giving the go-ahead for a solemn funeral for the deceased Catholic head of state in the semi-private Chapel of the Countess Matilda in the Vatican Palace, Benedict felt it prudent to seek assurances from the Italian Government, via Baron Monti, that it would maintain law and order during the course of the proceedings.[68]

In these circumstances, as Garzia demonstrates, though direct, informal relations between Italy and the Holy See usually remained good, the Roman Question had once again become a real issue in their relationship, after years of merely ritual protests.[69] Moreover, the Roman Question had returned to the international agenda. The Spaniards, hoping to exploit their former links with Benedict in an attempt to play a major role in international affairs once more by hosting a peace conference in Madrid, also offered the Pope 'sanctuary' in the Escorial in May 1915.[70] Benedict turned down the offer: in fact, he never intended to leave Rome and certainly the situation in Rome at that time in no way warranted it, though there is evidence of plans being drawn up for such a contingency.[71] A more significant initiative was that of the Central Powers, who sought to exploit the revival of the Roman Question as a weapon against Italy. In October 1915, Matthias Erzberger, on behalf of the German Centre Party proposed that the Law of Guarantees should be amended to provide the Papacy with real territorial sovereignty over the Vatican and adjacent areas down to the Tiber, commutation of the financial obligations of Italy to the Papacy and international guarantees of the new order.[72] This found no favour in the Vatican. Indeed Gasparri felt compelled to distance the Vatican from this partisan initiative. In an interview with *Il Corriere della Sera* on 28 June 1915 he insisted that the Holy See was not interested in foreign schemes but rather that it expected 'an appropriate resolution of its situation not from foreign arms but from the triumph of those sentiments of justice which it is hoped will become stronger in the Italian people in accordance with their real interests'.[73]

Though it was not appreciated at the time, this declaration would later make a negotiated solution of the Roman Question possible. But it was too late in preventing the Italian government from striking a decisive diplomatic blow against the Vatican. In the autumn of 1914, Sonnino had become alarmed by evidence that the Vatican was determined to get to the peace conference, by further evidence that the victorious Central Powers would use that conference to impose a solution of the Roman Question upon Italy and by an earlier, ingenious plan of Erzberger's for resolving the Roman Question and avoiding Italian intervention.[74] In response, he insisted upon inserting into the Treaty of London signed with the Entente Powers, a clause ruling out the possibility that a papal representative could participate in an eventual conference: 'France, Great Britain and Russia shall support any such opposition as Italy shall make to any proposal in the direction of introducing a representative of the Holy See in any peace negotiations or negotiations for the settlement of questions raised by the war.'[75] News of this clause reached the ears of Benedict and Gasparri in January 1916, but was not confirmed until the Bolsheviks published the texts of all the secret treaties they had found in the foreign office archives in Petrograd in December 1917.[76] Until the last, however, various members of the Italian government, including Salandra, Sonnino and Orlando, persistently denied the existence of the clause, which did nothing to strengthen Benedict's trust in them.[77]

While Italy had remained neutral, the bulk of Italian Catholics had also preserved a neutralist stance. That stance can be explained by a number of factors. There was a vein of stubborn Catholic intransigence whose sympathies inevitably lay with Catholic Austria rather than with the masonic, democratic and Protestant or Orthodox powers of the Entente.[78] Another principled element in Catholic neutralism was the objection to Italian intervention on the grounds of the 'Just War' theory: clearly, Italian intervention against Austria could not be justified on the grounds of defence.[79] But this feeling was restricted to a small part of the Catholic clergy and intelligentsia: the main source of opposition eventually came from the grass roots of the Catholic movement, and in particular from the Catholic peasantry who, like their Socialist counterparts, knew only too well that in the event of war they would provide the 'trench fodder'. Not surprisingly, the leading figure among Catholic peasants, the MP Guido Miglioli, remained a neutralist to the bitter end.[80] The neutral stance of the Papacy itself was a very powerful influence on Italian Catholics, but when the Italian Parliament voted for intervention in May 1915, Catholics were deeply split, with some leading Catholic figures like the priest Luigi Sturzo and the MP Filippo Meda opting for war. In response to this situation, Giuseppe Dalla Torre, by now the national president of the Unione Popolare, the precursor of the future Catholic Action organization, followed his instructions from the Vatican and laid down an official Catholic line: 'All support for the war, but no responsibility for it.'[81] This did not make the Church popular with the interventionists, who included the vociferous, violently anti-clerical Futurists and former extreme Left elements, most notably Benito Mussolini. Equally, Benedict XV was not happy with the more markedly pro-war, patriotic tone of some Catholic associations and clergy.[82] It was a difficult, confused situation. Italian intervention had undermined his peace hopes and efforts, but the patriotic enthusiasm of Italian Catholics could also very easily compromise the Vatican's neutrality in the eyes of the Central Powers: *L'Osservatore Romano* displayed a predictable coolness to the announcement of the entry of Filippo Meda into the Boselli 'national' government in 1916.[83] Meda's appointment was meant to signify the inclusion of even the Catholics in a government of 'national solidarity', but Benedict insisted that 'Meda only represents Meda' – a rather unrealistic attitude in the circumstances.[84] On the other hand, he complied when asked by the Italian government to mobilize the support of bishops and clergy for the war effort, and in particular for government loans.[85] Ironically, the contribution of Italian Catholics to the patriotic cause was never enough to satisfy most interventionists, and particularly their press. Their hostility towards Benedict, and Vatican policy generally, would reach its height in November 1917 after the cataclysmic Italian defeat at Caporetto when, paradoxically, Catholic commitment to the war effort was most obvious and complete.

The Gerlach Affair

At the beginning of 1917, Benedict was faced by a scandal, 'the Gerlach Affair', which threatened to seriously damage Italo–Vatican relations and thoroughly undermine the credibility of his neutralist stance. Italian police investigations, following the blowing up of the Italian battleship *Leonardo Da Vinci* in Taranto harbour in August 1916, and of the *Benedetto Brin* in Brindisi harbour a year earlier, eventually led to the Vatican, to the door of Mgr Rudolph Gerlach, papal secret chamberlain.[86] Gerlach was accused of being the leading light in an Italian espionage ring, with the role of financier and link to German and Austrian intelligence. It was bad enough that someone so close to the Pope should be accused of such activities, but it was also alleged that he had maintained contact with his intelligence bosses via the Vatican diplomatic courier and brought the funds for the spies into Italy by that same means.[87]

Inevitably, a number of quite fantastic stories were spun around the figure of Rudolph Gerlach, especially at the time. Apart from being described as a having led the life of a sexual libertine in Vienna, with Cardinal Agliardi, then nuncio, as his companion,[88] he was accused of having been 'planted' in the Vatican by German intelligence long before the war,[89] of trying to set up a refuelling base for German submarines on the Calabrian coast,[90] and it has been suggested that he was not even a priest – but there is not, in fact, a scrap of evidence to support any of these claims.[91] Nor does there appear to have been very much truth in the formal charges against him, even though he was convicted when the case against him and his fellow-defendants came to trial, and sentenced to life imprisonment with hard labour.[92] Much of the case against him rested on the testimony of a renegade priest Mario Tedeschi who claimed to have had close relations with Gerlach, but whose credibility as a witness was badly damaged by the fact that he was unable to recognize his photograph: his evidence was later cancelled from the court records and he was subsequently prosecuted for perjury.[93] One of the other accused, Valente, withdrew the charges he made against Gerlach, but the court ignored this development.[94] Papers in the Vatican archives confirm Gasparri's claims that Gerlach's correspondence with Muhlberg, the Prussian minister to the Vatican, Ritter, the Bavarian minister, and Erzberger was, as he and the Vatican always maintained, innocent, being part of

Benedict's diplomatic and humanitarian efforts, but that does not rule out the possibility that he was also using the correspondence for other, illicit purposes.[95]

Solid evidence that he was involved in the plot to blow up the battleships or that he was truly a spy is strangely lacking, though Erzberger's biographer claims that he was in German pay.[96] At most, it would seem likely that Gerlach did act as a paymaster for two anti-interventionist, Italian newspapers, *Il Bastone* and *La Vittoria*. There is even less evidence that he had used the Vatican for espionage purposes; indeed, the military tribunal in its final judgement made a point of saying that the Vatican as such was not involved in his spying activities.[97] The fact that Gerlach was allowed to leave Italy in January 1917, being escorted to the Swiss border by Italian police before the trial opened, suggests that the Italian authorities were anxious to limit the embarrassment to the Vatican, but also that they suspected he would have been able to make a very creditable defence had he been present at his trial.[98] On the other hand, his conviction and sentence satisfied both Allied governments and Italian anti-clericals.

The Gerlach Affair attracted a lot of criticism of Benedict, both from outside and within the Vatican, casting doubt upon the soundness of his judgement. De Salis claimed that Gerlach's appointment owed much to his ingratiating contacts with Benedict when the latter came to Rome to receive the red hat in May 1914 and for the conclave three months later.[99] Peters confirms this and he also describes Gerlach as 'one of his [Benedict's] most intimate friends'.[100] Gerlach was undoubtedly one of Benedict's closest personal assistants but it is unlikely that he was a 'friend' given the Pope's very formal relations with his entourage. It would seem, however, that Gerlach's cheerful, engaging personality was a comfort to Benedict, overriding his natural prudence.[101] De Salis backed up his argument against Benedict by claiming that a number of leading Vatican personalities, including Cardinal Merry Del Val, had warned him against appointing Gerlach to his service, or keeping him on after the Italian entry into the war, claims which are confirmed by Carlo Monti.[102] In Benedict's defence it should be said that in the four years that Gerlach had spent in

Rome, from 1910 to 1914, before he met Benedict, he had given no cause for concern to his superiors, and had progressed rapidly from the Capranica to the Academy of Noble Ecclesiastics, where he was appointed student prefect, and was made a judge of the Tribunal of the Rota in 1911.[103] Peters makes the point that under the 'rigoristic' rule of St Pius X and Cardinal Merry Del Val, no one on whom the merest breath of suspicion fell would have lasted long in the Vatican and its associated institutions and educational establishments.[104]

Benedict was also criticized for standing by Gerlach. He believed firmly and unshakeably in Gerlach's innocence; in one of his letters to Gerlach in April 1917, just before his trial opened in Rome, he wrote, 'I send you my blessing with my old and unchanged affection',[105] and as late as 1919, Benedict reaffirmed his belief in Gerlach's innocence by making him a domestic prelate.[106] Leading Vatican personalities, including Cardinals De Lai and Gasparri, and the Sostituto, Mgr Tedeschini, were unhappy with the Pope's obstinacy in the matter, and De Lai urged that 'the Holy See separate its cause from that (of Gerlach); given his indiscretions and lack of common sense, the Holy See will probably suffer badly'.[107] Yet Benedict's instincts were not entirely incorrect. For example, his suspicion that Gerlach had been convicted by a 'masonic sanhedrin' was borne out by both Orlando and Boselli, Italian prime minister at the time of the affair: the latter actually admitted to Monti that there were too many masons on the military tribunal which tried Gerlach.[108]

Despite the benevolent attitude of Benedict, Gerlach did not make things easy for the Vatican after his exit from Italy. His withdrawal to Switzerland was bad enough: as Benedict himself remarked, that country was regarded as an 'espionage centre'.[109] To make matters worse, in March Gerlach went to Germany and Austria where he made much-publicized visits to the King of Bavaria, the German and Austrian Emperors and Hindenburg, who all treated him as a hero and bestowed decorations on him, as a result of which people began to think that he really was a spy.[110]

The Gerlach Affair illustrates very graphically all of the difficulties of Benedict's relationship with Italy during the war; indeed, the period from January to July 1917 was the one in which that relationship reached its lowest ebb. The affair brought out the worst in Benedict, his obstinacy, his notorious irascibility and not a little paranoia. At its height, in early June, Monti recorded that he found the Pope 'very excited, he told me that he had decided not to receive me again as the representative of the government, with which he resolved to have no further relations'.[111] It is also indicative of the tension at that time, that Monti felt obliged to warn the Italian Prime Minister that if there were any attacks on the Vatican in the wake of the Gerlach trial the Catholic associations would rise *en masse* against the government, though it has to be said that there was remarkably little criticism of the Vatican in the Italian press.[112] On the other hand, despite the brave and untiring efforts of Monti, Italo–Vatican relations remained volatile throughout the period of hostilities between Italy and Austria-Hungary, periodically erupting into tension over such matters as the departure of the ambassadors of the Central Powers, Palazzo Venezia, Article 15 of the Treaty of London, the speeches of Government ministers, especially the blatantly anti-clerical one of Bissolati at Cremona in 1915,[113] and attacks on the Pope in the anti-clerical press. It is not surprising, therefore, that Benedict dug his heels in over the Gerlach Affair: he tended to see it as a part of a masonic, anti-clerical plot and refused to be bullied. There was always a little anti-masonic paranoia on the part of both Benedict and his Secretary of State, but it was not entirely unjustified by events. Nor was their hostility to Sonnino, the half-Jewish, half-Protestant and completely irremovable Italian Foreign Minister, unjustified either. According to Orlando, 'Sonnino is the systematic opponent of any proposal made in the Council of Ministers in favour of the Holy See.'[114] Orlando also admitted that though many would have liked to remove Sonnino from his post, it was impossible.[115] It was in these very difficult circumstances that Benedict and Gasparri were forced to conduct their diplomacy during the First World War.

Notes and references

1. 'Benedictus PP. XV, Ad Universos Orbis Catholicos', *La CC*, 1542, 19 September 1914, I–IV.
2. As quoted in Carlen (ed.), IV, p. 146.
3. Ibid.
4. Ibid., pp. 144–5.
5. Ibid.
6. AAES, Italia, 1427, fasc. 569, 'Imparzialità della S. Sede', memorandum by Gasparri (no date).
7. Zivojinovic (1978), p. 4.
8. ASV, SS, Guerra, 1914–18, rubrica 244, fasc. 63/64.
9. As quoted in Leslie, p. 214: this book also chronicles the indefatigable efforts of Gasquet and his colleagues to offset German and Austro-Hungarian influences in the Vatican, especially in the period before Italy's entry into the war in May 1915.
10. As quoted in Epstein, p. 121.
11. Monticone, p. 9.
12. Leslie, pp. 213–14.
13. Ibid.
14. Zivojinovic (1978), pp. 12 and 13.
15. See Epstein, Appendix II, pp. 408–9.
16. *Diario*, II, p. 3, 3 January 1917, where Monti says that Benedict told him the bulk of Peter's Pence came from first the United States and then from Germany.
17. As quoted in Hachey (ed.), p. xx.
18. Zivojinovic (1978), p. 12.
19. Rumi (ed.) (1990), p. 22, also makes the point that there was traditionally a close personal relationship between the Popes and the Habsburg family in the nineteenth century: 'The archdukes of the various branches of the Habsburgs grew up in comparative familiarity with the Pope: from Vienna came ingenuous poetry and hand-knitted goods and Rome replied with medals and objects of personal devotion.'
20. Randall, p. 13.
21. Quoted in Hachey (ed.), p. xx.
22. *Diario*, I, p. 416, 9 August 1916.
23. Vistalli, p. 39.
24. Garzia, p. 68.
25. Poincaré, pp. 305–6.
26. Garzia, 14.
27. Ibid., p. 68; Leslie, p. 225.
28. Loiseau (1956), p. 100 and May 1956, p. 54.

29. Garzia, p. 61.
30. Panzera, p. 323.
31. Gregory, p. 87.
32. Garzia, pp. 17 and 20.
33. De Salis, report on his mission, in Hachey (ed.), p. 7.
34. AAES, Stati Ecclesiastici, 1316, fasc. 455, 'Libri diplomatici pubblicati da vari Stati belligeranti, Libro bianco tedesco sulle crudeltà delle truppe russe contro i civili e i prigionieri di guerra tedeschi'.
35. Ibid. This file contains fifteen such remonstrances from the various belligerents, plus from one neutral, Holland.
36. The Holy See did possess at this time two major tribunals, the Segnatura and the Sacra Rota, but both were, of course, competent only in canon law, and not civil/public law of any kind.
37. AAES, Stati Ecclesiastici, 1316, fasc. 455, Germania–Inghilterra–Austria–Francia–Belgio–Olanda, 1914–1918, 'Libro tedesco sulla neutralità violata dal Belgio'.
38. Van Der Kiste, pp. 102–17.
39. AAES, Stati Ecclesiastici, 1427, fasc. 569, 'Imparzialità della S. Sede', p. 9.
40. Ibid., 1369/1372, fasc. 517, minutes of meeting of 16 August 1916; the Italian historian Luigi Salvatorelli, pp. 9–10, was of the same opinion: 'It was difficult for the Vatican to try to act as a moral arbiter in the conflict. The Vatican was liable to find itself utterly cut off from one side or another.'
41. As quoted in Peters, p. 121.
42. Ibid.
43. *Diario*, I, p. 189, 19 January 1915; Morozzo Della Rocca (1996), p. 563.
44. Ibid., p. 564.
45. Ibid.
46. For a detailed account of the 'Intervention Crisis' in Italy, see Seton-Watson, pp. 413–50.
47. ASV, SS, Guerra, 1914–1918, rub. 244, fasc. 29, Gasparri to Scapinelli, 12 January 1915.
48. Seton-Watson, p. 449.
49. Garzia, p. 20: according to Hachey (ed.), p. xvii, the Vatican feared for the effects of Italian intervention on the flow of Peter's Pence.
50. ASV, SS, Guerra, fasc. 258, Gasparri to Scapinelli, 17 January 1915.
51. Ibid.
52. ASV, SS, Guerra, 1914–1918, fasc. 29, Erzberger to Benedict, 8 March 1915.
53. Ibid., letter of Salandra to Gasparri.
54. Seton-Watson, p. 448.
55. Chadwick (1986), pp. 114–24.

56. For the text see Pollard (1985), Appendix I.
57. *Diario*, I, p. 219, 24 January 1915.
58. Stehlin (1974), p. 421.
59. Garzia, p. 61.
60. *Diario*, I, p. 437, 30 August 1916.
61. Ibid.
62. AAES, 953, 343–4, Roma, 1918–1920, 'Ospizio di S. Maria dell' Anima e Campo Santo confisca'.
63. There are numerous references in the *Diario* to the exemptions which Monti was asked to obtain; see for example volume I, pp. 212–3, 20 March 1915.
64. Felice, pp. 169–77.
65. *Diario*, I, p. 241, 4 July 1915.
66. Ibid., I, p. 293, 1 December 1915.
67. Stehlin (1974), p. 420.
68. AAES, Italia, 879, fasc. 316, 1916, 'Cappella papale per i funerali dell'Imperatore d'Austria'.
69. Garzia, p. 105.
70. Ibid.
71. AAES, 'Italia e Principato di Monaco', 1369/1372, 517, pro-memoria of 10 August 1917.
72. Epstein, pp. 144–5.
73. As quoted in Dalla Torre, p. 1292.
74. Epstein, pp. 144–5.
75. As quoted in Grenville, pp. 24–7.
76. Seton-Watson, p. 449.
77. *Diario*, I, p. 339, 28 January 1916.
78. Dalla Torre, p. 1294.
79. Ibid.
80. For an account of the behaviour of Italian Catholics during the Intervention Crisis, see Scoppola, pp. xli–xlii.
81. As quoted in De Rosa (1954), p. 423.
82. Molinari, p. 429.
83. Meda, p. 56.
84. See Benedict's annotations of the *L'Osservatore Romano* article of 14 September 1915, in ASV, SS, 1916, rub. 165, 857, 313.
85. *Diario*, I, p. 315, 1 January 1916.
86. The best, most succinct and up-to-date account of the Gerlach affair is to be found in Alvarez (1996); for contemporary accounts, see De Salis, Report on My Mission, PRO, FO, 7671/c15334/8227/22, in Hachey (ed.), pp. 18–19 and *The Times*, 8 August 1917, p. 16, 'The Italian Spy Trial'.
87. *The Times*, ibid.

88. Dillon, p. 11.
89. *Diario*, II, pp. 76–7, 1 May 1917.
90. Ibid.
91. Interview with the Della Chiesa family, October 1996.
92. *The Times*, 8 August 1917, p. 16.
93. Ibid.
94. *Diario*, II, p. 120, 21 June 1917.
95. AAES, Italia, 1917–1918, 930, fasc. 335, letter of Gerlach to Benedict, 17 May 1917.
96. Epstein, p. 163.
97. *The Times*, 8 August 1917, p. 16.
98. De Salis report, in Hachey (ed.), p. 19.
99. Ibid., p. 18.
100. Peters, p. 132.
101. Ibid., p. 127: The file on a young seminarian, Diana, recommended to the pope by his sister, Countess Persico, in AAES, Stati Ecclesiastici, p. 152 and Monti's references to him in his *Diario*, II, pp. 202–4, 10 November 1917, pp. 208–9, 16 November 1917, p. 356, 16 July 1918 and p. 359, 30 July 1918 all suggest that Benedict in his lonely 'imprisonment' was a little indulgent towards personable and plausible young men.
102. De Salis report, in Hachey (ed.), p. 19: Monti, II, p. 135, 16 July 1917.
103. AAES, Italia, 1917, 893–4, fasc. 323, contains assorted papers relating to his curriculum vitae.
104. Peters, p. 129.
105. AAES, Italia, 1917, 893–4, fasc. 326, 4 July 1917.
106. Ibid., 12 March 1919.
107. *Diario*, II, p. 105, 2 June 1917.
108. Ibid., II, p. 92, 11 May 1917.
109. AAES, Italia, 1917, 893–4, 326. letter of 17 April 1917.
110. Ibid., letter from Mgr Sardi, nuncio in Munich, 16 March 1917: as this file demonstrates, the Gerlach Affair was to haunt the Vatican for several years. In April 1924 Gerlach wrote a thinly veiled blackmail letter, threatening to publish Benedict's letters to him. He was only finally persuaded to burn it in December of that year.
111. *Diario*, II, pp. 108–10, 7 June 1917.
112. Ibid., II, p. 120, 22 June 1917.
113. Ibid., I, pp. 494–501, 30 October and 2 November 1916.
114. Ibid., II, 13 August 1918.
115. Ibid.

5

Humanitarian relief and peace diplomacy

It took some time for Benedict and Gasparri to develop the confidence and the contacts necessary to embark on serious peace diplomacy. During the first year of the war, they dedicated their diplomatic energies to the relief of suffering on all sides, among both soldiers and civilians. By the middle of 1915 they came to believe that the Papacy could and must now play an effective peace-making role. As a result, they moved beyond public appeals for peace to active peace diplomacy, a diplomatic offensive, as Garzia has described it,[1] which culminated in the 'Peace Note' of August 1917 (see pp. 123–8). Even after the bitter disappointment of seeing the Note scorned and rejected by both sides, Benedict did not give up. Though he did little for some months after the Note, he returned to an active policy in November 1917, after the catastrophic Italian defeat at Caporetto, when he sought to negotiate with Vienna on Italy's behalf. A year later, when the boot was on the other foot, when the Austrian Empire faced total defeat, he engaged in increasingly urgent diplomatic efforts to save it from collapse. All his efforts were fruitless, leaving the Vatican an impotent bystander when the First World War came to an end in November 1918.

The Vatican's humanitarian work

Christmas 1914 marked the point at which Benedict first sought to intervene directly in the war, by appealing to the belligerent powers to accept a twenty-four-hour cease-fire in celebration of the

1. The Della Chiesa family in 1862. From left to right: Giacomo, Mother, Baccino, Gianantonio and Giulia. Father behind.

2. Giacomo and family in 1902. Back, second from left, Baccino, Mother, Giacomo. Far right, Giulia. Bottom left, her husband Pino Persico.

3. Gioacchino Pecci, Pope Leo XIII (1878–1903)

4. Cardinal Mariano Rampolla, Secretary of State to
Leo XIII and Giacomo's mentor

5. Giuseppe Sarto, Pope Pius X (1903–1914)

6. Cardinal Raphael Merry Del Val, Secretary of
State to Pius X

7. Cardinal Pietro Gasparri, Secretary of State to
Benedict XV and Pius XI (from 1922 to 1930)

8. The consecration of Giacomo Della Chiesa as bishop in the Sistine Chapel, 1907

9. Archbishop Della Chiesa visiting a mountain parish, 1908

10. The coronation of Benedict XV in the Sistine Chapel, 6 September 1914

11. French prisoners of war brought to Switzerland by Benedict XV

12. British prisoners of war brought to Switzerland by Benedict XV

13. Benedict XV in his study in the Vatican

14. The French diplomatic delegation in the Vatican for the canonization of
Joan of Arc in 1921

15. Benedict XV on his deathbed, January 1922; his friend Carlo Monti is on his knees, third from right

16. The tomb of Benedict XV in the crypt of St Peter's Basilica

birthday of the 'Prince of Peace'. His efforts were not successful: though he received a sympathetic hearing from the British, German and Austro-Hungarian governments, the French and Russians said no. It was his first major disappointment, his first rebuff, but he was to experience many more of them in the future, and they were to be increasingly bitter and disillusioning. This failure notwithstanding, early in the New Year, on 10 January, he published his 'Prayer for Peace' which he urged the bishops to commend to their clergy and faithful.[2] The reception of this prayer in the Catholic world demonstrated the extreme difficulty of the Vatican's position during the war. In both Belgium and France clergy, and even bishops, insisted on interpreting the purpose of the prayer in a manner tailor-made to fit the patriotic intents of their countries.[3] And one bishop actually went so far as to change the text of the prayer, adding the words 'On conditions honourable to our Fatherland'.[4] What possible chance was there of developing mutual comprehension among Catholics of the two warring camps in these circumstances?

Of all the papal initiatives of this time, the one which was to bear most practical fruit was the decree published in *L'Osservatore Romano* of 23 December 1914, providing for 'spiritual and material assistance to prisoners'.[5] Even though the Vatican had already begun some relief operations earlier, out of this decree developed a vast array of papal humanitarian relief measures throughout the course of the war, and afterwards, which was comparable in extent to the great work of the International Red Cross. The main thrust of this humanitarian endeavour was obviously the welfare of prisoners of war. By the spring of 1915, an organization called the Opera dei Prigionieri had been set up in the Vatican, located in the offices of the Secretariat of State, and by the end of the war it had dealt with a staggering 600,000 items of correspondence, including 170,000 enquiries about missing persons, 40,000 appeals for help in the repatriation of sick POWs and the forwarding of 50,000 letters to and from prisoners and their families.[6]

As the conflict developed, Benedict's first priority was to alleviate the condition of sick, wounded and invalid POWs in the camps, and to provide them with chaplains (of all faiths) and other services; in this regard, the visits of local bishops and clergy, and of the papal nuncios in Brussels, Munich and Vienna, to the POW camps was very important.[7] The latter also inevitably involved the Vatican in negotiations over the condition of prison camps and the facilities provided there, as well as delicate questions of the maltreatment of prisoners.[8] Particular attention was devoted to young soldiers who had been wounded and captured in their first battle – in September 1916, Benedict received an especially heart-rending letter on this subject from a Mme Dumas, a widowed mother in the town of Nevers in France.[9] There was also the special case of the fathers of large families.[10] Another small but neverthe-less important group were civilian internees, especially French and Belgian;[11] the problems of humanitarian relief and moral condem-nation of the actions of the military authorities became hopelessly intertwined when it was a case of civilian populations deported *en masse*, such as in Belgium in 1915. Nevertheless, the Germans agreed to halt Belgian deportations thanks to the intervention of Benedict and the nuncio in Munich, Mgr Aversa.[12]

Switzerland rapidly became a major centre of the Vatican's relief humanitarian operations. The government of that neutral country was very anxious to assist in the Pope's various projects for assistance to POWs and a succession of Vatican special envoys, first Mgr Marchetti-Selvaggiani and later Mgr Maglione (who became cardinal Secretary of State to Pius XII) took up residence in Freibourg and Berne to co-ordinate these joint efforts, and they were assisted by Count Santucci, a leading member of the 'black' aristocracy and president of the Banco di Roma.[13] The presence of the Prussian, Bavarian and Austro-Hungarian legations in Lugano, following their departure from Rome, also made this papal 'pres-ence' especially useful. By January 1917, 26,000 POWs and 3,000 civilian detainees had been given the opportunity to convalesce in hospitals or sanatoria in Switzerland.[14]

The negotiations for these relatively modest operations were not easy, but those for the exchange of prisoners between the two sides were extremely difficult and long-drawn-out, frequently breaking down due to mutual suspicion.[15] The most difficult of all exchanges to arrange seem to have been those between Italy and Austria-

Hungary – the Vatican never succeeded in bringing Italian or Austro-Hungarian POWs to Switzerland, and in February 1918, Maglione was still negotiating to obtain the release of sick Italian prisoners captured at the battle of Caporetto five months before: he did not succeed.[16] The Vatican had almost as much difficulty brokering a truce to permit the burial of the dead on the Italo-Austrian front line in December 1915.[17] The Italians' record of looking after the interests of their captured soldiers during the First World War was not a good one.[18] A major motive for opposing repatriation of POWs on both sides was the fear that such a measure would breed defeatism among soldiers at the front: Sonnino was particularly obdurate about this.[19]

Both during and after the war (see pp. 147–8), one of Benedict's major concerns was the fate of children. In October 1916 he addressed an appeal to the clergy and laity of the United States for money to help feed the children of Belgium.[20] But feeding the famished was not restricted to children; the Vatican was involved in a number of operations aimed at providing foodstuffs for populations in or behind the war zones. To quote a few examples, Lithuania, Montenegro in both 1916 and 1917, Poland in 1916, Russian refugees in 1916 and Syria and Lebanon from 1916 through to 1922.[21] In the latter case, Benedict's efforts were once again obstructed by Sonnino.[22] Count Giuseppe Dalla Torre, a leading Catholic layman and editor of *L'Osservatore Romano*, wrote of this operation, 'the Christians of Syria and the East, subject to diseases, famine and oppressive maltreatment, recognized in him [Benedict] their most effective protector'.[23] The very specific reference to 'Christians' in that quotation was not accidental: the Vatican's relations with The Sublime Porte, the Ottoman Government in Istanbul, had not been good for a long time, but they deteriorated further during the course of the war, due to the Turks' treatment of Christian populations in their empire and most particularly, the massacres of the Armenians, who were considered disloyal. In April and May 1915 a campaign of what would now be called 'ethnic cleansing' was launched against the Christian, mainly Armenian, populations of Anatolia. In July, the Apostolic Delegate in Constantinople, Mgr Dolci, was instructed to protest against the massacres; the governments of Germany and Austria-Hungary were also asked to bring pressure to bear on their ally to stop the killings, and Benedict himself sent an autograph letter on 10 September to the Sultan who, in his role as Caliph of Islam, was, like the Pope, a world-wide religious leader.[24] The Pope's intervention had only limited success; by the end of the war it was estimated that over a million Armenians had died, either killed outright by the Turks, or as a result of maltreatment or from starvation.[25]

In a comment on the role of Benedict XV during the First World War, the leader of the future Italian Catholic party, Fr Luigi Sturzo, made the point that moral theology took a long time to catch up with the horrors unleashed by the new technology of warfare.[26] But it was not merely theology which had to catch up, men's imaginations took some time to come to terms with the appalling human effects of mines, submarines and aerial bombardment. Benedict was particularly revolted by the effects of the latter on civilian populations, which were very evident in and around the battle zones of north-eastern Italy, especially Venice, Treviso, Padua, Trieste and Pola. From early 1916 onwards, Vatican diplomacy accordingly devoted much attention to pleading with the military authorities to desist from these 'barbarous' practices.[27] It had only limited success, despite the support of Orlando who suggested a thirty-kilometre 'air-raid-free zone': there continued to be bombardments of even 'open cities' right until the end of the war.[28] Benedict was truly prodigal in his efforts to relieve suffering on all sides during the war. In the process, he spent an enormous amount of money – eighty-two million lire – and nearly bankrupted the Vatican.[29] He got little in the way of reward during the course of the conflict: on the contrary, as we have already seen, he was attacked from all sides. Ironically, the lasting monument to his humanitarian efforts came not in any European state, but in Turkey of all places: in Istanbul a statue was erected in his honour, even before the end of the war.

Papal peace diplomacy

The publication of the Apostolic Exhortation, 'To the Belligerent Peoples, and their Rulers', of 28 July 1915, marks a turning point in the development of Vatican policy during the course of the war; it was at this stage that Benedict and Gasparri committed themselves to active diplomacy in the cause of peace: 'a peace offensive' that would culminate in the famous 'Peace Note' of August 1917.[30] Their decision to do so at this point was determined by two factors: Italy's entry into the war was, as has been seen, causing serious problems for the Holy See, and the fact that it was clear the belligerent powers were unable or unwilling to initiate peace moves themselves.

The Exhortation, written to commemorate the first anniversary of the outbreak of the war, contained an apocalyptic warning of the dangers of not seeking a negotiated peace: 'Abandon the mutual threat of destruction. Remember, Nations do not die; humiliated and oppressed, they bear the weight of the yoke imposed upon them, preparing themselves for their come-back and transmitting from one generation to the next a sad legacy of hatred and vendetta.'[31] The phrase 'Nations do not die' was one of Benedict's most evocative and memorable, and was followed by a very explicit invitation to the belligerents to go to the negotiating table:

> It is not true that this conflict cannot be resolved without the violence of arms . . . Why not from this moment consider with a serene conscience the rights and just aspirations of peoples? Why not commence in good will an exchange, direct or indirect, of views with the purpose of keeping in mind as far as possible those rights and those aspirations and thus put an end to this conflict, as has happened in other circumstances? Blessed be he who first raises the olive branch of peace and extends his right hand to the enemy offering reasonable conditions for peace. The equilibrium of the world and prosperity and secure tranquillity of nations rest on mutual benevolence and the respect of the

117

rights of and dignity of others, rather than on a multitude of armies and a formidable ring of fortresses.[32]

The reference to an 'indirect' as well as direct exchange of views was clearly intended as a hint that the Holy See would be willing to assist in the making of secret contacts.

In fact, Benedict and Gasparri had already actively engaged in a quite sustained peace 'offensive', that is they had striven to preserve the peace between Italy and Austria-Hungary throughout the whole period of the former's neutrality, August 1914 to May 1915. After the failure of that episode in Vatican diplomacy, some prompting to resume their efforts and extend their scope must have come from the awareness that the Pope was increasingly being seen by a variety of groups as a major force for peace. In May 1915 the Pope received a delegation from the Dutch Roman Catholic State Party to discuss the possibility of a peace conference at The Hague.[33] A month later came the visit of the American women peace activists, Jane Adams and Alice Hamilton Balch who, fresh from their own 'peace' conference at The Hague, set out to visit the European heads of state, including the Pope: they recorded with some surprise the enthusiasm, informality and cordiality of the reception which they received from Benedict.[34] In this same period began the succession of approaches from Jewish groups and individuals in both France and America, pleading for the Pope to intervene in defence of Jews being maltreated in Russia or in territories under Russian occupation.[35] Shortly before the publication of the Exhortation, the Vatican had been involved in an attempt to assist in bringing about a separate peace between Germany and Belgium and France. It conveyed an offer, on behalf of Germany, to restore Belgian independence and sovereignty, and to negotiate the future of Alsace-Lorraine with France.[36] Cardinal Mercier's reply to the suggestion that he should pass the offer on to his government was a decisive 'no', and Mgr Baudrillart, the head of the prestigious Catholic Institut de France, and also the author of the French reply to the declaration of the German Catholics of 1914, made it clear that such a proposal was wholly inopportune.[37] Benedict blamed the failure of this *démarche* on the intransigence of the British.[38] After the failure of this, the first major peace initiative since Italian intervention, Benedict desisted from major peace efforts until the autumn of the following year. In the meantime, he intensified his efforts to relieve suffering and to denounce the war, like the impassioned plea of his consistorial allocution of 15 December 1915 against 'the fatal war on land and sea'.[39]

The peace initiative of the Central Powers

December 1916 marked a watershed in the First World War, a moment when the increasing futility of the military stalemate induced one side at least – the Central Powers – to seriously consider a negotiated peace. The German peace initiative came, as was to be nearly always the case during the First World War, at a time of relative strength – the Central Powers had knocked Romania out of the war at the end of November and captured Bucharest at the beginning of December. On the other hand, during the Brusilov offensive in June 1916, the Russians had driven the Austro-Hungarian armies back to the Carpathian mountains, threatening the collapse of the Habsburg Empire; indeed, it would have collapsed but for repeated German intervention.[40] In consequence, the government in Vienna was even more dependent than ever upon its German ally, and subservient to it: in effect, its satellite. The death of the Emperor Franz Josef of Austria and the accession of his nephew Karl I to the Habsburg throne that same November represented a substantial change in the Austrian position. Henceforth, though young and inexperienced, the new Emperor would become increasingly anxious to negotiate his way out of the war in order to escape what seemed to be the war's inevitable consequence – the collapse of the Empire. This latent division between the policies of the two Central Empires would provide both the Vatican and the Entente Powers with considerable opportunities for peace diplomacy in 1917 and 1918.

Meanwhile, Germany took the peace initiative. On 12 December, separate and different notes were handed to both the United

States Chargé d'Affaires in Berlin, and to Cardinal Gasparri in the Vatican.[41] The latter was conspicuous for the deliberate echoes of the language which the Pope himself had used in all of his pronouncements on peace but most notably in the Apostolic Exhortation of July 1915, and concluded by saying: 'The Imperial Government is firmly confident that the initiative of the four Powers (Germany, Austria-Hungary, Bulgaria and Turkey) will find a friendly welcome on the part of His Holiness, and that the work of peace can count upon the precious support of the Holy See.'[42] The work of peace could, of course, always count upon the support of the Holy See, nevertheless, the German peace note received a rather qualified welcome in the Vatican. The problem was that it contained nothing in the way of suggestions for heads of discussion, or even less, possible concessions: nothing concrete at all. Benedict and Gasparri were by no means convinced of the usefulness of the initiative, and it is clear that they were made to understand by De Salis that Britain and France would not welcome any support that they gave it.[43] Peters concludes that 'Benedict realised that if he offended the Entente Powers now, any future efforts would be met with antagonism'.[44] With the palpable unenthusiasm of the Vatican's eventual response to the note, and its unhappiness at the declaration of unrestricted submarine warfare, following the Allies' rejection of the German Peace Note, there was a decided cooling in the relations between the Vatican and Berlin which was not to change until Benedict issued his own Peace Note in August 1917.[45]

The entry of the United States into the war

Shortly after the German note was published, on 20 December 1916, the US President Woodrow Wilson made his own appeal for peace. The key sentence in the note – 'The President is not proposing peace; he is not even offering mediation. He is merely proposing that soundings be taken in order that we may learn, the neutral nations with the belligerents, how near the haven of peace may be for which all mankind longs with an intense and increasing longing'[46] – is strongly reminiscent of Benedict's own appeal of July 1915, but had no more success in achieving its goal, coming too soon after the rejected German peace initiative. On 24 December, *L'Osservatore Romano* came out in support of Wilson's initiative, but privately Gasparri was less enthusiastic.[47] Within just over four months of his note Wilson had broken off relations with Germany. In the meantime, as indeed it had been doing for some previous time, the Vatican strove to avert the breach.

The cause of tensions between Germany and the United States was the former's adoption of submarine warfare, against both enemies and neutrals alike. As J. A. Salter points out, the First World War 'was as much a war of competing blockades, the surface and submarine, as of competing armies. Behind these two blockades the economic systems of the two opposing countries were engaged in a deadly struggle for existence.'[48] To the British and French naval blockade of their coasts, the Central Powers, chiefly Germany, replied with submarine warfare, and the Germans eventually decided upon the introduction of unrestricted submarine warfare, sinking without warning. As the sinkings took their toll and anger stirred in America, Benedict had tried to intervene. His attitude towards both the blockade and submarine warfare was a complex one. He regarded both as essentially immoral, and both as probably violations of international law. He was almost certainly right. Hardach argues:

> Such procedure (sinking without warning) was clearly contrary to established international law, but so, too, was the unrestricted blockade of the Central Powers by the Allies from March 1915 onwards. Hence during and after the war, the Germans tended to regard the one as offsetting the other under international law. But to all save the Germans there was a marked distinction between the confiscation of goods and the sinking without warning of ships, together with their helpless crews and passengers.[49]

In the autumn of 1915 Gasparri had denounced 'the appalling and immoral submarine warfare' and condemned Germany's U-Boat campaign to the Canadian bishop, Mgr MacNally.[50] On the other hand, there was a feeling in the Vatican that the USA was not an impartial neutral, that it was helping one side – the Allies – against the Central Powers, and for largely selfish reasons. Certainly, the United States was effectively committed to the Allies because of economic ties.[51] Benedict particularly deplored the United States' arms trade with Britain and France, especially when it was carried on in passenger vessels, thus providing an excuse for their sinking by the Germans. As early as April 1915, in an interview published in a pro-German New York newspaper, Benedict had called upon the United States to enforce an arms embargo against both sides.[52] In 1916, the Pope went so far as to claim that the arms trade was 'contrary to the law of nations': though he was a lawyer by training, strictly speaking his judgement was wrong.[53] Even so, there is no evidence to support Zivojinovic's claim that the Vatican believed the sinking of passenger ships which carried arms was justified.[54]

The Vatican's hope that, despite the increasing tensions with Germany, the United States would remain neutral were based on the plausible assumption that the German and Irish Catholic groups in America would continue to influence public opinion in a neutralist direction. It also had reason to believe that United States Jewish opinion, which was hostile to Russia, could also be mobilized in support.[55] Thus Benedict regarded Wilson's proposal for a 'League for Peace', on 28 May 1916, as a sop to Irish and German voters.[56] The Vatican urged restraint after the sinking of the *Arabic* in 1915 and Zivojinovic grudgingly admits that when on 1 September 1916, the German Ambassador Bernstorff told the United States Secretary of State Lansing that passenger liners would not be attacked, 'The Pope was credited by some for this concession on Germany's part'.[57] As late as February 1917, Benedict was prepared to be a go-between in an attempt to seek both the end of the blockade and of submarine warfare.[58]

The United States declaration of war in April 1917 was greeted with dismay and perplexity in the Vatican. Commenting on the sour response of *L'Osservatore Romano*, the *Tablet* declared rather patronizingly, 'These are not easy matters for the Roman mind to grasp', but at least it had the decency to admit that 'Had not the

President as short a time ago as last Christmas sent out the great peace message?'[59] He had indeed, and A. J. P. Taylor, speaking of Wilson's decision, says, 'It was ironical that he abandoned neutrality just when his mediation might have achieved some purpose at last.'[60] Gasparri was rather more cynical about Wilson's decision, claiming that it had been prompted by an overweening desire to be present at the peace conference.[61] For Benedict, the American decision was another tragedy, threatening to prolong the war even further.

The papal Peace Note of August 1917

Though the United States entry into the war might have seemed to make the prospect of peace even more remote, by the summer of 1917 there were factors in the general situation which suggested that some peace initiative at this point might have had success. Since the beginning of the year there had been tentative approaches on both sides. The brother-in-law of the Austrian Emperor, Prince Sixtus of Bourbon-Parma, had sought to open a channel of communication on his behalf with the French,[62] an initiative which had received support from the Vatican.[63] By February 1917 there were rumours of developing talks between representatives of Britain and France, and Austria-Hungary in Switzerland. Carlo Monti repeatedly asked both Benedict and Gasparri about the truth of these rumours and about alleged Vatican involvement in them: both repeatedly denied the rumours, but some evidence suggests that they might have been thrifty with the truth in their answers to Monti.[64] It seems unlikely, however, that the Vatican was actively involved in these talks because Cardinal Bourne, Archbishop of Westminster, told Benedict that any peace initiative on the Pope's part would displease Britain.[65]

The contacts which did take place were indicative of increasing war-weariness in both camps. The Russian Revolution of February was an instructive example of what could happen under the strain of war – economic, social and political breakdown. These were just the sorts of evils which Benedict and Gasparri, and others like

Erzberger and Karl I, had been warning about. The mutinies among French troops following the failure of Nivelle's offensive in the spring of 1917 brought home to the Allies the grave risks they now faced. Again, by the summer of 1917, various international congresses were putting on the pressure for peace negotiations. In February Catholic MPs from various countries had met to discuss peace in Switzerland;[66] in Stockholm, representatives of Europe's Socialist parties met to talk peace and there were rumours of a secret masonic congress dedicated to that end.[67] All these developments must have weighed on Benedict's mind. As Taylor says, 'The Summer of 1917 saw the only real gropings in Europe towards peace by negotiation.'[68]

The most promising and interesting of all the aspects of the situation in the summer of 1917, and the one which undoubtedly influenced Benedict most in his decision to publish a 'Peace Note' in August, was the situation which had developed in Germany. Though militarily Germany was in a strong position, at home the war effort was potentially threatened by unprecedented parliamentary dissent. Led by Matthias Erzberger, a 'respectable' majority emerged in the Reichstag which passed a 'peace resolution' in July.[69] Erzberger was in a uniquely powerful position for a civilian politician in wartime Germany. A major exponent of the Catholic Centre Party, he had run the country's propaganda and intelligence-gathering operations abroad, including Italy.[70] In early 1915 he had been sent on two missions to Italy to dissuade her from entering the war, and in the course of them had established contact with the Vatican, meeting Benedict on two occasions, and had been instrumental in securing the consent of the German High Command to Benedict's request for a truce on the Nieuw Chapelle battlefield in order to bury the dead.[71] By the summer of 1917, Erzberger had been converted from an 'annexationist' to a 'disannexationist' viewpoint and was the Vatican's white hope in Germany, the man it believed who would work as its agent of peace within the Empire. Aside from his parliamentary influence, Erzberger had already demonstrated the influence which he could exercise within the Imperial Government by his success in securing prisoner exchanges at Benedict's request.[72]

Monticone talks about the 'German origins' of Benedict's Peace Note.[73] In one sense he is right: Benedict believed that Germany was the key to a successful peace process. Unlike the Allied Powers, Germany and Austria-Hungary were in control of large areas of occupied territory, most especially Belgium, whose restitution was for the Allied Powers the *sine qua non* of any settlement.[74] Benedict therefore began from the premise that only the indication of a willingness on Germany's part to evacuate occupied territory would persuade the Allied Powers to come to the negotiating table. Benedict and Gasparri made careful preparations for what was to become their major peace initiative. In May, in anticipation of a 'peace note', Benedict was in contact with the Emperor Karl and Empress Zita of Austria-Hungary[75] and sent Mgr Pacelli as nuncio to Bavaria, and therefore effectively papal representative to Germany in place of Aversa who had died the previous month.[76] During the course of several conversations with Chancellor Bethman-Hollweg and the Kaiser himself, Pacelli hammered out heads of discussion on which Germany would be prepared to negotiate peace:

1. General limitation of armaments
2. Establishment of international courts
3. Restoration of the independence of Belgium
4. Alsace-Lorraine and other such territorial questions were to be settled by agreements betweens the countries concerned

It was on this that Benedict based his own Peace Note. The problem was that by August Bethman-Hollweg had been ousted by Hindenburg and Ludendorff and replaced by Michaelis, a colourless bureaucrat who more or less did their bidding.

In content, Benedict's note of 1 August (actually sent to the governments of the belligerent powers on the 15th) was a considerable improvement upon both his own previous pronouncements, and the German and American notes of the previous December. It did not content itself with vague references to 'exchanges of views' or 'the rights and just aspirations of peoples'. It set out, systematically, proposals for bringing the war to an end and securing a just and enduring peace:

1. A simultaneous and reciprocal decrease of armaments
2. International arbitration
3. True freedom and community of the seas
4. Reciprocal renunciation of war indemnities
5. Evacuation and restoration of all occupied territories
6. An examination in a conciliatory spirit of rival territorial claims[77]

Belgium, northern France and the German colonies were explicitly mentioned by name under no. 5, and no. 6 talked equally explicitly of 'territorial questions . . . pending between Italy and Austria, and between Germany and France'; in addition, Benedict went beyond the *status quo ante bellum* by insisting on the need to examine 'the remaining territorial and political questions, and particularly those which concern Armenia, the Balkan states, and the territories which form part of the former kingdom of Poland'.[78] This was the first time during the course of the war that any person or power had formulated a detailed and practical schema for a peace negotiation.

The responses to the Peace Note were disappointing. The initial Allied response was summed up by an article in *The Times*. Headed 'German Peace Move', the article went on to say, 'More peace proposals' have been put forth. This time they emanate from the Vatican'.[79] The British Government was, in fact, slow to respond, sending only a letter of acknowledgement. The French never replied at all, combining their resentment of Britain's unilateral action with their usual suspicion of the Papacy: Clémenceau dubbed Benedict's plan as 'a peace against France'.[80] Of all the Allied Powers, Italy was the most overtly and publicly hostile. Its reply came from Sonnino in a debate on foreign policy in October in the Italian Senate where he dismissed the Pope's proposals as inadequate.[81] Sonnino's hostility was motivated by a number of factors. In the first place, his intelligence sources had convinced him that the German High Command were not really serious about giving up Belgium, which was eventually proved to be the case.[82] He was also concerned that in any detailed negotiations over territorial questions, Italy's claims to the *terre irredente* would be brushed aside because of Italy's lack of military progress. The double-dealing of Britain and France earlier in the year make this a plausible scenario. Finally, Sonnino was tenaciously opposed to any increase in international prestige and profile which a successful peace initiative would bring the Pope, fearing that Article 15 would be set aside by his allies, and that Benedict would be allowed a representative at the talks, if not the presidency of them. The reaction of the Central Powers was equally disappointing. Despite the Emperor Karl's genuine support for Benedict's initiative, given the hopeless dependence of the Habsburg Empire upon German military support he was obliged to follow the lead given in Berlin. What was most striking was that the replies of the Central Powers omitted all mention of territorial questions.[83] The problem was that real bargaining power lay with the German High Command, Hindenburg and Ludendorff, the Kaiser and the Prussian military caste. They were not inclined to budge: as Kennedy points out, in the summer of 1917, especially after the success of the German U-Boat offensive in the Atlantic and the failure of the Russian offensive on the Eastern Front, 'Germany seemed on the point of victory.'[84] Benedict had overestimated the power of civilian politicians like Erzberger, and underestimated that of the military. Erzberger was actually prosecuted for treason after his conciliatory Ulm speech in 1917.[85]

It was precisely the need to crush the power of German militarism which Woodrow Wilson gave as his reason for rejecting the practicability of Benedict's proposals in the letter he sent which effectively served as the official reply on the part of the Allied governments. Wilson argued that Germany simply could not be trusted: 'We cannot take the word of the present rulers of Germany as a guarantee of any thing that is to endure',[86] and he implied that only a change of regime in Germany in a democratic direction would provide the necessary preconditions for peace.[87] As O'Neill says, 'the [President's] Note very clearly closed the door to the initiation of peace in the near future . . . the other replies to the Pope's Note cease to have interest in the face of Mr. Wilson's answer. They came as an anti-climax.'[88]

By the spring of 1917, Wilson had already emerged as the

dominant figure on the Allied side, and therefore as the future leader of the world, and this was confirmed by his reply to the papal Peace Note of August. As such he would brook no rivals. This Calvinist idealist, who was 'convinced of his own moral and intellectal superiority', was also notoriously anti-Catholic (though not at election time), and tended to see all Europeans as parochial and unenlightened, including Benedict.[89] According to Zivojinovic, Wilson's 'Peace without Victory' speech of January 1922 swept Benedict and his peace efforts aside.[90] The only 'victory' which the Pope could claim over the President was a moral one: the famous 'Fourteen Points' speech made by Wilson in January 1918 was so close in content and formulation to Benedict's note that the only conclusion to be drawn is that it was heavily inspired by it.[91]

The Pope and his Secretary of State were inevitably bitterly disappointed by the responses to the Note and the ultimate failure of their initiative: Benedict told one of his friends that it was the bitterest moment of his life when he heard of the rejection of the Note by Wilson.[92] Though there were many positive responses from bishops, clergy and laity throughout the world, there were equally many hostile ones. A preacher in the church of La Madeleine, Paris, exclaimed, 'Holy Father, we do not want your peace.'[93] The hardest of all to swallow were the responses which the Note elicited in Benedict's homeland: in Naples he was denounced as 'the German pope'.[94] Posterity has been kinder to the papal peace initiative of August 1917. Enrico Serra, the distinguished Italian diplomatic historian, for example, has remarked that:

> it seems legitimate to conclude, on the basis of the tragic military events which followed, that the note was anything but premature. So much so that France and Britain decided to make contact with Vienna, while the new Italian prime minister, V. E. Orlando, proposed to establish direct [diplomatic] relations with the Holy See.[95]

Caporetto

The failure of the Peace Note was soon overshadowed by events in Italy; in late October and early November 1917 Italy suffered a catastrophic defeat at the hands of the Austro-Hungarians, backed by German forces. Within less than three weeks, the Italians were driven back from their positions on the river Isonzo, on the far side of the Austro-Hungarian frontier, over 120 miles to the river Piave, and only succeeded in stabilizing the exposed northern end of that line with great difficulty. In the rout, they lost nearly 300,000 men, not to mention precious stores and guns.[96] In this great national crisis, the Church, and especially the rural clergy of the Veneto region, were called upon to play a vital role to restore morale. On 12 November, the Italian Prime Minister, Vittorio Emmanuele Orlando, asked Benedict to order the bishops to tell the people of the front-line areas to stay put, in order to diminish the stream of panic-stricken civilian refugees who were hampering the efforts of the Italian armies to re-group.[97] In fact, information reached the Vatican that in areas on the line of retreat of the Italian forces, both Italy's military and civil authorities behaved badly, often abandoning their posts; in the resulting chaos, and amidst widespread looting by Italian troops, the local bishops and clergy were often the only focus of authority.[98] Behind the lines, bishops and clergy were often also the main providers for those same refugees, church property being used for these as well as military purposes.[99] Benedict showed great patriotic concern, and his feelings were inspired in part no doubt by the fact that the estate of his sister Giulia lay only eight kilometres behind the Piave. And as Carlo Monti noted in his diary, the Pope was also afraid for his only nephew, Pino, who was fighting at the front; unknown to Benedict, Monti tried several times, unsuccessfully, to persuade the authorities to send him to the rear.[100] As Benedict noted with a certain irony, the same Italian ministers and officials who had often been responsible for obstructing his humanitarian efforts for prisoners, etc., now besieged the Vatican with requests for information about their sons or nephews taken prisoner by the enemy: 'You would not believe how many people are turning to us to have news.'[101]

Sonnino's hostility to the Peace Note, and indeed all papal peace initiatives, did not prevent the Italian Ministry of Foreign Affairs from seeking to use Vatican diplomacy to extricate Italy from her perilous predicament after Caporetto. On 14 November, the Secretary-General of the Ministry urged on Sonnino the necessity 'to take advantage of the Vatican, whose close links with Germany at the time of the papal note of last August we know about. The Vatican could be able to guarantee the word of the enemy sovereigns.'[102] When Gasparri was asked his opinion on this proposal he replied that Italy could not expect much more the *parecchio* of Giolitti (i.e. that which Giolitti believed Italy could have obtained from Austria-Hungary in 1915 simply by remaining neutral, which was a lot – *parecchio*), because things had changed since then.[103] By the end of the month the situation at the front had settled itself, and the Italian government abandoned its initiative. But Vatican diplomacy was still needed to help Italy: Benedict sought to persuade Germany and Austria-Hungary not permanently to annexe the Italian territory which they had conquered in October and November.[104] By the New Year, despite the reinforcements from her allies, Italy's plight was such that the Italian Finance Minister, Francesco Nitti, was again seeking the Vatican's good offices to negotiate a separate peace with Austria-Hungary (see p. 132).

There is about the Italian defeat at Caporetto a certain element of hubris. Just at the moment that the offensive of the Central Powers was getting under way on the Isonzo front, Gasparri, on the Italians' behalf, had been taking soundings with the Emperor Karl about a peace based on the cession of Trento in exchange for an Italian colony.[105] Later that month Orlando asked Benedict to tell Germany not to wage war upon Italy, as she was doing with such effect at that time: Gasparri in reply pointed out that 'Italy should not have declared war on Germany and Victor Emmanuel III should not have visited Alsace-Lorraine . . .'.[106] In fact, Benedict and Gasparri showed considerable sympathy towards Italy throughout the conflict, and it could even be said that the Vatican's policy of impartiality towards the belligerents was temporarily abandoned for the sake of Italy when Gasparri gave warnings to Nitti about an imminent Austro-Hungarian offensive in 1917.[107]

Though in the long term, the rallying of Catholic clergy and laity to the patriotic cause was to do a great deal of good for Church–State relations in Italy, at the time some Italian authorities and newspapers showed scant gratitude or even recognition of the fact. In early 1918, both Prime Minister Orlando and the Vatican were contacted by a number of bishops in the front-line areas protesting about numerous cases of their clergy being prosecuted for defeatism, spying and contacts with the enemy.[108] Another victim of Italian suspicion and paranoia in the wake of the Caporetto defeat was Giuseppe Dalla Torre, head of Italian Catholic Action, who was later investigated by the 'Commission of Inquiry into Caporetto' for encouraging defeatism.[109] More seriously, the interventionist and anti-clerical press, returning to their longstanding accusation that Benedict was a pawn of the Central Powers, and in search of a scapegoat for Caporetto, cited the Peace Note as having spread defeatism among the Italian troops at Caporetto.[110] The more malicious changed the Pope's regnal name from Benedetto XV (meaning 'blessed') to Maledetto XV (meaning 'accursed'). And British newspapers took up the cry; The *Morning Post* and *The Times* blamed the lack of resistance at Caporetto on Benedict.[111] Of course, Benedict's famous condemnation of the 'useless slaughter' in the Peace Note could just as easily have affected the morale of the armies of the Central Powers as well as those of Italy, France or Belgium.

The disintegration of the Habsburg Empire

By the beginning of 1918, Benedict's worst fears about the wider consequences of the war were being realized. The Bolsheviks had carried out their revolution and civil war was spreading throughout Russia. Unrest was also spreading in the belligerent states, especially the Central Powers. In a letter to the Emperor Karl, Benedict warned about the increasing influence of subversive elements in all the countries at war.[112] Karl hardly needed to be told; he had his own problems. Widespread strikes, a naval mutiny in Dalmatia and open agitation among the various minority nationalities for 'self-determination' were beginning to tear his empire apart.[113] But even at this stage all was not lost: the Entente Powers, for example, remained convinced that the survival of Austria-Hungary would still be essential to the maintenance of the post-war balance of power. In the same letter to Karl, Benedict therefore urged upon him the view that the only way out of the desperate situation in which the Habsburg Empire found itself was to seek peace at once, by appealing to President Wilson: 'In the present international situation, it is not England or France but the President of the great American Republic alone: only he can bring about peace or the continuation of the war, and he wishes to dictate the peace in the time that remains of his presidential term.'[114]

Who said that Benedict was old-fashioned, out-of-touch, ignorant, prejudiced and blind to the importance of the United States? The Vatican's peace diplomacy continued into April when Gasparri reiterated to Nitti the need for peace negotiations between Italy and Austria-Hungary, but without success.[115] In August, Benedict had resolved not to engage in any further initiatives,[116] but the autumn brought a different situation, the impending collapse of Austria-Hungary. As late as October 1918 Benedict was still seeking to persuade Orlando of the continuing validity of the original Entente view, now somewhat eroded by events, that it was necessary to preserve Austria-Hungary.[117] Yet it is also clear that both Benedict and Gasparri were pragmatists: when they saw that it was impossible to save the Habsburg Empire they turned their attentions to Poland, arguing that this overwhelmingly Catholic state would provide a more than adequate substitute as a bulwark against both Germany and Russia.[118]

Conclusion

It can be argued that the failure of Benedict's peace diplomacy was due principally to three powers, Britain, the USA and Germany.

Britain repeatedly made it clear via its envoys to the Vatican that it did not welcome the Pope's peace efforts. As De Salis explained to Gasparri, the British were not only fighting for Belgium, but for Sterling as well.[119] In other words, they were engaged in a struggle for economic supremacy with Germany, not to mention naval mastery. They might consider a negotiated peace with Austria-Hungary, but a 'draw' with Germany was out of the question, whatever the cost. France and, even more so, Italy were effectively clients of Britain. However much they might resent that status, they were obliged out of economic weakness to follow the British line; and Sonnino had his own good reasons for not wanting Benedict's impartial mediation.

The USA, or at least Wilson, was determined to play the role of arbiter in the conflict, whether it was at peace or war. Crusading, anti-European idealism and Wilson's international ambitions were the driving forces behind American policy towards the war, and her attitude towards Benedict's peace efforts. It was, therefore, pretty clear from the beginning of 1917 that unless a papal peace initiative elicited strong and practical support from the European powers at war, Wilson would oppose it. Britain, in its turn, after the American entry, was not prepared to gainsay Wilson's policy because of its dependence on the USA for any hope of winning the war.

In the case of Germany, the calculation by her military commanders after the failed Brusilov offensive was that Russia could be pushed into capitulation, thus opening up vistas of territorial acquisitions in Poland, the Baltic States and western Russia that were in fact largely realized by the Treaty of Brest-Litovsk of March 1918. This powerful temptation to return to the policy of the *Drang nach Osten*, the imperialistic and colonizing drive to the East, coupled with the very correct perception that the survival of the Prussian military monarchy in an age of mass politics would require more than a negotiated 'stalemate' peace, ruled out accepting papal mediation in August 1917. The fact that 1917 was the four-hundredth anniversary of the start of the Lutheran Reformation did not augur well for the success of papal efforts in Protestant Germany anyway. And, of course, Austria-Hungary was capable of no independent response at all, utterly tied as she was to Germany.

Faced by these brutal realities, Benedict's patient, gentlemanly diplomatic efforts were to no avail. Zivojinovic has argued that Benedict was old-fashioned, out of touch and irrelevant, and J. D. Gregory has claimed that the Vatican was 'a fifth-rate diplomacy'.[120] But these were not the reasons for the failure of Benedict's effort; in any case, both claims are highly contentious. The turbine of modern, mass, total warfare produced forces that were not susceptible to a diplomacy based essentially on morality, on Catholic social doctrine, however much that doctrine might be in tune with the aspirations of other peoples, and even the principles of Wilsonianism. What Benedict was ultimately fighting against was nationalism (and militarism) in a variety of forms, and his failure to save Austria-Hungary was ultimately due to that as well.

Perhaps the cause of the failure of Benedict's peace diplomacy was more fundamental than all the explanations advanced so far. His was a fragile, high-risk strategy which depended absolutely upon the Vatican's ability to convince its diplomatic interlocutors of its impartiality and neutrality. But what are impartiality and neutrality? How could the Vatican under Benedict be truly impartial and neutral? Certainly, many politicians and journalists, and consequently sections of the population, in the warring countries had serious doubts about the impartiality and neutrality of the Vatican during the First World War. In the Entente countries that scepticism was widespread and in the case of France, it was deliberately fostered by anti-clerical propaganda hostile to the Vatican. The machinations of French representatives and journalists in Rome did much to put the Vatican in a bad light in the eyes of French.[121] The interviews which Benedict gave to the French journalist Latapie in June 1915, and to the American pro-German journalist Weygand in April of that year were particularly damaging.[122] There was rather less hostility towards the Vatican in the Central Powers, though Germany was prone to periodic waves of anti-Vatican feeling, the most notable example being when the Te Deum was sung in all Roman churches (except St Peter's) to celebrate the British liberation of Jerusalem from the infidel Turks in December 1917.[123]

Just how justified these doubts about the impartiality and neutrality of the Vatican were during the war hardly matters: they were the unfortunate reality in which Benedict had to conduct his diplomacy. But it also has to be said that some attitudes and actions of the Vatican during the war did justify these doubts, like its suspicions towards Italy, its sympathy towards Austria-Hungary and its preference for a peace based on the *status quo ante bellum*, which was increasingly at odds with the war aims of the Entente Powers. There were even moments when the Vatican very clearly abandoned its self-imposed neutrality. One was the episode in which Gasparri gave a warning to Italy about an impending Austro-Hungarian military offensive, and another was even more serious than that. In April 1916, Gasparri, presumably with Benedict's blessing, sought to persuade the German High Command to make special efforts to halt the Russian advance on Constantinople.[124] Though the initiative was aborted half-way through, Morozzo Della Rocca, an Italian historian very sympathetic to Benedict, asks, 'Was this true neutrality?'[125] Of course it was not.

The lesson of Benedict's peace efforts would appear to be that, though entirely sincere in their aims, i.e. to relieve suffering and stop the war, they were undermined by the hard reality that the Vatican had its own agenda and its own interests. The Papacy is a moral and religious power, not a secular and territorial one. Even so it has its own interests which can be at odds with those of other powers and thus ultimately make it impossible to be entirely impartial. But what alternative was there to Benedict's high-risk policy? He could, perhaps, have pursued his humanitarian relief efforts, and made moral condemnations of the horrors and atrocities of war, and scrupulously abstained from any diplomatic involvement. This was the alternative which Merry Del Val, who opposed Benedict's strategy throughout the war, would undoubtedly have followed. But such an approach would never have been acceptable to Benedict; he was temperamentally incapable of being so passive in the face of events. His charity and courage and above all his sense that duty obliged him to act, forced him to follow the policy which he did, with all its risks and dangers, its contradictions and its limited chances of success.

Though it failed to stop the war, Benedict's peace diplomacy eventually bore its fruits. In the short term, it gave an immense boost to the diplomatic standing and influence of papal diplomacy, which was to be of great importance in the post-war period. In the longer term, it laid the foundations for a new peace-making role for the Papacy which has been continued by the majority of Benedict's successors, most notably Pius XII at the beginning of the Second World War, John XXIII during the Cuban Missile Crisis, Paul VI during the Vietnam War and John Paul II during the Gulf War.

Notes and references

1. Garzia, pp. 106–7.
2. A copy of prayer is to be found in AFDC, 'Libretto usato dal S. Padre Benedetto PP XV nella Basilica Vaticana per la preghiera della pace'.
3. Peters, p. 124.
4. As quoted in ibid.
5. L'Osservatore Romano, 23 December 1914.
6. Dalla Torre, pp. 1289–90 and Jankowiak, p. 221: according to Peters, branches of the Opera were eventually established in Germany, Switzerland and Austria.
7. AAES, Stati Ecclesiastici, 1401, fasc. 535–6, 'Visite di Mons. Valfré di Bonzo ai prigionieri italiani nei campi di Mathausen e Katzehan'. The nuncio at Munich was responsible for visits to German prisoner-of-war camps.
8. Ibid.
9. ASV, SS, Guerra, 1914–1918, rub. 244, fasc. 8, 22452, letter to Pope, 26 September 1916.
10. Ibid., 24154, letter to Pope, December 1916.
11. See AAES, Italia, 1369/1372, fasc. 517, and AAES, Stati Ecclesiastici, 1340, 492, 'Belgio-Germania, Per la liberazione dei civili belgi detenuti in Germania'; Cardinal Hartmann was asked by the Vatican to mediate with German authorities on their behalf.
12. The Tablet, 4 April 1917.
13. Panzera, pp. 321–2.
14. Ibid.

15. Ibid., p. 323.
16. Ibid.
17. *Diario*, I, pp. 308–9, 17 December 1915.
18. Procacci, p. 156.
19. *Diario*, II, pp. 324–6, 21 and 24 May 1918.
20. *The Tablet*, 21 October 1916.
21. AAES, Stati Ecclesiastici, 1329, fasc. 484, Lithuania, 1915–1916, 'Soccorsi della S. Sede in favore dei Lituani provati dalla guerra, sussidi'; 1415, fasc. 561–2, Montenegro, 1916–17. 'Vettovagliamento della popolazione', and 1418, fasc. 562–6, Siria-Libano, 1916–1922. 'Vetto-vagliamento della Siria e del Libano'. From the correspondence in these files it is clear that, as always, hostility between belligerent powers made negotiations for humanitarian work very difficult.
22. *Diario*, II, pp. 363–4, 13 September 1918.
23. Dalla Torre, p. 1290.
24. J. D. Gregory of British Legation to the Holy See to Grey, PRO, FO, 371, 152040, 16 October 1915. See also ASV, SS, Guerra 1914–1918, rub. 244, f. 64, 1915–16, Correspondence between Benedict XV and Sultan Mohamed V, and A. Riccardi, 'Benedetto XV e la crisi della convivenza multireligiosa nell'Impero Turco', in Rumi (ed.) (1990), pp. 83–128.
25. Riccardi, p. 89.
26. De Rosa (1977), p. 183.
27. See the correspondence with the Austrian and German governments in AAES, Italia, 843, fasc. 308–10, 'Bombardamenti di città indefese' and *Diario*, I, pp. 242–4, 7 July 1915 and p. 339, 28 January 1966.
28. Ibid.
29. Lo Bello, p. 63.
30. Garzia, pp. 106–7.
31. *La CC*, 66 (1915), vol. 3, 7 August 1915, p. 259.
32. Ibid.
33. Zivojinovic (1978), p. 48.
34. Adams, pp. 12–19.
35. Korecs, p. 340 and Zivojinovic (1978), p. 22.
36. *Diario*, I, pp. 250–1, 17 July 1915.
37. Garzia, p. 111.
38. *Diario*, ibid., p. 251.
39. *La CC*, 66, 3 (1915).
40. Kennedy, pp. 337 & 339.
41. O'Neill, pp. 689–90.
42. Ibid., p. 691.
43. O'Neill, p. 696.
44. Peters, p. 141.

45. Monticone, p. 13.
46. O'Neill, p. 694.
47. *Diario*, I, p. 525, 16 December 1916.
48. Salter, p. 1.
49. Hardach, p. 37.
50. Spadolini, p. 178 and Zivojinovic (1978), p. 51.
51. Kennedy, p. 349: 'The dependence of US exporters on European markets had made Washington far less neutral towards Germany.'
52. Wiegand interview, Zivojinovic (1978), p. 46.
53. Leslie, p. 242.
54. See Bruti Liberati, p. 132.
55. Korecs, p. 341.
56. *Diario*, I, p. 379, 29 May 1916.
57. Zivojinovic (1978), pp. 50 and 70.
58. Epstein, p. 127.
59. *The Tablet*, 21 April 1917.
60. Taylor, p. 42.
61. *Diario*, II, p. 67, 7 April 1917.
62. Poincaré, p. 68.
63. *Diario*, II, p. 33, 13 February 1917.
64. Ibid., II, pp. 35–7, 13 February 1917.
65. Ibid.
66. Panzera, p. 333.
67. Serra, in Rumi (ed.) (1990), p. 59.
68. Taylor, p. 42.
69. Epstein, pp. 173–4.
70. Ibid., p. 163.
71. Ibid., pp. 119–20 and 126–7.
72. Ibid., p. 126.
73. Monticone, p. 14.
74. Ibid.
75. Rumi (ed.) (1990), p. 40.
76. *Diario*, II, p. 85, 17 April 1917.
77. As quoted in O'Neill, pp. 822–3.
78. Ibid.
79. *The Times*, 15 August 1917.
80. O'Neill, p. 823.
81. Garzia, p. 167.
82. For the replies of the Central Powers see ASV, SS, Guerra, 1914–1918, rub. 244, fasc. 79, protocol 5482.
83. *Diario*, I, Appendice Generale, doc. 15.
84. Kennedy, p. 347.
85. Epstein, p. 281.

86. O'Neill, p. 825.
87. Ibid.
88. Ibid., p. 825.
89. Taylor, p. 43.
90. Zivojinovic (1978), p. 63.
91. Serra, in Rumi (ed.) (1990), p. 61.
92. See Zivojinovic (1978), p. 39.
93. As quoted in Morozzo Della Rocca (1996), p. 550.
94. ASV, SS, Guerra, 1914–1918, rub, 244, fasc. 82, letter from S. Castellano, 28 August 1917.
95. Serra, in Rumi (ed.) (1990), pp. 59–60.
96. *Diario*, II, p. 214, 23 November 1917.
97. Ibid., II, p. 206, 12 November 1917.
98. Ibid., II, pp. 215–18, 25 and 26 November 1917.
99. Ibid., II, p. 215, 25 November 1917.
100. Ibid., II, p. 197, 4 November 1917 and p. 203, 23 November 1917.
101. Ibid., II, p. 205, 10 November 1917.
102. DDI, Quinta Serie, vol. IX, documento 438, 14 November 1917.
103. Ibid., document 233, Gasparri a Nitti, 14 December 1917.
104. Benedict and Austrian annexations PRO, FO, De Salis.
105. *Diario*, II, pp. 187–8, 26 October 1917.
106. Ibid., II, 1914, 31 October 1917.
107. Warning re offensive. Margiotta-Broglio (1963), p. 349.
108. See for example, ASV, SS, Guerra, 1914–1918, letter of the Bishop of Padua to Orlando, 18 February, 1918 Portogruaro.
109. AAES, Stati Ecclesiastici, 216, 49301, Vol. VI, 93–100.
110. *Diario*, II, p. 306, n. 98.
111. AAES, Stati Ecclesiastici, 216, 49301, Vol. VI, 93–100.
112. Rumi (1990), p. 40, letter of 28 February 1918.
113. Cornwall, p. 118.
114. Rumi (ed.) (1990).
115. *Diario*, II, p. 388, 25 October 1918.
116. Ibid., II, p. 362, 7 August 1918.
117. Ibid., II, p. 388, 25 October 1918.
118. Ibid., II, p. 390, 27 October 1918.
119. Ibid., II, p. 39, 22 February 1917.
120. Zivojinovic, p. 13 and Gregory, p. 89.
121. Hachey (ed.), p. 18.
122. *Diario*, I, pp. 236–7, 26 June 1915.
123. Ibid., II, 15 December 1917.
124. Morozzo Della Rocca (1993), p. 550.
125. Ibid.

6

Peace and its problems

On the first day of December 1918, Benedict issued a new encyclical *Quam Iam Diu* in which he welcomed the respite brought to Europe by the Armistice of the previous month, and called upon Catholics to pray that the coming peace conference would bring 'a just and lasting peace'.[1] This was a tall order in a continent ravaged by more than four years of war, where starvation persisted, in part because of the continuation of the Allied blockade, and which would experience economic, social and political breakdown. In the spring and summer of 1919, the statesmen at the Versailles Peace Conference laboured to resolve the momentous and often intractable issues with which they were confronted, in particular to reach a territorial settlement in the wake of the collapse of four empires, the Ottoman, Hohenzollern, Habsburg and Russian. Meanwhile, Europe's problems got worse. Influenza began to sweep through central Europe, killing more civilians on a world-wide basis than the war itself, rapid demobilization fuelled the rising tide of political violence in many states, and the Bolshevik threat became more and more of a reality.

Benedict and Gasparri were sharply critical of the peace which eventually emerged from Versailles and were afraid that its inadequacies exposed Europe and the Middle East to the continuing threat of war. They were not entirely wrong in this. The fundamental cause of the defects of the Versailles Peace Settlement, in their eyes, was that it was not based on Christian principles. It was easy to criticize the handiwork of the statesmen at Versailles, especially in retrospect, and many did, but as King Albert of the Belgians said, 'What would you have? They did what they could'.[2] Nevertheless, the peace settlement left Benedict and the Roman Catholic Church with many problems, as well as a number of unexpected opportunities.

Benedict and the Peace Conference

Probably the greatest defect of the Versailles Peace Conference in Benedict's eyes was quite simply the fact that he or his representatives were excluded from it, as Sonnino had intended. Though both Benedict and Gasparri had persistently denied that they wanted a place at the conference table for the Holy See,[3] it is now clear that those denials were as false as the denials of Sonnino that Article 15 of the Treaty of London excluded that presence. In 1916, an article was published in the prestigious Italian journal *Nuova Antologia*, written by Umberto Benigni, regarding the eventual Peace Conference and the participants in it. Benedict saw the draft of the article and gave instructions on how it should be modified. In his comments, he observed that the article gave the game away, 'it makes it too obvious that its [the article's] principal objective is to encourage the idea of the participation of the Holy See', and suggested that, as a start, the article should argue that 'all powers not interested in dividing the spoils should, nevertheless, have a right to participate, then to introduce the question of the admission of the neutral powers, as a matter of principle, not even to mention the Papacy'.[4] Curiously, when the article was eventually published, it ignored all of his suggestions and followed a different, more direct tack arguing that if the Kings of England and Prussia and the Czar, who were all heads of their own churches, and the Sultan, Caliph of Islam, were entitled to attend the Peace Conference, then so was the Pope.[5] It is doubtful whether Benedict's subtle modifications to the article would have had much effect anyway, and in 1917 and 1918 the Vatican was obliged to wage a concerted diplomatic campaign in the hope of inducing the Allies to abandon Article 15. Strong representations were made to the British Government to persuade it of the injustice and inappropriateness of Article 15, an attempt which initially at any rate had some chance of success since Foreign Secretary Balfour had shown sympathy for the Vatican's claims.[6] An attempt was also made to persuade Cardinal Gibbons to lead an American Catholic press campaign against papal exclusion from the Peace Conference, but he declined on the grounds that the position of Catholics in the United States was too delicate.[7] Gasparri also sought to mobilize the neutral powers, most especially faithful Spain,[8] and as a last desperate throw an attempt was made to get Cardinal Mercier added to the Belgian delegation to the Conference in the hope that the outstanding international eminence of the Belgian prelate could be used to raise matters of interest to the Holy See.[9] All these efforts failed, but it is indicative of just how seriously the Italian government took them that Sonnino waged an equally vigorous diplomatic counter-offensive.[10]

Benedict's comments on the original draft of the *Nuova Antologia* article demonstrate that he feared that exclusion from the Peace Conference would damage the prestige and authority of the Holy See.[11] The Papacy had been represented at the Vienna Peace Congress of 1814–15, and Cardinal Consalvi, the Secretary of State, had succeeded in obtaining entry to the inner circle of powers and in negotiating the restoration of the Papal States for his master, Pope Pius VII.[12] Benedict could not seriously have expected that Gasparri could do the same at Versailles, but the exclusion of the Papacy from the Hague Conferences of 1897 and 1899, due to Italian intervention, still rankled and the Vatican's participation in the Peace Conference would have been a tremendous boost to its international prestige. In the event, exclusion was no great diplomatic defeat because *none* of the neutral powers, including Spain, Holland and Switzerland – the other neutrals most heavily involved in peace attempts – were admitted to the conference, thus saving the Holy See a major loss of face. When matters that really touched upon the Vatican's interests came up at the conference, like the future of the German missions, the despatch to Paris of Mgr Cerretti, the new Sostituto, ensured that behind-the-scenes diplomacy obtained for the Holy See what it desired.[13] Indeed, Cerretti's success in protecting the German missions demonstrated that the Holy See was recognized as the sovereign, international Catholic authority by the Great Powers. As for the Roman Question, it is clear that Cerretti made far more progress in his clandestine talks with Orlando (see Chapter 7, pp. 167–9) than could have been secured in open conference; indeed, even to have raised publicly the issue in such circumstances would have set progress back for years by alienating Italy.

Benedict and the peace settlement

Exclusion from the conference almost certainly spared Benedict and Gasparri a lot of other problems. It is hard to see how the Vatican could have maintained its position of impartiality between the powers if it had taken part in the conference when controversial matters of war guilt, disarmament, reparations and, particularly, territorial changes were being discussed and decided: it would have been even more difficult if it had actually signed the peace treaties.[14] As we shall see, much of the Vatican's post-war diplomatic prestige and room for manoeuvre was built precisely upon its distance from the peace settlement. One of the most difficult of issues facing the conference in 1919 was that of Italian claims to parts of the Adriatic coast of the former Habsburg dominions, most especially Fiume (Rijeka), an issue on which Orlando felt compelled to abandon the conference in the summer of 1919. Gasparri was extremely unsympathetic towards the Italian claims. In a conversation with Carlo Monti he argued forcefully that the Italians were unrealistic and that it was better that they 'give up their claims to a few shoals in the Adriatic and seek ample compensation in Asia Minor, where we could have in abundance those raw materials which we lack and for which we depend on foreign imports'; he also argued that the acquisition of Bolzano, with its German-speaking majority, was a mistake.[15] The merest hint of such feelings in public would have had a disastrous effect upon Italo-Vatican relations.

But there were far bigger issues on which the views of Benedict and Gasparri diverged radically from those not only of Italy but also of the other Allied powers. The matter of most important concern was the 'German question'. In April 1918, Gaparri had expressed his and Benedict's view that one of the most dangerous consequences of the likely dissolution of the Habsburg Empire was that it would leave Germany more powerful than ever; furthermore, with the gains made in the Treaty of Brest-Litovsk with the Russian Bolshevik regime, to the already seventy million Reich Germans would probably be added thirty million Germans in the Baltic States and Austria/Bohemia.[16] This perception was very much in line with the traditional policy of Rampolla, of whom, of course, Benedict and Gasparri had both been pupils. In November 1918, Gasparri reiterated his fear that Italy and France would be unable to contain the new German 'colossus' and that the 'successor states' to the Austro-Hungarian and Russian empires would not be able to oppose it either.[17] In fact, as a result of Germany's defeat, in the short term the pendulum swung in favour of French hegemony over Europe, an adjustment to the European balance of power which was equally unacceptable to the Vatican. In particular, *L'Osservatore Romano* and *La Civiltà Cattolica* repeatedly stated their objections to the Allied treatment of Germany: according to the Jesuit journal, the Treaty of Versailles 'humiliated Germany'.[18] The Vatican objected in particular to the 'War Guilt' clause, the size of reparations and Allied attempts to bring the Kaiser to trial as a 'war criminal'. Gasparri made strenuous efforts to prevent the latter, using Cerretti to lobby the statesmen at Versailles, with some success.[19] He also also argued strongly that the size of the reparations bill imposed upon Germany was too harsh and would threaten a quick return to economic stability in Europe.[20] The Vatican was to pursue its efforts to mitigate the effects of reparations throughout the 1920s, and attempted to mediate in the Ruhr crisis of 1923 which was precipitated by the decision of the Germans not to continue payments.[21]

Another problem for Benedict in the post-war peace settlement was the application of Wilson's principle of 'National Self-determination'. In his various appeals for peace during the war, Benedict had demonstrated his unease with the phenomenon of emerging nationalist forces; indeed, on a copy of the Peace Note of August 1917 he wrote: 'The principle of nationality is good thing when it is free; bad when it is imposed. On the basis of the principle understood in this sense, which means the principle of the aspirations of the peoples, so-called territorial questions should be regulated.'[22] The Jesuit journal took this thinking a stage further when, in 1919, it entitled an important article on national self-determination 'On the Just Aspirations of Peoples'.[23] In other words, no national ethnic group had an automatic right to self-determination and the nation state was not necessarily preferable to a multi-ethnic, dynastic state like the Habsburg Empire. Ultimately, the Vatican's attitude towards emerging nationalities would be determined by essentially pragmatic considerations. Thus, when faced with the force of events – the declarations of independence by the Poles, Czechs and other subject nationalities of the Habsburg Empire – in a public letter to Gasparri in November 1918 Benedict announced that he had told the nuncio in Vienna to establish friendly relations with all 'the various nationalities of the Austro-Hungarian Empire who constituted themselves into independent states'.[24]

But at the same time, in private, Gasparri expressed an opinion that was not popular in the Allied countries, that is that the creation of the successor states was not a good thing because they could not be self-sufficient, they would be vulnerable to the Bolshevik menace (a fear that had also prompted worries about too harsh a treatment of Germany), and that they would tend to fight among themselves, which history proved only too painfully to be correct.[25] There were bitter disputes over the rights and treatment of minorities, and over boundaries: the most Catholic of the new states, Lithuania and Poland, engaged in repeated armed clashes over the Vilnius Question in 1919 and 1920. Benedict, who had supported Polish claims to nationhood in his Peace Note of August 1917, and made the point to Monti in October 1918 that as a resurrected Poland would serve as a strong bulwark both against the Bolsheviks and Germany,[26] he felt obliged to urge moderation in Polish demands after the end of the war.[27] Benedict and Gasparri had particular reservations about the emergence of Yugoslavia (the Kingdom of the Serbs, Croats and Slovenes, as it was originally called). If they did not support extravagant Italian claims in the

145

Adriatic, they were equally unhappy about the domination of two Catholic peoples – the Croats and the Slovenes – by an Orthodox one, the Serbs. In January 1919, Gasparri actually despatched an emissary to Zagreb with the task of impeding this union, but it was too late.[28] Benedict went so far as to express the opinion that the Slavs in general were less intelligent but more numerous than other races.[29] In fact, despite the deep ethnic tensions in the new state, the treatment of Croatian and Slovene Catholics by the Belgrade government gave few grounds for complaint on the Vatican's part.[30]

The most characteristically 'Wilsonian' feature of the Versailles Peace Settlement was the creation of the League of Nations: the American President had insisted that the Covenant of the new world body be inserted at the beginning of the Treaty of Versailles. Italy was very anxious about the possibility that the Vatican would seek to join the League and in May 1919, Orlando sent Monti to find out: Benedict gave a very non-committal answer.[31] In fact, there is no evidence that the Holy See was invited to join or even sought admission. If their attitude in 1929, when the question of the Holy See joining the League was raised after the establishment of the sovereign, independent State of the Vatican City, is anything to go by, then Britain and France would have opposed its admission in 1920.[32] The USA would surely not have supported the idea either: in June 1919, a certain Senator Sherman made a speech claiming that, 'twenty-four of the forty Christian nations are spiritually dominated by the Vatican, thus the Pope wishes to rule the world through the League': the speech was dismissed by other senators, but President Wilson would have been too wary of the strong Protestant lobby in the United States to have ever countenanced Vatican involvement in the League.[33]

The Holy See's exclusion from the League was one of the reasons for the hostility of the Vatican organs towards it. In June 1920, commenting on Benedict's encyclical De Pacis, the Jesuit fortnightly, Civiltà Cattolica, strongly attacked the League, claiming that the themes of the encyclical 'have got nothing in common with that mockery, the so-called "League of Nations" . . . which is the expression of an atheistic and utilitarian policy, with its harsh exclusions and odious presuppositions, where the Holy Name of God has no place and where the rights of Christ and his Church receive no recognition'.[34] The article also condemned *'the primacy of egoistic and nationalistic* [original italics] considerations' in international politics, and concluded by declaring that, 'No, the Pope does not approve of either exclusivisms or imperialisms, or of the other excesses of nationalism and patriotism'.[35] It was a comprehensive condemnation of the policies followed by the Allied powers since the end of the war. Though Benedict's encyclical was rather less forceful in its language than this article, calling for nations to 'unite in one league, or rather a family [of] peoples', as if the League did not already exist, it cannot be doubted that the Jesuit journal was faithfully expressing Benedict's deepest feelings.[36]

In the encyclical Benedict once more appealed for world-wide disarmament and implicitly endorsed the idea of European integration. According to Mizzi, 'The first, hesitant mention of the possibility of European unification in a pontifical document is to be found in the encyclical *Pacem Dei Munus*, 1920.'[37] But the core of the encyclical was Benedict's lament that the peace settlement was not built on the Christian principles of justice, and above all, charity.[38] Benedict argued that because of the absence of charity – Christian love – latent hostilities between peoples continued and that there could be no real reconciliation and therefore no lasting peace. The chief target of his concern was undoubtedly the relationship between France and Germany, which was to deteriorate badly in 1923 with the Ruhr crisis. Benedict's reference to charity was more than just an appeal for Christian love among nations, it also encompassed the practical application of that love, i.e. charitable works: 'stretch the bonds of charity', he declared, and he went on to remind his readers that: 'we see immense areas utterly desolate, uncultivated and abandoned; multitudes reduced to want of food, clothing and shelter; innumerable widows and orphans bereft of everything . . .'.[39] Benedict was as active in seeking to relieve this suffering as he had been during the war. He himself gave donations on several occasions,[40] and the Vatican raised five million lire alone to relieve the Russian famine in 1921.[41] He had a particular concern for children, and issued two separate encyclicals, *Paterno*

Diu Iam in 1919 and *Annus Iam Plenus* in 1920, in which he appealed for funds to relieve the distress. Perhaps the most enduring monument to his charity is the Save the Children Fund, to which he gave strong public support after it was established in 1919.[42] It was thanks to this support that collections for the children of Eastern Europe were taken up in Catholic, Anglican and other churches on 28 December 1921, the feast of the Holy Innocents.[43] On his death in 1922, the founder, Eglantyne Jebb, paid tribute to Benedict's work: 'Pope Benedict XV has died before the world has recognised the magnitude of the debt which it owes to him for his championship of the world's children.'[44]

Palestine, Zionism and the Vatican

With the exception of Russia, which the Allied Powers never managed to settle, its fate being decided in the civil war between the Bolsheviks and the various 'White' forces, the most difficult problem which faced them was the fate of the former Ottoman Empire. Their endeavours to settle its future, in the Treaty of Sèvres, failed because of the emergence of Kemal Ataturk, who successfully resisted the attempts of both the Greeks and the Italians to carve up substantial parts of Asia Minor. What the Versailles Peace Conference did settle, however, was the future of the Turkish Middle East where League of Nations mandates to govern were accorded to France for Lebanon and Syria, and to Britain for Palestine, Transjordan and Iraq. But the French were far from satisfied with this division of the spoils, and it was into the cauldron of Franco-British rivalries, and the resulting intrigues around the final settlement of Palestine in particular, that Benedict and Gasparri were drawn in the immediate post-war period. And it has to be said, that the Vatican was not averse to stirring the pot, indeed it added another ingredient by encouraging the Italians to get involved. In 1919 and 1920, three cardinals, one British, one French and one Italian, visited Palestine in turn, each being used to serve the interests of his home country. What was at stake was influence. The French sought to preserve the liturgical honours accorded their representatives in services of the various churches, in virtue of the 'protectorate' which they had exercised over the Christians under the Turkish regime: with the latter's fall, the protectorate, and the honours, lapsed but French governments refused to abandon them, and so the Vatican was dragged in to make a decision, in favour of the French, much to the annoyance of the Italians, who had hoped to acquire some of the former French influence.

Above and beyond striving to avoid being entangled in great power rivalries, the Vatican had two major concerns in Palestine – the administration of the holy places and the future of the Christian, especially the Catholic, minority. The factor which seemed to threaten the Vatican's interests in both cases was the 'Balfour Declaration' of 1917 which, following the British liberation of Jerusalem from the Turks, committed the British government to the setting up of a 'Jewish Homeland' in Palestine.[45] Very quickly, Benedict and Gasparri became convinced that an augmentation of the Jewish presence in Palestine posed a threat to Catholics' interests there. A particular fear of the Vatican was that the advent of British rule signified a take-over by the Jews of the administration in Palestine. In fact, there is no evidence that the proportion of Jews in the administration outstripped their presence in the population at large,[46] but the fear was not allayed by the appointment of a Jew, Sir Herbert Samuel, to be High Commissioner (governor) of Palestine. In the circumstances, it seems to have been a singularly tactless move on the part of the British, certainly not one likely to inspire confidence in the impartiality of their administration towards the various ethnic and religious groups in the country. Samuel tried to pre-empt Vatican hostility by making a visit to the Pope in July 1920, but the attempt clearly failed. Benedict was not convinced by Samuel's protestations of impartiality.[47] The Vatican had hoped that an international body would be set up to deal specifically with matters relating to the holy places, but the British rejected this idea in favour of continuing the set-up under the Turkish administration whereby representatives of the various religious groups acted in a consultative capacity.[48] This was not a satisfactory solution for Benedict. In his allocution of March 1919, he warned that 'it would be a terrible grief to Us and for all Christian faithful if infidels were placed in a more prominent position: much more if those most holy sanctuaries of the Christian religion were given into the charge of non-Christians': the reference to 'infidels' was clearly aimed at the Jews and Muslims.[49] In the end, the Vatican accepted the British proposal, with a proviso that all disputes over rights in the holy places would be ultimately settled by British courts.[50]

The wave of Jewish migration that followed the establishment of British rule intensified Vatican fears for the future of Palestine as a whole. There was, first, the fear that many of the Jewish immigrants from Europe would bring with them Bolshevik tendencies; after all, were not many of the leading Bolsheviks – Leon Trotsky in Russia, Kurt Eisner in Bavaria and Bela Kun in Hungary – Jews? And in the latter case, the Church had been persecuted under the short-lived Soviet regime.[51] The influx of Jews also seemed to threaten an unwelcome modernization in broader terms: in March 1921 Benedict protested against the alleged plans of Jewish businessmen to build 'leisure complexes' near sacred sites, such as Mount Carmel and the Church of the Holy Sepulchre.[52] There were already fears that wealthy Jews, or Jews backed by American finance, would buy out Christian and Muslim landowners.[53] It was not only the Jews, however, whom Benedict feared. In his March 1919 allocution, he warned that 'non-Catholic foreigners, furnished with abundant means . . . are there spreading their errors'.[54] What he was worried about were British and American Protestant groups who appeared to be 'buying' converts by offering free education to Catholic and Orthodox Christians. By 1919, the Vatican must have begun to regret the passing of the Turkish administration which had been celebrated by the ringing of Church bells in Rome in December 1917.

The arguments over Palestine demonstrated the strong vein of anti-Semitism in the Italian Church, and especially in the Jesuit order, which came out in *La Civiltà Cattolica*'s comments on events in the Holy Land, and on the Pope's pronouncements on them, like the claim in March 1919 that Palestine was 'falling into the hands of the enemies of Christian civilisation'.[55] A year later it was even more blatantly anti-Semitic: 'The Jews are distributing their money inside the closed circle of the tents of Israel, using it to dominate Christians . . . The Jews are seeking to accumulate their money by taking it from Christians, regarding it as their legitimate right as chosen people to take possession of the spoils of Egypt.'[56] There is no evidence that Benedict attempted to restrain this crude anti-Semitism, but the overall thrust of Vatican policy on Palestine was anti-Zionist rather than anti-Semitic. Benedict's concern, uttered in his allocution of June 1921, was that the Jews would 'obtain a position of preponderance and privilege in Palestine', and that, conversely, 'the situation of Christians in Palestine has not only not improved but has even become worse'.[57] As Sergio Minerbi has recognized, Benedict's policy boiled down to this: 'The Great Powers must guarantee the rights of Catholics, although without impairing the rights of Jews and also without giving Jews any privileges'.[58] Gasparri's position was sharper and clearer, presumably because he felt able to speak with more freedom than the Pope. Even before the end of the war, he told the Belgian Ambassador that what he feared was the establishment of a Jewish state, with consequent damage to the rights of other, especially Christian, religious groups.[59] The policy which Benedict and Gasparri accordingly adopted towards Zionism was more or less the one which the Vatican followed until very recently, that is until it decided in 1992 that, in the aftermath of the Gulf War, recognition of the State of Israel was the only way to defend those rights.

The Vatican's policy over Palestine during the pontificate of Benedict XV must have caused a great deal of disappointment for many Jews world-wide because in 1915 and 1916 the Vatican appears to have given its backing to the 'Deloncle Plan' for a Jewish 'homeland' in Poland, a proposal which received some support among Jews in France and the United States, though not in Britain.[60]

Benedict and Ireland

In May 1917, in a conversation with Carlo Monti, Gasparri made a very revealing statement: 'The Holy See absolutely cannot afford to get on the wrong side of England which gives the broadest freedom to Catholics: it would be the end of Catholicism in England.'[61] He was undoubtedly exaggerating the dangers of such a rupture to British Catholics, but what was true was that the Vatican could not afford poor relations with the British Empire, in whose various dominions, protectorates and colonial territories there were very substantial numbers of Catholics. Moreover, following the United States withdrawal from world affairs in 1920, Britain had become the world superpower, extending its influence further as a result of colonial gains in the Versailles peace settlement. And this was undoubtedly the reason why Benedict and Gasparri found the 'Irish Question' to be one of the most troublesome they ever faced and why they handled it with the greatest of care and delicacy.

Given the especially close historical ties between the Papacy and Irish Catholicism – as Bella points out, there was never any major schism or heresy in the history of the Irish church[62] – one would have expected a strong degree of support for Irish nationalism in the Vatican. Certainly, there was no lack of supporters of Irish nationalism in Rome and Italy. Apart from the fact that both of the new political movements in Italy in the post-war period, the Catholic Partito Popolare and Mussolini's Fascio di Combattimento, demonstrated strong sympathies for Irish nationalism,[63] the Irish ecclesiastical community in Rome was characterized by a strong element of support, with Mgr Hagan of the Irish College at its head.[64] In addition, the Irish diaspora in Australia, New Zealand, Canada and the United States, especially some of its leaders, like Archbishop Mannix of Melbourne, also showed strong support for the Irish cause, and lobbied the Vatican accordingly.[65] But the position within the Vatican itself was rather different. L'Osservatore Romano was initially quite hostile, which is not surprising. Benedict was not enamoured of the idea of national self-determination *per se* so the Irish were not treated differently from, say, the Czechs before 1918, nor the United Kingdom of Great Britain and Ireland from the Habsburg Empire. It is also clear that the attitude of the Vatican organ was swayed by suspicions that Sinn Fein had Bolshevik leanings.[66] On the other hand, though Benedict never seems to have treated Catholic Ireland with the same solicitous concern as Catholic Poland, he and Gasparri were clearly sympathetic to the plight of the Irish,[67] and this came out in the pages of *La Civiltà Cattolica*: in December 1920, the Jesuit journal expressed support for proposals for peace, but urged that the link with the British Crown and the defence of the British Empire had to be guaranteed.[68] But other forces were at work to counter them. Within the Curia itself, the influence of Benedict and Gasparri was balanced by that of their old enemies, Merry Del Val and De Lai, on whose side that English super-patriot, Cardinal Gasquet, also played a supporting role. From afar, Cardinal Bourne of Westminster also lobbied the Vatican on Britain's behalf.[69] The Vatican was also aware of the deep divisions between the older and younger clergy in Ireland, thanks to the report by Mgr Cerretti in December 1918.[70] And then there was the British envoy, who was continually being urged by the Foreign Office to press the British case, sometimes with scarcely veiled threats that Britain would break off relations if the Vatican did not comply with its wishes.[71]

The Vatican's policy towards Ireland seems to have followed that of the Irish episcopate: it was less than enthusiastic about either the Easter Rising of 1916 or the morality of the hunger strike of Terence MacSwiney, Lord Mayor of Cork, which led to his death in 1920.[72] The Irish bishops were initially divided, but conscription, the summary execution of Irish nationalists after the Rising and the activities of the Black and Tans during the Anglo-Irish War won increasing sympathy among them for the nationalist cause. The Vatican was expected, and of course encouraged, by the British to condemn the Irish nationalist movement, but refrained from doing so: it is unlikely that Benedict and Gasparri ever seriously contemplated such action.[73] Instead, in April 1921, Benedict published a letter to the Irish bishops, appealing for peace. The genesis of the letter was a complex one. Following an inconclusive outcome to the debate on the direction of Vatican policy towards Ireland in the Congregation for Extraordinary Ecclesiastical Affairs, in which Merry Del Val had asked for a moral condemnation of the violent, terroristic methods of Sinn Fein, without calling for the same for the equally violent methods of the British auxiliaries, the Black and Tans, Benedict and Gasparri commissioned a secret report on the Irish situation which recommended a pacific approach by the Pope.[74] Archbishop Mannix also appears to have influenced the Vatican in this direction, though the content of Benedict's letter to the primate of Ireland, Cardinal Logue, could not have satisfied his partisan instincts.[75]

In his letter, Benedict followed the policy which he had maintained throughout the First World War, benevolent impartiality, coupled with practical suggestions for a peace process and a call for Catholics to engage in charitable work in relief of the devastation and suffering in Ireland, setting an example by donating 200,000 lire.[76] The reasons why he took this stance are obvious: a genuine horror of war and desire for peace, an unwillingness to divide the various Catholic communities of the British Empire by taking sides and a concern not to stir up anti-Catholicism in Britain. The British Empire was the world in microcosm: the Irish conflict a minuscule version of the Great War. The core of his message was his heart-felt statement: 'We hope, and we implore the parties in conflict to bring to an end the fury of this war as soon as possible so that a stable peace and a sincere determination of the spirits will conquer the great flame of envy.'[77] The appeal had a mixed reception in Britain and Ireland: it heartened the majority, without satisfying the extremists on either side, or even the Irish 'lobby' in Rome.[78] The letter came at a critical moment; opinion in Britain and the British Empire was shifting against government policy because of the atrocities of the Black and Tans. Peace negotiations between representatives of the British government and the Irish Dáil suddenly and unexpectedly led to agreement in December 1921, and one of the last acts of Benedict's pontificate was the despatch of congratulatory telegrams to both sides on the signing of the Treaty.[79] Benedict was lucky to be spared the further horrors of the civil war between Treatyites and anti-Treatyites which broke out shortly after his death.

Vatican diplomacy at the end of Benedict's reign

At the death of Benedict, the diplomatic standing of the Holy See had been transformed. In simple, mathematical terms, whereas at his election in September 1914 the Vatican had relations with only 17 states,[80] in January 1922 that number had risen to 27.[81] Three of the world's major powers – Britain, France and Germany – were now represented at the Vatican and a fourth, China, would also have been, but for the intrigues of the French (see p. 202). Three of the new states which had established diplomatic relations in Benedict's reign had done so during and/or because of the war – Britain, Holland and Switzerland. Most of the rest were creations of the peace – the so-called 'successor states'. So the Holy See was the beneficiary of developments – the rise of nationalism and collapse of multi-ethnic dynastic states, the Habsburg Empire in particular – which Benedict had deplored and sought to prevent. In fact, Benedict and Gasparri adapted quickly and successfully to the post-war territorial set-up in Europe. By the end of Benedict's reign the Vatican had established relations with all of the successor states to the Habsburg Empire. Other new states, even predominantly or overwhelmingly Protestant states like Estonia and Finland, hurried to obtain recognition from one of Europe's oldest powers.[82] Even the embattled Bolshevik regime in Russia was anxious to win *de facto* recognition from the Vatican in 1921 (see p. 200)

On 28 June 1919, the German Reich established diplomatic relations with the Vatican. This abandonment of the old system whereby the states of Prussia and Bavaria were represented in Rome and the Vatican in Munich was one of the clearest signals of the new standing of the Holy See in the post-war world. The fledgling German democracy, the Weimar Republic, needed the support of the Vatican if it was to mitigate, or at least delay, the effects of the territorial losses in West Prussia, Upper Silesia and on the Belgian border, decreed by the Versailles Treaty, and if it was to prevent the temporary transfer of the Saar, under the same Treaty, from being made permanent.[83] According to Stewart Stehlin, the Vatican wished to avoid precipitate action in the realignment of diocesan boundaries and its concern for the rights of minorities was crucial to the limited success of German policies.[84] Weimar Germany might be said to have enjoyed a 'special relationship', the Vatican's benevolent attitude being determined by the pro-German sentiments of Mgr Pacelli, the nuncio first in Bavaria and then in Berlin, and by Benedict's sense of justice, by his desire to see the balance of power re-established in Europe, and by his anxiety that Germany should function as a bulwark against communism. The Vatican even tolerated a governmental alliance between the German Catholic Centre Party and the Social Democratic Party. Such an alliance would have been unthinkable and impossible between their Italian counterparts, but was essential in order for Weimar democracy to survive. But Pacelli drove a hard bargain: 'nothing for nothing' might have been his motto. The Vatican's recognition of the Weimar Republic was bought at a cost that would not finally become apparent until after Benedict's death, a new concordat with Bavaria, which was intended to be the model for the rest of the German Reich, and which extracted maximum advantage for the Church.[85]

The Vatican's improving relations with Germany gave the final impetus to the French to re-establish the diplomatic links broken off in 1905. A major obstacle was Clémenceau's pressing demand for the replacement of the bishops in Alsace-Lorraine, restored to France at the end of the war. As Gasparri pointed out, such demands were not legal: the incumbent bishops had not resigned and the territorial transfer had not been ratified by a peace treaty. He was under no illusions about the nature of the eventual agreement: 'a return to the concordatory regime with presentation of bishops has assuredly gone for ever'.[86] The canonization of Joan of Arc in June 1920 provided a felicitous prelude to a resumption of relations, with French representatives being received in the Vatican. But the path to a normalization of relations had not been easy; in particular, despite the conservative, even Catholic, nature of the 'Horizon Bleu' Chamber elected in 1918, there was a lot of resistance to the step in France.[87] There was also some ambiguity of attitude in the Vatican as well. As late as January 1920, Gasparri was warning Monti that a resumption of links with France could have its drawbacks: a French Ambassador at the Vatican would continually be demanding things.[88] Though Benedict XV, unlike his predecessor, tacitly accepted the operation of the *associations cultuelles*, the prospects for an end to the separation of Church and State in France and for a definitive solution of the vexed question of the religious orders did not seem good at the end of his reign. Nevertheless, the exchange of envoys, with Cerretti being sent to Paris as proof of the importance in which the Vatican held the posting, was a great achievement of Benedict and Gasparri's diplomacy, its crowning triumph in the post-war period and a reversal of the mistakes of Pius X and Merry Del Val. It was also a result of the war: the unhesitating and unstinting Catholic support for the patriotic *union sacré* of all Frenchmen. Thus, it seemed that there was a real chance that Leo XIII's policy of *ralliement*, of Catholics accepting the Republic and working inside its institutions, would finally bear fruit under his pupils, Benedict and Gasparri. In broader terms, the resumption of relations with France, and also with Portugal, suggested that at last the great wave of Liberal anti-clericalism unleashed by the French Revolution was, perhaps, at last ebbing. Perhaps, only perhaps, because in Mexico the persecution of the Church by the revolutionary regime seemed to be intensifying.[89]

But the success of Benedict's diplomacy should not be calculated solely by the numbers of states with which the Vatican had relations or the importance of those states. After the war, and as a result of that policy, the Vatican had become a new force in international affairs. It is significant in this respect that heads of state and government from the most variegated countries beat a path to Benedict's door in the years of peace. In 1919 the great President of the United States deigned to honour Benedict with his presence, as did the president-elect of Brazil and the Emir Feysal of Hejzad (now Saudi Arabia).[90] The following year saw the visits of the chancellors of Austria and Germany, and 1921 those of the sovereigns of Denmark and the crown prince of Japan; the visit of the Belgian king and queen was prevented by Benedict's death. And in 1921 the Empress and the Regent of Ethiopia sent a delegation to greet Benedict and present him with gifts: a most extraordinary act of recognition from a lost, far-away land.[91]

Not everyone in the Vatican approved of the successes which Benedict had achieved in international affairs in the post-war period, and especially of his efforts to ensure a lasting peace. Merry Del Val was particularly critical. Writing to his friend Cardinal O'Connell, Archbishop of Boston, in November 1921, Merry Del Val lamented the

> prevalence of too much politics, worldly diplomacy and intrigue that are hardly in keeping with the lofty ideals of our mission, nor profitable to the best interests of God and his Church. Here, alas, we come up against it at every step, all day and every day . . . We are drifting . . . Surely at a time when the world has lost its bearings and is anxiously seeking that which we alone are able to provide, we should not drift ourselves, or appear to juggle with principles, but hold up the lesson of light as God gave it to us and refrain from the tactics of human politics.[92]

No one could seriously claim that Benedict had failed to give a moral lead to the statesmen and peoples of the world, or that he had 'juggled with principles'. On the contrary, he had repeatedly set before the world the Christian principles on the basis of which alone, he believed, a just and lasting peace was possible. Under Benedict, the Vatican had escaped from the international isolation in which Pius X and Merry Del Val had left it in 1914, and both during and after the war the Vatican had re-asserted its moral and diplomatic influence, forcing powers, great and small, to take notice of it, and obliging some to establish or re-establish relations with it, in furtherance of their most essential national interests. This was one of Benedict XV's greatest achievements.

Notes and references

1. Carlen (ed.), IV, pp. 161–2.
2. As quoted in Marks, p. 23.

3. Garzia, p. 139.
4. AAES, 1369/1372, memo, undated; comments in Benedict's hand.
5. *Nuova Antologia*, 1 March 1916, 'Il Papa e il congresso di pace'.
6. Pollard (1990), p. 211.
7. Zivojinovic (1978), p. 140.
8. ASV, SS, Guerra, 1914–18, fasc. 70, 14480, Gasparri to nuncio in Madrid, 15 December 1918.
9. For the Mercier 'episode', see Garzia, pp. 198–205.
10. DDI, Quinta Serie, vol. X, doc. 547, Sonnino to ambassadors in Paris and Rome, 23 March 1918 and doc. 730, 22 May 1918, Sonnino to ambassador in Washington.
11. AAES, 1369/1372, Benedict's memorandum on the *Nuova Antologia* article.
12. Hales, pp. 81–2.
13. De Marco, pp. 77–8.
14. *Diario*, II, p. 467, 24 April 1919.
15. Ibid.
16. Ibid., p. 299, 20 April 1918.
17. Ibid., pp. 395–6, 9 November 1918.
18. *La CC*, 71, 2 (120), p. 506.
19. Stehlin (1994), p. 6.
20. Ibid., p. 3.
21. See Stehlin (1983), ch. V.
22. Cited in Morozzo Della Rocca (1996), p. 552.
23. *La CC*, 71, 1 (1919), p. 451.
24. Ibid., 69, 4 (1918), p. 341.
25. *Diario*, II, pp. 391–2, 5 November 1918.
26. Ibid., p. 390, 27 October 1918.
27. Morozzo Della Rocca (1996), p. 552.
28. *Diario*, II, p. 432, 28 January 1919.
29. Ibid., p. 438, 13 February 1919.
30. Alexander, pp. 2–6.
31. *Diario*, II, p. 474, 30 May 1918.
32. Pollard (1985), p. 85.
33. ASV, DAUS, V, p. 97, telegram of 21 June 1919 from Bonzo to Gasparri.
34. *La CC*, 1920, 2, p. 567, 19 June 1920.
35. Ibid.
36. Carlen (ed.), IV, p. 174.
37. Mizzi, p. vi.
38. Carlen (ed.), IV, pp. 170–1.
39. Ibid., p. 174.
40. *Diario*, II, p. 567, 26 December 1920.
41. Molony, p. 103.

42. Norton, p. 283.
43. Ibid., p. 281.
44. As quoted in ibid.
45. Minerbi, pp. 117–20.
46. Ibid., p. 150.
47. *Diario*, II, p. 563, 27 July 1919.
48. Minerbi, pp. 89–90.
49. *La CC*, 70, 2 (1919), p. 8.
50. Minerbi, p. 89.
51. *La CC*, 72, 2 (1921), p. 519.
52. Ibid., p. 87.
53. Minerbi, p. 153.
54. *La CC*, 70, 2 (1919), p. 4.
55. Ibid., p. 12.
56. Ibid., 71, 3 (1920), pp. 42–3.
57. As quoted in Minerbi, p. 44.
58. Minerbi, p. 149.
59. Ibid., p. 19.
60. See ASV, DAUS, V, 82/3, Scatola 67, Deloncle, and AAES, 1335, fasc. 488, especially the memorandum on the 'Lugano Pact', no date. *Diario*, II, p. 88, 10 May 1917.
61. *Diario*, II, p. 88, 10 May 1917.
62. La Bella, p. 5.
63. Keogh, pp. 34 and 49.
64. Ibid., p. 49.
65. See ASV, DAUS, V, 82/3 for the file of letters about Ireland received by Apostolic Delegate in Washington, Mgr Bonzano.
66. Keogh, p. 40.
67. Ibid., p. 83.
68. *La CC*, 71, 3 (1920), p. 97.
69. Keogh, p. 40.
70. AAES, Stati Ecclesiastici, 1350, Italia 1915–1924, vol. III, 'Missione di Mons. Cerretti a Parigi, Londra, Washington e scambio di corrispondenza', Cerretti–Gasparri, 9 December 1918.
71. La Bella, pp. 62–3.
72. Ibid., pp. 128–9.
73. Ibid., pp. 174–5.
74. Keogh, pp. 67–70.
75. Ibid., p. 75.
76. Ibid., p. 69.
77. As quoted in La Bella, p. 175.
78. Ibid.
79. Keogh, p. 69.

80. Austria-Hungary, Prussia, Bavaria, Russia, Spain, Monaco, Belgium, Serbia, Brazil, Peru, Colombia, Argentina, Bolivia, Honduras, Chile, Costa Rica, Dominican Republic.

81. The Russian envoy disappeared after the Revolution and the Prussian envoy with establishment of relations with the Reich. The Austria-Hungarian envoy was replaced by envoys for the two separate states. Yugoslavia replaced Serbia. Czechoslovakia, Romania, Portugal, Britain, Switzerland, Holland, Poland, Lithuania, Luxembourg and France all established relations after 1914.

82. For example, Estonia; see *La CC*, 70, 2 (1919), p. 279.

83. Stehlin (1994), p. 9.

84. Ibid.

85. Ibid.

86. *Diario*, II, pp. 337–8, 3 June 1918.

87. Marchese, pp. 319–21 and 351–5.

88. *Diario*, II, p. 529, 30 January 1920.

89. *La CC*, 71, 4 (1920), p. 103.

90. Ibid., 70, 2 (1919), p. 265.

91. Ibid., 72, 1 (1921), pp. 175–6.

92. As quoted in Fogarty, p. 219.

7

Benedict XV and Italy, 1918–1922

Benedict's homeland presented him with both promising opportunities and grave problems in the years following the end of the
First World War. First of all, there seemed to be reason for
believing that a resolution of the Roman Question was a realistic
prospect. The emergence of the Partito Popolare Italiano (henceforth PPI or the Popolari) also suggested that Catholics, with their
programmes of economic and social reform based on the Church's
social teaching, would have a powerful influence on Italy's future
development. On the other hand, in the aftermath of the war there
appeared in Italy, as in other parts of the devastated and disrupted
continent, the threat of revolution and the painful, violent reality
of serious political and social disorder, which would take its final
form in the emergence of Fascism. Thus, in the last years of his
pontificate, Benedict was obliged to dedicate himself to the pursuit
of social peace, just as he had struggled to bring peace among the
nations between 1914 and 1918.

The First World War transformed the relationship between Italy
and the Papacy. In part, this was the result of the steady, quiet
diplomacy of Benedict's friend Carlo Monti who managed to
smooth things over, despite the constant, and sometimes bitter,
arguments over such matters as Palazzo Venezia, Article 15 of the
Treaty of London, the Pope's unfortunate newspaper interviews and
the anti-clerical outbursts of Italian politicians and newspapers.
He ensured that a much warmer, more relaxed and co-operative
spirit prevailed between the governing bodies of the two powers at
the end of the war than had been the case at the beginning. To
give but one example of the new relationship: in May 1920, the

Italian government offered, without any prompting on the Vatican's part, a gift of four hundred rifles with which to equip the Vatican Palatine Guard, one of the Pope's 'armed forces'.[1] Such a gesture would have been inconceivable in the pre-war period, when Giolitti, the author of the famous aphorism that Church and State in Italy were 'two parallels that should never meet', was the dominant figure in Italian politics. The cordiality of relations between the Vatican and a succession of Liberal prime ministers, Orlando, Nitti, Bonomi and even Giolitti himself, was one of the novelties of the Italian post-war political scene. In December 1920, King Victor Emanuel even sent his condolences to Benedict on the death of the latter's brother, Giannino.[2]

The war accelerated processes of change that were wider and more radical than those on the strictly diplomatic/political level. As Pietro Scoppola has observed, the war radically altered the position of Catholics in Italian society and politics.[3] The support of at least some Italian politicians for Intervention, and the participation of the Italian Catholic masses, especially the peasantry, in the war, combined with the patriotic mobilization of both the Catholic clergy and lay organizations in the war effort, removed once and for all the anti-patriotic, anti-Italian stigma which had been attached to Italian Catholics since the Risorgimento. Some diehard anti-clericals, especially revolutionary Interventionists like Benito Mussolini, might continue to inveigh against the Church, but they did so with increasingly less conviction especially since their fellow Interventionists, the Nationalists, had been moving in a Catholic direction since before the war, anxious to enlist Catholic and Church support for their vision of a strong, authoritarian Italian State with imperial ambitions.[4] Much, though by no means all, anti-clerical venom still sprang from the revolutionary Left which, however, was discredited in the eyes of many by its militant neutralism, pacifism and 'defeatism' during the course of the war. There was also an obstinate residue of masonic anti-clericalism in the old Italian political class, especially among Republicans and Democratic Liberals, which would effectively impede further progress in the process of reconciling the Papacy and Italy during Benedict's lifetime. Nevertheless, on 9 November Church and State in Italy came together in a unprecedentedly official way when the Cardinal Vicar of Rome celebrated a solemn Te Deum for the Italian victory over Austria in the Church of Aracoeli, in the presence not only of the mayor of Rome and government ministers, but of HRH the Duke of Genova, Lieutenant General of the Kingdom, in the absence of the King who was still at the front. Monti's account of a reception in Rome for Bishop Endrici of Trento, whose internment by the Austrians had made him a national hero, the very symbol of Catholic, patriotic Italy, also records that it closed with cries of 'Long live the King!', 'Long live Italy!', 'Long live the Pope!'[5]

The new *détente* between Italy and the Vatican had an international dimension. Monti made systematic attempts to align the policies of the Vatican and Italy in some areas of international relations, most notably Anatolia and the Middle East generally, for the intended benefit, it has to be said, primarily of Italy. Thus he sought to encourage the 'planting' of Italian missionaries in the territories of the former Ottoman Empire and to enlist Vatican support against French pretensions in Syria and Lebanon (see Chapter 8). Another key area for Italy after 1918 was the Adriatic, and more specifically the new north-eastern provinces which Italy acquired under the terms of the Versailles Peace Settlement. The new Italian authorities faced problems with the local Slav clergy almost from the moment they arrived: the Bishop of Trieste, for example, refused to sing a Te Deum in his cathedral to celebrate the Italian take-over.[6] As Monti's diary shows, the resistance of the local clergy and even bishops to the authorities' policy of 'Italianization' of the large Slav minorities provoked serious disputes which the Vatican attempted to settle. In January and February of 1919, the row over Italian treatment of the recalcitrant bishop of Spalato (Split) was so serious that it led to a brief rupture in relations between the Vatican and Italy.[7] There were further problems over the behaviour of the bishops of Trieste and Veglia in 1920.[8] The German-speaking minority in the newly acquired province of Trento also posed a problem, which the Italian authorities sought to resolve by transferring the Germans in the diocese of Trento to that of Bressanone, and by removing Trento itself from its subordination to the archiepiscopal see of Salzburg and making it immediately subject to the Holy See.[9] These problems were not satisfactorily resolved during Benedict's pontificate, nor even after the signing of the Concordat between his successor and Mussolini in 1929. The problem of recalcitrant German and Slav clergy rumbled on long afterwards, and was only effectively dampened down by the complete removal of Slav and German bishops.[10]

From Benedict's point of view, a major benefit of improved relations with Italy was an amelioration of the working conditions of the Vatican and its offices. In general terms, Vatican officials were now treated with more respect and consideration than they had been in the past, cardinals, leading ecclesiastics (including Mgr Tedeschini) and lay members of the Papal Court being given diplomatic number plates for their vehicles in December 1918, for example.[11] The 'guarantees' and 'immunities' of the Law of Guarantees were now being transformed into real, 'extra-territorial' privileges for the Holy See. The amicability in the relations between the 'two Romes' also manifested itself in matters that pertained more directly to the life of the Church within the Kingdom of Italy itself. The fact that Carlo Monti was Director-General of the Fondo per il Culto not only meant that damaging disputes about appointments to benefices, and most especially to bishoprics, could now be avoided, but that the Vatican was automatically consulted on wider ecclesiastical matters within the competence of the State. In particular, the Vatican was consulted on two major issues affecting the life of the Italian Church: the first was consideration of establishing a *congrua*, that is a payment to parish priests to supplement the revenues from their benefices which had been seriously diminished by wartime inflation.[12] The decision to do so, as Jemolo points out, 'meant that another bastion of Liberal ecclesiastical policy fell unnoticed – namely the principle of "no state subsidies for religion"'.[13] The second was the proposal to expropriate the endowments from which these revenues were derived.[14] As Monti argued, to have proceeded in the latter case would have been to commit a seriously ungenerous act, given the patriotic behaviour of the clergy during the war.[15] In both cases, the outcome was satisfactory. In 1919, the Holy

See's own financial position, precarious at the best of times, was threatened by the Italian government's decision to tax all earnings from interest and dividends. The unprecedentedly good relations between Gasparri and the first post-war Prime Minister, Nitti, eventually ensured that the Vatican's investments continued to be exempt, in accordance with the terms of the Law of Guarantees.[16] A not dissimilar measure was proposed by Prime Minister Giolitti in 1920, to have all stocks, bonds and shares registered in the name of individuals, which would have been especially burdensome for religious houses whose heads were often ageing: at each death of the person in whose name the titles were registered, death duty would have had to be paid. Once again, Gasparri was able to persuade the government to exempt the Church's holdings from this provision.[17]

There was nearly always a quid pro quo, even a strictly financial one, for these 'favours': from the beginning of 1919 onwards, the Italian government sought the Vatican's support for a new war loan.[18] As time passed, the demands grew. In January 1920, Schanzer, the Italian Finance Minister, was putting pressure on the Vatican to instruct its envoys in North and South America to mobilize support for the loan from Italian immigrant communities[19] and in February Benedict agreed that various Vatican organs, including the administration of the Apostolic Palaces, would subscribe several millions of lire to the new loan.[20] Thus began a process, which was consolidated by the financial arrangements attached to the Lateran Pacts of 1929, which would bind the finances of the Vatican to those of the Italian State.

The attempt to resolve the Roman Question

Given the transformation of relations between Italy and the Holy See, and the obvious reservoir of good will on both sides, why was a resolution of the Roman Question not achieved in Benedict's reign, and especially in the aftermath of the war, which was undoubtedly a very propitious time for it? Even before the end of 1918, there were strong expectations in Italy, and to a lesser extent in international circles, that a comprehensive agreement between the Pope and the Italian State was not far off[21] and a growing belief in more restricted, Italian governmental circles that the unofficial relations with the Vatican carried on by Carlo Monti would be transformed into official, diplomatic ones at any moment.[22] On the Vatican's side, there was certainly a very strong desire to reach a settlement, much thought and discussion had gone into ways of achieving it[23] and Carlo Monti himself had a powerful ambition to bring it about.[24] The casual evidence would suggest that Benedict's ideas about a solution of the Roman Question changed during the course of his reign. In 1916, he told Monti that he did not want ownership of the Vatican palaces, etc., let alone territorial sovereignty, nor 'internationalization' of the Law of Guarantees, i.e. guarantees by the powers to maintain it.[25] This statement may have been solely prompted by the Vatican's need to disassociate itself from speculation being raised in the German Catholic press about precisely these questions at that moment in time, and also from Erzberger's earlier schemes (see Chapter 4). On the other hand, Benedict's opposition to 'internationalization' was consistent throughout the war, the reason given being, as he pointed out to Carlo Monti, that such an arrangement would result in the replacement of one 'master', Italy, by several, that is other powers.[26] By the end of the war, however, there is evidence that both Benedict and Gasparri were beginning to favour some element of territorial sovereignty in any solution of the Roman Question, and that even 'internationalization' was beginning to look like a attractive prospect to them.[27] This change of tack may have been prompted by the Palazzo Venezia incident which seemed to suggest the dangers to the Holy See of being merely a 'guest' of the Italian State on the latter's property (see p. 99).

The Cerretti–Orlando talks, 1919

For a brief few days in the spring–summer of 1919, the Roman Question came close to being resolved. In fact, Monti had sounded out the prospects for talks with Orlando on Gasparri's behalf as early as December 1918.[28] There is also evidence that Gasparri made his own private soundings with Nitti.[29] But real progress came in May when, as a result of an almost chance conversation between Mgr Kelley (later Bishop of Oklahoma City) and the Italian Prime Minister Orlando, in Paris, negotiations were opened for a settlement.[30] Kelley managed to persuade Orlando that Italy's hopes of succeeding to the position of leading Catholic power, following the demise of the Habsburg Empire, depended upon a settlement with the Holy See.[31] With Orlando's approval, Kelley travelled to Rome, where he presented himself to Gasparri. The Cardinal Secretary of State and Benedict responded rapidly and favourably to Orlando by despatching Mgr Cerretti, the Under-Secretary of State for Extraordinary Ecclesiastical Affairs, to Paris with an outline plan for an agreement: the ostensible reason for Cerretti's visit to the Peace Conference was the question of the future of German missions.[32] The essence of Cerretti's bargaining position consisted of a) territorial sovereignty over the Vatican, and possibly some adjoining areas and b) international guarantees. According to Jemolo: 'It did not advocate any financial contribution on the part of Italy, nor any modifications of the Italian juridical system . . . but it spoke in general terms of an eventual Concordat that would restrict the application of ecclesiastical laws.'[33] This gradualist approach, first seeking to remedy the defects of the Holy See's legal position so painfully revealed by the war, before tackling the thorny issue of Italian ecclesiastical laws, was a sensible one in view of the dogged commitment of Liberal politicians like Sonnino to the 'fetish' of State jurisdiction over the Church. During the course of the negotiations, Cerretti expressed his optimism at the likely reaction of the Italian people to a settlement. Orlando was more realistic:

If, Orlando told Mgr. Cerretti, the cataclysmic happenings of the past four years are succeeded by an epoch-making event such as the solution of the Roman Question, we may find that the shock delivered to the organism has brought the patient to the verge of what I would almost describe as nervous prostration . . .

Therefore, all things considered, it might be better to await the signature of the peace treaty before opening negotiations.[34]

Further progress in the talks was prevented by the fall of Orlando's government in June. In any case, though, as he himself claimed, he could probably have squared the King, who was a notorious anti-clerical, it is doubtful whether Orlando could have carried his cabinet colleagues with him on any agreed package, owing to the opposition of Sonnino, and it is even more unlikely that he could have got such a package through Parliament at this stage. The secret of the talks was very carefully kept: not even Carlo Monti was informed. Cerretti did not give up. In November 1921 he tried to interest Monti in what he described as a 'San Marino' solution of the territorial dimension of the Roman Question.[35]

The 1919 talks reveal just how much good will there was in Italy at this time, and also Benedict's willingness to try all avenues to reach a settlement. Not surprisingly, therefore, secret discussions continued under both Nitti in 1920 and Bonomi in 1921, though without any successful outcome.[36] Italy's steadily deteriorating parliamentary political situation, set against a background of Socialist, and later Fascist, violence in the north and centre pushed relations with the Vatican, always a contentious issue, to the bottom of the government's priorities. The re-establishment of relations between the Holy See and France in 1920 must have resurrected hopes of a similar development in regard to Italy, but no such thing materialized. Benedict's own contribution to the attempts to reach an agreement is to be found in his encyclical *Pacem Dei Munus Pulcherrimum* (On Peace and Christian Reconciliation) of May 1920. In it, the Pope made a significant relaxation of the intransigent papal boycott of the Italian State. In a section entitled 'Papal Concession', Benedict noted that good relations between nations were 'maintained and fostered by the modern custom of visits and meetings at which the Heads of State and Princes are accustomed to treat of matters of special importance'.[37] He therefore decided to relax the ban imposed by his predecessors on the visits of Catholic sovereigns and heads of state to Rome, while taking the opportunity to reiterate his demand, 'now that peace is made among the nations that "for the Head of the Church, too, an end may be put to that abnormal condition" which in so many ways does such serious harm to tranquillity among peoples'.[38] The ground had been prepared beforehand with great care; in particular, Gasparri himself had negotiated the niceties of the protocol of such visits with Nitti, and publication of the encyclical was delayed while the question of the resumption of relations with France was finally resolved.[39] According to Monti, 'the impression created by the document has been enormous'.[40]

Benedict was not to see 'peace' with Italy in his lifetime: he probably never expected it, though he certainly strongly desired and strove for it. And no matter how many concessions he might make in pursuit of that end, he maintained his dignity and defended the sacrosanct rights of the Holy See in the face of the dispute with Italy, until the end. When Count Santucci, a leading member of Rome's 'black' aristocracy, was made a member of the Italian Senate in October 1919, the Vatican was clearly at a loss to know how to deal with the situation.[41] Two years later, Mgr Pizzardo, the new Sostituto, forwarded a request from Prince Colonna, who as one of the princely 'Assistants at the Papal Throne' occupied the number two lay position in the Papal Court, and was therefore one of the most eminent of all the 'black' nobility, that he be granted permission to make a formal visit to the Spanish Ambassador to the Quirinale on the occasion of the wedding of the Ambassador's daughter. Benedict wrote on the note 'Negative . . . only a private and simple visit!!'[42]

Benedict and the PPI

The post-war relationship between Italy and the Vatican was also strongly influenced by the emergence of a 'Catholic' party – the PPI – in 1918. The presence of a political party of Catholic inspiration in the Italian parliament inevitably complicated relations between the Vatican and the Italian government, and in part helps to explain the failure of the democratic regime to resolve the

Roman Question. The emergence of the PPI was another consequence of the First World War and the role which Italian Catholics
played in it. Leading figures from the Catholic movement like
Luigi Sturzo and Filippo Meda felt that Italian Catholics had
politically come of age, that they were now mature enough to play
a direct role on the political stage. As Federico Chabod has stated:
'The most notable event in Italian history in the twentieth Century
[. . .] was the official return of the Catholic masses to Italian
political life.'[43] It is arguable whether any section of the Italian
masses had played a political role before 1913 (when universal
adult male suffrage was introduced), but certainly the entry of the
PPI on to the Italian political stage was to have enormous
consequences for both Church and State in Italy.

Gasparri later claimed that, 'The PPI emerged as a result of a
process of spontaneous generation without any political intervention on the part of the Holy See, neither for nor against.'[44] This
statement is strictly speaking true, though it is also a trifle
disingenuous. It is a well-known fact that no Italian Catholic at
this time could make a major political act without the consent of
the Vatican. The emergence of a party of Catholics was a revolutionary act which upset all of the established bases of the Vatican's
policy towards the involvement of Catholics in Italian politicial
life, the ground rules for this having been set in Pius X's reign.
Though, because of the war, there had been no Italian general
elections since 1913, the rules were clear: Catholics could only
stand as candidates and vote in elections under the guidance of the
bishops and the local branches of Count Gentilone's Unione
Cattolica Elettorale (see Chapter 2), and in parliament, Catholics
were expressly forbidden to form a political party according to the
injunction 'Cattolici deputati non deputati cattolici' (untranslatable).[45]
The electoral activity of a Catholic-inspired political party was
impossible without the complete lifting of the *non expedit* decree
issued by the Sacred Penitentiary in 1864, in other words without
the approval of the Vatican.

So Benedict was presented with an interesting dilemma in the
late autumn of 1918 when leading Italian Catholics, grouped
around Luigi Sturzo, expressed their desire to form a 'Catholic'

political party and sought the Pope's permission to do so. On the advice of Cardinal Ferrari of Milan, Sturzo and Santucci went to see Gasparri. According to Molony, Gasparri said that the Vatican would raise no objection so long as the Church and Catholic Action were not involved: 'Gasparri even accepted the theoretical possibility of some sort of alliance with the Socialists instead of the Liberals.'[46] It was a very theoretical possibility given the ideological gulf between the Socialist Party and Italian Catholics. When asked by Sturzo to raise the *non expedit*, Gasparri replied that only the Pope could do that.[47] On the basis of this understanding, the PPI was launched by Sturzo and his friends. In January 1919, the Vatican dissolved the Unione Elettorale as no longer serving any useful purpose and this was taken as a signal by various Catholic organizations, the bulk of the Catholic press, and thousands of the parochial clergy and the Catholic laity to adhere to the party.[48]

For Benedict, the major assurance of the probity of the new party was the presence at its head of Luigi Sturzo. The fact that Sturzo was a priest does not seem to have worried Benedict at this time, though it was later to be used as a stick by both Liberal politicians and the Fascist leader Mussolini with which to beat the Vatican. In fact, priests rose to become leaders of Catholic parties in a number of countries in Europe in the inter-war years: Mgr Seipel in Austria, Mgr Kaas in Germany and the wretched clerico-Fascist, Mgr Tiso in Slovakia. Benedict had known Sturzo when he was Sostituto, and the story goes that it was he who gave the Sicilian priest permission to accept the post of deputy mayor in his home town, 'for the public good' in 1905.[49] Such was Benedict's esteem for Sturzo that in 1914 he appointed him Secretary-General of the Unione Popolare, the main organization of the Italian Catholic movement. Though Sturzo opted for Italian Intervention in 1914, seeing in it an opportunity to finally create a truly united Italian nation, united that is, morally and culturally, and to challenge the existing Liberal political class, he did not criticize Benedict's Peace Note of 1917.[50] According to De Rosa, Benedict had a particular affection for Sturzo, and until the end of his own life in 1959 Sturzo always said Mass on the anniversary of the Pope's death.[51] Benedict and Sturzo had much in common: both suffered exile (in Sturzo's case, outside of Italy) and both had to bear the pain and bitterness of the failure of their best efforts and sacrifices in great causes.

Benedict was an extremely interested spectator as the PPI took form in early 1919, establishing groups in both the Senate and Chamber of Deputies, and drawing up its programme. This was for the Pope the ultimate test of the new party's probity. Sturzo opted for 'aconfessionalism', that is the deliberate disassociation from the Church, opening its membership to all regardless of religion, which in Italy meant that its non-Catholic members were rare birds indeed. But the programme was clearly inspired by Catholic, religious principles. According to a carefully planted 'Nota' in the Jesuit organ *La Civiltà Cattolica*, the programme had the Pope's *nihil obstat*,[52] indeed there is a possibility that some aspects of the programme were modified to conform with Benedict's ideas, particularly those relating to the Church. It is clear from the Vatican Archives that Benedict and Gasparri wished to consult widely for opinions on the PPI programme, but they were overtaken by events and there was only time to sound out the opinions of the bishops of the Veneto region of north-eastern Italy. Most of the bishops welcomed the new party, seeing in it a new and more efficacious form of Catholic social action: only Cardinal La Fontaine, Patriarch of Venice, was unhappy, arguing that the PPI would to be an embarrassment to the bishops.[53] Gasparri took further advice from the noted French Catholic social thinker, Mgr Pottier, on what attitude the Church should adopt towards democracy.[54]

When Padre Enrico Rosa, the editor of *La Civiltà Cattolica*, submitted the draft of his Nota for Benedict's comments, in his reply the Pope only expressed reservations about two items of the PPI's programme, the one which called for the identification of paternity and the extension of the franchise to women. As far as the latter was concerned, the Pope took a pragmatic line. Though it seems likely that he did not approve of women's suffrage in principle, on the grounds that it would take them out of their 'natural sphere', he declared that, 'The totality of social conditions in our times renders it [votes for women] a social necessity in some countries, that is in order to counter the generally subversive votes of the socialists with the supposedly conservative votes of women.'[55] It is at this point that a certain divergence of attitude towards the PPI between Benedict and his Secretary of State became apparent. Benedict was prepared to suspend judgement on the party and its policies, as he explained in the letter 'until it [the PPI] has given a practical demonstration of what it stands for'.[56] And no doubt the passsage in the Nota which expressed the hope that 'interference from government, banks and newspapers closely connected to the government would not upset the equilibrium of the party and its broad moral programme'[57] was also inspired by Benedict. Gasparri was never to show such sympathy and understanding of the difficulties of the position in which Sturzo and the party were to find themselves.

But the Pope and his Secretary of State were united in their attitude to one policy of the PPI, the one which related to the Church and the Roman Question. The PPI programme had said very little about this problem, restricting itself to the following rather bland statement in Point VIII: 'Freedom and independence of the Church in the full development of its spiritual authority. Freeedom and respect for the Christian conscience considered as the foundation and safeguard of the life of the nation, of the liberties of the people and of the continuing development of civilisation in the world.'[58] The statement aroused the wrath of such *integristes* as Fr Agostino Gemelli, founder of the Catholic University of Milan and later a close adviser of Pius XI and Francesco Olgiati, who quickly constituted a 'right-wing' faction inside the PPI. It also caused disappointment inside the Vatican.[59]

Worse was to come. In his speech to the first congress of the PPI in Venice in March 1919, Sturzo took up a clear position on the Roman Question:

If today there exists a territorial question between Church and State, then we must respond by saying that for us the unity of Italy is sacred. Nor are we prepared to accept the internationalization of the law of guarantees which would violate the sovereignty of the State. Once the territorial dimension has been excluded from any Church and State dispute, it is the duty of every Italian to help resolve it.[60]

It was less than helpful for the Vatican that the PPI leader was publicly committing his party to a policy which constituted a repudiation of the absolutely minimum negotiating position of the Vatican, and precisely at a time when negotiations were going on in Paris between Cerretti and Wilson. Benedict was unhappy with Sturzo's statement,[61] and Gasparri expressed this unhappiness in a very firm letter to the Sicilian priest: 'The way in which the dispute [between the Holy See and Italy], that is the way of giving the Holy See effective liberty and independence . . . the party [the PPI], individual Catholics, and even more importantly priests, must leave to the interested parties, that is to the Holy See and the Italian State . . .'[62] Sturzo would not have known of the negotiations in Paris, and probably did not know of the negotiations that were to continue under Nitti, but Benedict and Gasparri must have felt that his public stand at Venice did not augur well for parliamentary ratification of any negotiated solution of the Roman Question.

On 16 November 1919 Italy held its first general elections under both universal male suffrage and proportional representation. Only five days before, the Vatican had announced the lifting of the *non expedit*: it had certainly taken its time to do so. According to the judgement of the Sacred Apostolic Penitentiary, 'because the *non expedit* was a positive law of the Church relating to a very specific situation, it should be abandoned for a greater and universal good, that is to save society from an anti-Christian and anarchic threat . . .'; furthermore, it declared that it was licit to support and vote for the PPI because it was 'inspired by Christian principles . . . and is no threat to Christian doctrine or morality'.[63] The Penitentiary further affirmed that it was 'not necessary for successful candidates to swear an oath of obedience to the Church and . . . and in the present case for many reasons it would be dangerous'.[64] It would indeed have been dangerous, giving the impression that the deputies and senators of the PPI were the servants of the

Church, which was exactly the accusation being made against them by their enemies. As one of the leading historians of the PPI has commented: 'Without Vatican tolerance, the PPI would have had to struggle for electoral support, but with Vatican sanction in the official sense it would have ceased to be what Sturzo wanted it to be – an autonomous political party.'[65] Nevertheless, the Vatican reserved to the bishops the right to object to the programme of a local candidate and to that person himself.[66]

Though Gasparri was privately elated at the outcome of the elections, claiming that if women had had the vote the Popolari would have won three hundred rather than the hundred seats they did win in the Chamber of Deputies,[67] he was already showing signs of concern about the party's conduct. In essence, the problem was that the emergence of the PPI on to the parliamentary stage rather complicated the direct interlocutory relationship which the cardinal had established with the leading Liberal politicians, largely through the mediation of Carlo Monti. As a result of the electoral success of the PPI, the Liberals had lost many seats and the Nitti government was consequently facing a crisis. Gasparri, in a conversation with Monti, agreed with him that in the circumstances of the time a crisis would have had 'grave consequences and for that reason he has given instructions to Don Sturzo in this sense'.[68] A few days later the conversation, and the Secretary of State's assurance, was repeated.[69] Precisely what form those 'instructions' took, by whom they were conveyed and what effect they had, we do not know. It is difficult to see how he could have given 'instructions' to a party with which he claimed the Vatican had no links. If he did give such instructions, he certainly did not do so face to face because he never saw Sturzo again after the meeting in December 1918. Gasparri seems to have tied himself too closely to the old Italian political class, especially to Francesco Nitti. Benedict displayed more prudence and circumspection in his attitudes towards Italian politics, a quality which Monti appreciated. Recording a conversation with the Pope in June of 1920, Monti wrote: 'Gasparri . . . though he is an able, if somewhat crude, diplomatist and a distinguished canon lawyer, does not understand internal politics very well.'[70]

Staring into the abyss: the threat of social revolution

But by the spring of 1920, Benedict had more reason to share Gasparri's anxieties about the PPI. The Secretary of State believed that 'the direction taken by certain tendencies in the Party and the admission of untrustworthy elements . . . give rise to grave concerns'.[71] What Gasparri was referring to was the *estremista* faction led by the Cremonese peasant leader, Guido Miglioli, who had sought to change the PPI's name to 'The Party of the Christian Proletariat' at the 1920 Congress in Venice.[72] Miglioli had supporters in the Catholic or 'white' peasant leagues in other parts of northern Italy, like Bergamo and Verona. Their militant tactics in the struggle with the landowners over tenancy agreements and sharecroppers' contracts,[73] and their support for co-operation with the Socialists led them to be called the 'white bolsheviks' and aroused Benedict's concern. In a letter to Mgr Marelli, Bishop of Bergamo, in March 1920, Benedict warned against the adoption of the Socialist methods of class struggle by the diocese's Catholic trade union organization, the Ufficio di Lavoro: 'Those who are responsible for such an institution . . . must above all keep in mind and follow scrupulously that doctrine of Christian wisdom built around social science, set out in the memorable encyclical *Rerum Novarum* and other letters of the Apostolic See', and he went on to advise the bishop not to hesitate, if he felt it necessary, to remove the organization's officers.[74] As a result of the Pope's intervention, the bishop expelled the radical Catholic trade unionist, Romano Cocchi, a supporter of Miglioli, from the Ufficio di Lavoro and sacked two priests in charge of it.[75]

Benedict issued no great encyclicals on Catholic social doctrine during the course of his pontificate, certainly nothing as coherent or complete as Leo XIII's *Rerum Novarum* or Pius XI's *Quadragesimo Anno* (1931). But his letter to the Bishop of Bergamo constitutes a comprehensive restatement of his, and the Church's, established teaching on the Christian ethics of industrial relations. Underlying his teaching was the belief that 'distinctions between social classes are of the natural order and in consequence are the will of God', and the resulting need of the poor to resign themselves to their lot.[76] He utterly rejected, therefore, the theory and practice of class war, and with them socialism, which he explicitly described as 'the enemy'. On the other hand he reiterated the legitimacy of the right of workers to organize themselves in unions and to bring about an improvement in their material situation.[77] He had, after all, given his blessing to the creation of a Catholic trade union organization – the Confederation of Italian Labour, which emerged almost simultaneously with the PPI in 1918: by late 1920 it had one million members. While stressing the need for the poor to remember their duties as well as their rights, he asserted that the 'better off should regulate their interests with the proletariat more by equity than right', and he reminded the clergy of their obligation to educate their parishoners in the pursuit of these goals.[78] He concluded with an appeal for 'social peace': 'The cause of truth and justice cannot be defended by violence or disorder':[79] exactly the same judgement he had made about the war.

The Bergamo episode was emblematic of a much bigger, more serious and developing situation: the pre-war militancy of the working class, which Benedict had witnessed as Archbishop of Bologna, had in the post-war period become general, affecting sections of the Italian Catholic movement as well. Under the influence of the radicalism born out of the experience of trench-warfare, and the example of the Bolshevik Revolution in Russia, Italy in the early 1920s witnessed an upsurge of militancy on the part of unionized workers and peasants, the so-called 'Red Two Years', marked by protests against rent and price rises, strikes, occupations of the factories and land, many of which were accompanied by acts of violence.[80] The bitter class warfare that developed frightened both Catholics and Liberals, and to some extent divided the Catholic movement, most especially the PPI, and the clergy, for the Catholic peasant leagues, like those in Cremona, Bergamo, etc., could sometimes be as militant and instransigent, if not more so, than their Socialist counterparts, and they were often led by priests. Violent agitations in the countryside of the Veneto region prompted Benedict to address a letter to its bishops formulated in much the same terms as the one to the Bishop of Bergamo.[81] It may also have been prompted by a letter which his sister Giulia forwarded to him from a local priest deploring 'the unfair and immoral' contracts imposed on the landlords by the white leagues.[82] As a result of these events, Catholic landowners and businessmen, and the middle classes generally, drew closer to their Liberal counterparts, and when their leaders, Nitti, Giolitti and Bonomi, appeared unable to stem the tide of militancy, some of them eventually turned to Fascism.[83]

In August of 1920, when the threat of revolution in Italy had reached its height in the Occupation of the Factories in the major northern Italian cities, Benedict once more took up his pen, this time in the form of a *motu proprio* ostensibly motivated by the fiftieth anniversary of the proclamation by Pius IX of St Joseph as Patron of the Universal Church, but since that was not due until December 1920, it is legitimate to believe that he was inspired by more immediate events. In the *motu proprio*, he first of all voiced his concerns about the decline of the family, which he attributed to the effects of the war, and reminded his readers of the example which the Holy Family offered to Catholics.[84] He then turned once again to the problems of class hatred and class warfare 'which today is desolating a not so small part of Europe'.[85] This last statement was the result of the reports he was getting from Mgr Achille Ratti, his nuncio in Poland, of the horrors of Bolshevik rule and civil war in Russia, which would soon extend to Poland when the Red Army invaded that country in September, of Nuncio Pacelli who witnessed the short-lived Soviet in Bavaria and information about the persecution of the Church under the Soviet in Hungary. Finally, he condemned the utopian dreams of 'a universal republic' and 'absolute equality' among men.[86] Monti says that Benedict told him he was preparing an encyclical on Communism.[87] It never appeared, but this document may certainly be regarded as a good substitute: it is also significant that it was directed to the whole Catholic world, that is the universal Church, and not just to Italy.

The failure of the PPI to adopt what was regarded as a satisfactory strategy in the local elections of May and October 1920 was another factor leading to divisions in the Catholic movement in Italy, and the estrangement of the party from the episcopate in large areas of northern and central Italy, and ultimately from the Vatican itself. Though the tide of Socialist violence and militancy was soon to ebb, and was to be replaced by the threat and reality of violence from the Fascists, that was not apparent in the summer and autumn of 1920, when the Socialists seemed to be carrying all before them. The necessity for a united 'clerico-moderate' electoral front against the Socialists seemed, therefore, to be an absolute imperative, but Sturzo and the PPI executive had agreed on a policy of 'intransigence', that is an absolute refusal to enter into such alliances. The memory of the way in which Gentilone had allowed the Liberals, especially Giolitti, to shamelessly use Catholics as voting 'fodder' in the pre-war period was undoubtedly a powerful influence on Sturzo's decision; he wanted to ensure that the PPI did not become a bag of votes into which the Liberals could dip at will.[88] But that was not much help for local bishops and clergy facing the Socialists – which in some areas meant violence directly against priests and the Church. According to Molony, seven Catholics died as a result of Socialist attacks at Sestri, Mantua and Siena where, in the last-named, a church was attacked.[89] In a village near Bologna, a church was invaded at Midnight Mass on Christmas Eve and the congregation turned out into the street, and in other parts of Emilia two priests were killed.[90] For someone like the *integriste* Cardinal Boggiani of Genoa, the behaviour of the PPI in these circumstances was all too predictable, and Cardinal La Fontaine of Venice was not surprised either, though he did at least succeed in persuading the local section of the party into an alliance with Liberal-Conservatives in his see city.[91] Even someone as sympathetic to Sturzo as Cardinal Ferrari of Milan appealed to him to relax his intransigence for the sake of the peculiar needs of the Lombard capital.[92] Monti lamented what he called 'the indiscipline of the PPI in Bergamo and Bologna',[93] meaning their refusal to enter into 'clerico-moderate' alliances.

The outcome of the local elections of 1920 was a great success for the Socialists. But the PPI was also successful, even in areas where some of its more right-wing members broke ranks and entered into personal alliances with local Liberal notables.[94]

After those elections, it is clear that the PPI and the Vatican were drifting further and further apart, and this reflected a wider split inside the Italian Catholic world. The gulf between the two was emphasized by the appointment of Giuseppe Dalla Torre, national president of Italian Catholic Action, as editor of *L'Osservatore Romano*. The Vatican organ was severely critical of the PPI strategy during the local elections of both May and October, and under Dalla Torre's direction space was increasingly devoted to the activities of Catholic Action, at the expense of coverage of the party. In an interview with his friend Buonaiuti in September 1921, Gasparri revealed the full extent of the Vatican's disillusionment with the PPI. He also made it clear that he could see no hope for progress in relations between the Holy See and Italy in a political situation effectively dominated by that party, and he concluded ominously, by saying that as far as a solution of the Roman Question was concerned, 'We are still awaiting our man.'[95]

Benedict and the rise of Fascism

That man would turn out to be Benito Mussolini, former revolutionary Socialist, and by mid-1921 the *Duce* (leader) of a new political movement, Fascism, which was going from strength to strength. Founded in March 1919 as a radical, patriotic alternative to the neutralist Italian Socialist Party, the *fasci* were from the beginning characterized by a strong ex-servicemen's element and a consequently natural resort to the use of political violence. Until the middle of 1920, Fascism remained a small, minority movement – it won no seats in the November 1919 elections – largely restricted in geographical terms to the cities of northern Italy. Its programme also remained radical – anti-clerical, anti-capitalist and anti-monarchical. Its opportunity came in the wake of the Occupation of the Factories, when Fascism extended its established strike-breaking activities into a wave of reaction against the working-class movement. But the spectacular growth of Fascism in 1920 and 1921 took place, not in the big industrial cities, but in the small towns and countryside of northern and central Italy, in a rural and agrarian setting, rather than an urban, industrial one. Here the class war had not abated; on the contrary, the bitter conflicts over labour contracts, tenancy and share cropping agreements were reaching their peak, as we have seen. And the victories of the Socialists in the local election of 1920 created the impression that if the revolution had failed in the towns with the end of the Occupation of the Factories, it was about to triumph in the countryside.

Systematic violence by the Fascist squads against the various organizations of the working-class movement – Socialist party branches, trade union offices and above all the peasant leagues (Catholic as well as Socialist) – spread across northern and central Italy, with the result that by the summer of 1921 a virtual civil war reigned in many of these areas. Frequently the authorities, military, police and judicial turned a blind eye to Fascist activities,[96] and in some cases they helped them, on the grounds that Fascism was a healthy, patriotic reaction against the threat of Bolshevik revolution, a spectre that was, of course, also haunting other parts of Europe at that time. This feeling was undoubtedly shared by many Catholics, clerical and lay, but the Catholic press, and in particular L'Osservatore Romano, consistently deplored the spread of Fascist violence: on the eve of the May 1921 elections, its attitude to the Socialists and Fascists was effectively 'a plague on both your houses'.[97] The attitude of La Civiltà Cattolica towards Fascism was much more severe. At this time, the Jesuit journal was edited by Padre Enrico Rosa, a man whom Benedict appointed, and who was to persist in his anti-Fascism even after Mussolini had established his regime.[98] As early as January 1915, as agitation for intervention in the war mounted in Italy, La Civiltà Cattolica had attacked the doctrines of pre-war nationalism which were ultimately to form the central core of Fascist ideology from 1919 onwards, in particular castigating 'exaggerated nationalism', the obsession with state power and authority and the belief that war was the natural condition of mankind.[99] This stand clearly reflected the position which Benedict had taken up in his encyclical Ad Beatissimi of the previous September. As the tide of Fascist violence rose in the spring of 1921, *La Civiltà Cattolica* repeatedly condemned it.[100]

Benedict was able to follow the rise and spread of Fascist violence, especially against Catholic organizations, and even churches, in the reports from clergy and bishops which poured into the Vatican from the end of 1920 onwards. Bishop Rossi of Udine, for example, reported that following the victory of both Socialists and Popolari candidates in the May 1921 general elections in his area, Fascists from as far away as Trieste, Monfalcone and Ravenna took their revenge by instigating a reign of terror in the city and burning down the diocesan printing press.[101] According to Bishop Longhin of Treviso, in his own diocese, and in the provinces of Venice, Vicenza and Bassano, the Fascist squads, 'armed with clubs and hand grenades', carried a campaign of violence against both Catholic and Socialist organizations.[102] The Bishop of Padua, Pellizzi, said that the situation in his diocese was even worse.[103]

In the May 1921 elections, Mussolini and 35 Fascists managed to get elected to Parliament on the coat-tails of Giolitti, that is in a National electoral 'bloc' which the 'Grand Old Man' of Italian politics had created in order to defeat the Socialists. The PPI, true to its declared electoral intransigence, refused to join, and the Socialists won almost as many seats as before. The chief winner was Mussolini, who now set his sights on power, which inevitably involved major compromises in order to win the support of the Italian establishment. Sheer opportunism and the need to placate increasing numbers of supporters from the middle and upper classes led Mussolini to play down, and eventually abandon, both anti-capitalism and republicanism. A desire to win Catholic support prompted a similiar change in his attitude to the Church. In the Manifesto of the Fascio of 1919 proof of the anti-clerical sentiments of the majority of the first Fascists was given by a clause which demanded the confiscation by the State of all the endowment funds of the Italian Church,[104] and in November 1919, in an editorial in his own daily newspaper, Mussolini declared: 'there is only one possible revision of the Law of Guarantees and that is its abolition followed by a firm invitation to His Holiness to quit Rome'.[105]

But by the autumn of 1920, Mussolini had seen the light and

without abandoning any of his instinctive and lifelong anti-clericalism and atheism, the Fascist leader recognized the crucial importance of the Church in Italian politics, as he revealed in a letter to Gabriele D'Annunzio: 'I believe that Catholicism can be used as one of the greatest forces for the expansion of Italy in the world.'[106] And with the same opportunism which had motivated his other swings to the Right, Mussolini made a direct overture to the Church in his maiden speech to Parliament in June 1921, when he brazenly declared that 'Fascism neither preaches not practices anti-clericalism', and he followed this up with an offer of material aid to the Church in Italy if it would abandon its 'temporalistic dreams'.[107] This Damascene conversion seems to have cut little ice in the Vatican; neither of its major press organs, *La Civiltà Cattolica* nor *L'Osservatore Romano*, deigned to comment on the speech.

By the time that Benedict lay on his deathbed, in January 1922, Italy had become virtually ungovernable. Fascist violence continued to spread in the provinces, and in Rome government was paralysed by a parliamentary crisis, indeed the regime itself, the Liberal State, had effectively entered into crisis, a crisis that would not be finally resolved until after Mussolini took power following the March on Rome ten months later. Even in his last agonies, Benedict could not escape the problems of Italian politics: Giolitti appealed to the Vatican to persuade Sturzo to lift the veto on PPI participation in any government which he led.[108] His attempt failed; the Popolari would only accept the premiership of Facta, Giolitti's colourless lieutenant, and so Italy drifted further into chaos with yet another weak, coalition government.

Would Italian history have been different if Benedict had not died in January 1922? Would he have refused to accept the reality of Fascist power after the March on Rome, would he have refused to push the PPI aside and would he have refused to make a 'marriage of convenience' with Fascism as his successor was to do? The answer is almost certainly 'no' to all these questions. Though he was less eager to come to terms with Fascism than Achille Ratti, the future Pius XI – and it is also certainly true that *L'Osservatore Romano*'s attitude to Fascism radically changed after

Ratti's election in February 1922 – it is doubtful if Benedict could have resisted the drift of events in Italy from 1922 onwards. And though he would have found the prospect of doing a deal with the Fascists rather more distasteful than his successor found it, he would not have shrunk from grasping the opportunity to settle the dispute had he been offered it. His concern for the future of the Church in Italy, and above all his desire to establish true independence and liberty for the Holy See would have compelled him to make the sacrifice. The lines of Vatican policy towards the PPI and Italian politics generally had already been established by the end of his pontificate. The Vatican was disillusioned with the experiment in a mass 'Catholic' political party for which, it has to be said, it had never had a great deal of enthusiasm. The distancing of the Church from the party, which was undoubtedly to become more pronounced under Pius XI, who was rather less tolerant of independent-minded Catholic lay, and even worse, clerical politicians, than Benedict, was, nevertheless, an established part of Vatican policy by the end of the latter's reign. Equally, the increasing ecclesiastical emphasis on the importance of the work of Catholic Action, a Catholic organization strictly under the control of the Holy See and Italian bishops, had become a feature of Vatican policy long before January 1922. Indeed, one of Benedict's last public utterances included a lamentation of the fact that, as he saw it, the Catholic press in Italy did not give sufficient attention and coverage to Catholic Action.[109]

It seems likely, therefore, that had he lived, it would have been Benedict, and not Achille Ratti, who would have played, on behalf of the Catholic Church, a key part in the tragic destruction of nascent Italian democracy in the 1920s. Nevertheless, it is regrettable that he was used, posthumously, to damn the PPI and facilitate a *rapprochement* between the Vatican and Fascism when it came to power in 1922. On the eve of Mussolini's appointment as Prime Minister of Italy, *L'Osservatore Romano* published a letter from a parliamentary deputy who claimed to be a friend of Benedict, Stanislao Monti-Guarnieri, in which he reported the Pope as saying: 'The Pope has nothing to do with the Partito Popolare. I have not recognized it as a party and I do not wish to recognize it now so that I may disown it later.'[110] The editor of the paper, Giuseppe Dalla Torre, and the Cardinal Secretary of State, Gasparri, were clearly behind this letter, and it is all the more unfortunate that they should have traduced Benedict's memory in this way, for Monti-Guarnieri was regarded by Carlo Monti, who was truly Benedict's friend, as an extremely unreliable busybody.[111]

Notes and references

1. *Diario*, II, p. 540, 2 May 1920.
2. Ibid., p. 567, 26 December 1920.
3. Scoppola, pp. xlii–xliv.
4. Webster, p. 37.
5. *Diario*, II, p. 413, 18 December 1918.
6. Ibid., II, p. 398, 19 November 1918.
7. Ibid., II, pp. 27–31.1 and 3–8 February 1919, pp. 430–4.
8. Ibid., II, pp. 484–5, 2 August 1919 and p. 526, 9 January 1920.
9. Ibid., II, pp. 517–8, 21 December 1919.
10. Pollard (1985), pp. 91–103.
11. *Diario*, I, pp. 447–8, 8 August 1916 and II, 21 December 1918.
12. Jemolo, p. 166.
13. Ibid.
14. *Diario*, II, pp. 410–11, 19 December 1918.
15. Ibid., p. 411.
16. Margiotta Broglio, p. 385, Gasparri to Nitti, 4 April 1919.
17. *Diario*, II, p. 555, 19 June 1920.
18. Ibid., II, pp. 511–2, 10 December 1919.
19. Ibid., II, p. 526, 9 January 1920.
20. Ibid., II, p. 532, 1 February 1920.
21. Ibid., II, p. 403, 7 December 1918, p. 408, 14 December 1918 and p. 410, 19 December 1918.
22. Ibid., II, p. 422, 16 January 1919 and pp. 410–11.
23. See the voluminous files in Stati Ecclesiastici, 1350, Italia 1915–1924, on the 'Questione Romana', AAES.
24. *Diario*, II, pp. 403–5, 7 December 1918.
25. Ibid., I, pp. 415–6, 7 August 1916.
26. Ibid., I, p. 331, 20 January 1916.
27. Ibid., II, pp. 403–5, 7 December 1918, conversation between Monti and Gasparri.
28. Ibid., II, pp. 410–11, 19 December 1918.
29. Gasparri, p. 49.

30. Binchy, pp. 235–7.
31. Ibid., p. 235.
32. Ibid., p. 236.
33. Jemolo, p. 166.
34. Ibid., p. 167.
35. *Diario*, II, p. 568, 27 December 1921.
36. Jemolo, p. 167.
37. Carlen (ed.), IV, p. 174.
38. Ibid.
39. Gasparri, p. 187.
40. *Diario*, II, p. 552, 31 May 1920.
41. Ibid., II, p. 507, 18 November 1919.
42. AAES, Stati Ecclesiastici, 1914–1918, 1447–1448, p. 596, Pizzardo to the Pope, 28 November 1921.
43. Chabod, p. 43.
44. Gasparri, pp. 233–4, 267.
45. Pollard (1996), p. 76.
46. Molony, p. 16.
47. Ibid.
48. Pollard (1990), p. 78.
49. Mellinato, pp. 273–4, where he says that this event took place in 1899: this is impossible, Sturzo was not elected to public office until 1905; De Rosa (1977), p. 186.
50. De Rosa (1977), pp. 182–3.
51. Ibid., p. 394.
52. Mellinato, p. 275.
53. AAES, Italia, 1918–1921, 953–5, 346, 'P.P.I., Pareri dell'Episcopato Veneto sul programme sociale dei cattolici nell'ora presente', letter of 27 January 1919.
54. Ibid., p. 348, 'Mons. Pottier sulla questione del movimento democratico el il ruolo della Chiesa'.
55. Mellinato, pp. 277–8.
56. Ibid., p. 278.
57. *La CC*, 70, 1919, vol. 1, p. 276.
58. As quoted in Molony, p. 49.
59. Ibid., p. 51 and pp. 56–7.
60. *Corriere della Sera*, 27 March 1919.
61. *Diario*, II, p. 460, 6 April 1919.
62. As quoted in *Diario*, II, p. 462, n. 68.
63. AAES, Italia, pp. 954–5, fasc. 346, letter from Cardinal Giorgi to Gasparri, 13 November 1919, 40–42 (in confirmation of a previous verbal judgement).
64. Ibid., p. 42.

65. Molony, p. 66.
66. AAES, Italia, p. 955, fasc. 348, unsigned, undated memorandum in Gasparri's handwriting.
67. *Diario*, II, p. 508, 20 November 1919.
68. Ibid., II, p. 516, 13 December 1919.
69. Ibid., pp. 519–20, 24 December 1919.
70. Ibid., p. 556, 17 June 1920.
71. AAES, Italia, p. 955, fasc. 348, unsigned, undated memorandum in Gasparri's handwriting.
72. Molony, p. 61.
73. Foot, pp. 420–8.
74. *La CC*, 71, 1920, vol. 2, p. 104.
75. Cento Bull, p. 39.
76. *La CC*, ibid., p. 105.
77. Ibid., p. 101.
78. Ibid.
79. Ibid., p. 106.
80. Pollard (1998), p. 23.
81. Scottà, p. 452.
82. ASV, SS, Guerra, 1920, rub. 80, fasc. 1, Venice, 20 April 1920.
83. Pollard (1990), p. 40.
84. *La CC*, 21 August 1920, pp. 290–1.
85. Ibid., p. 293.
86. Ibid.
87. *Diario*, II, p. 491, 2 September 1918.
88. Molony, p. 84.
89. Ibid., p. 96.
90. Ibid.
91. Ibid., p. 85.
92. De Rosa (1974), p. 72.
93. *Diario*, II, p. 565, 7 November 1920.
94. Molony, p. 85.
95. As quoted in Molony, p. 102.
96. Pollard (1998), p. 35.
97. O'Brien, p. 39.
98. Pollard (1985), p. 141.
99. *La CC*, 16 January 1915, p. 129.
100. Ibid., 72, 2, 1921, p. 7 and 373.
101. Scottà, pp. 452–3.
102. Ibid., p. 460.
103. Ibid., p. 452.
104. Delzell (ed.), p. 13.
105. *Il Popolo d'Italia*, 18 November 1919.

106. As quoted in Margiotta Broglio, p. 52.
107. Scoppola (1971), pp. 52–3.
108. See Pollard (1985), ch. 2.
109. Molony, p. 108.
110. *L'Osservatore Romano*, 29, pp. 30–31, 1922.
111. *Diario*, II, p. 49, 10 March 1917 and p. 106, 7 June 1917.

8

Benedict XV, the Church and the world

All popes, even one like Benedict XV whose reign was so overshadowed by secular concerns, war and peace and the necessary papal diplomacy, must ultimately be judged by their record as supreme pastor of the Universal Church – their government of the Roman Catholic Church throughout the world, their promotion and defence of its interests, the efficient working of its hierarchy of charisms and functions and, above all, its expansion in the world in accordance with its self-proclaimed, historic mission, the evangelization of peoples.

Benedict and doctrinal orthodoxy

As has already been seen, one of Benedict's first concerns as Pope was to bring peace back to the Church after the anti-Modernist excesses of the previous reign (see Chapters 1 and 2). Though he was clearly not a Modernist himself, he rejected the methods that had been used by Pius X and his collaborators against the Modernists. But he had a no less elevated idea of the authority of his office than his predecessor. In *Ad Beatissimi* he talked of his role as 'the Common Father of all', and reminded his hearers of his unique office: 'Us to whom is divinely committed the teaching of the truth.'[1] He went on to say: 'Therefore it is Our will that the law of our forefathers should be sacred: "Let there be no innovation; keep to what has been handed down." In matters of faith that must be inviolably adhered to as the law; it may also serve as a guide even in matters subject to change but even in such cases the rule would hold: "Old things but in a new way".'[2] It would seem that Benedict was exercising his natural caution. He was both reiterating a warning against the pursuit of the dangerous novelties of Modernism, and leaving the door open to further discussion of less contentious issues: a fairly sensible policy and one which was in line with that which he had pursued as Archbishop of Bologna. He was making it clear that he would countenance no deviation from accepted doctrine, nor did he himself intend to exercise his infallible power to introduce doctrinal innovations. The most obvious one would have been in relation to the Marian cult, the next development of which eventually took the form of Pius XII's definition of the dogma of the bodily Assumption of the Blessed Virgin Mary in 1950. Given that Benedict had led both a Bologna diocesan and Italian national pilgrimage to Lourdes, the first Pope to do so, and that the apparition of our Lady of Fatima took place in 1917, such a step would have been entirely natural. But he seems to have been content with the 'deposit of the faith' as he had inherited it and as he understood it.

Spiritus Paraclitus, 1920

It is all the more significant, therefore, that Benedict was to devote his longest encyclical, *Spiritus Paraclitus*, of 1920, to the problems of biblical scholarship, for it seemed that such questions had been settled once and for all by Leo XIII's encyclical *Providentissimus Deus* of 1893, which asserted the full, divine inspiration of the Scriptures, their inerrancy, the rejection of the distinction between relative and absolute truth in them and of the suggestion that the Bible was not historical fact.[3] The warnings against Modernist interpetations of the Bible had been repeated by Pius X in *Pascendi Dominici Gregis* in 1907, and he had also set up a Pontifical Biblical Commission to hand down rulings on such matters. Benedict in his encyclical, which was ostensibly prompted by the recurrence of the anniversary of St Jerome, the father of the Church who devoted so much of his life to the study of Scripture, does more than just reiterate the line taken in *Providentissimus Deus*. 'The pope was more negative in tone in his dealings with modern advances than Leo XIII had been and more strongly defensive on the historicity of the Bible.'[4] The most likely explanation for Benedict's initiative in the field of biblical scholarship must be that he feared that his abandonment of the excesses of Pius X's anti-Modernist campaign might send the wrong signal; that it might be interpreted as condoning the errors which both Leo XIII and Pius X had previously condemned. Another possible explanation may be found in the fact that the debate about Darwin's theories of evolution had entered another, vigorous phase precisely in his reign. *La Civiltà Cattolica*, for example, devoted several articles to the question of 'Evolution or the Stability of the Species?' in 1919 and 1920 which, after presenting the scientific evidence both for and against, came out against evolution.[5] Perhaps Benedict felt it necessary to re-assert the divine authorship, and the inerrancy of Scripture in these circumstances. What was novel about his encyclical, however, was the stress on the need to make the scriptures available to the faithful, and not just the Gospels, which was what commonly happened in the Church at that time, but the whole Bible.[6] He strongly recommended the work of the Society of St Jerome, which was dedicated to just that end and which, he reminded his readers, he himself had founded.[7] In part, he was probably seeking to respond to the long-established Protestant allegation that the Roman Catholic Church kept the Bible from the people.[8] In this sense, *Spiritus Paraclitus* had positive results, but more broadly speaking its consequences were negative: it 'froze' Roman Catholic biblical scholarship until Pius XII reopened the subject with his encyclical *Divino Afflante Spiritu* of 1943.

If there was a substantial continuity and identity of policy in the field of biblical studies between the pontificate of Benedict and that of his predecessor, there were clearly many differences in other fields, and the most striking difference was undoubtedly in the field of liturgy. Benedict issued no decrees on liturgy or liturgical discipline such as those of Pius X, whose insistence on frequent communion for the laity and on early communion for children was undoubtedly the most important development since the Council of Trent in the sixteenth century. Benedict was content to leave things be in this field. In the broader one of Catholic devotion, his only major contribution was an intensification of the cult of the Sacred Heart of Jesus: indeed his reign marks the high point of the development of that cult. In May 1915, he had consecrated all the nations involved in the war to the Sacred Heart,[9] in May 1919 Spain was dedicated to the Sacred Heart with great pomp and ceremony[10] and in October the Basilica of the Sacré-Cœur was consecrated in Montmartre.[11] The new Catholic university instituted at Milan in Benedict's reign was also dedicated to the Sacred Heart. To crown all his efforts, in May 1920, Benedict canonized Mary Margaret Alacoque, the Visitandine who had done so much to spread devotion to the Sacred Heart in the seventeenth century. One of the few churches which he is known to have been responsible for building was dedicated to the Sacred Heart – the burial church of his predecessor Cardinal Svampa in a suburb of Bologna and the one church which he raised to the status of a minor basilica was the church of the Sacred Heart in Castro Pretorio, Rome. Yet even here, in the area of popular devotion, Benedict had to be on his guard against attempts to exploit the cult for nationalistic ends during the war and after. In particular, in 1919 he sought to prevent the ambitious and energetic Padre Gemelli from distorting popular devotion in this way.[12]

In 1912, Pius X had established an Italian text of the catechism, which also went into use elsewhere. A few years later Benedict launched his project for a new, universal catechism. The particular concern which he had had for the teaching of the catechism as Archbishop of Bologna was a necessity dictated by the obstacles to religious instruction which he encountered in the state schools of his diocese. But his interest in the catechism endured beyond his stay in Bologna. In 1919, in his constitution *Etsi Minime*, he declared: 'There is nothing more effective than catechetical instruction to spread the glory of God and to secure the salvation of souls.'[13] Two years earlier, in March 1917, Benedict began the process of creating a universal text of 'The Catechism of the Catholic Church', by setting up a commission 'for the compilation of the definitive text for a Catechism for the Universal Church'.[14] Much like the commission which had laboured to produce the

Code of Canon law, this commission was composed of experts but was to draw on the opinions of all the bishops.[15] In his letter to the papal representatives throughout the world, Gasparri claimed that the decision to establish a universal catechism was prompted by the 'horrible war still raging among the nations and the need to have clear, consistent teaching throughout the Catholic Church'.[16] Almost all the bishops welcomed Benedict's decision and deplored the confusion over existing texts.[17] But Benedict did not live to see the fruits of his initiative. In fact, the *Catechism of the Catholic Church* was not published until 1993.

The Code of Canon Law

One of the major events in Benedict's reign, and a landmark in the history of the Roman Catholic Church, was the promulgation of the Code of Canon Law on 27 May 1917: the Code actually came into force a year later.[18] It had been Pius X's idea to codify the very scattered and fragmentary sources of the public law of the Church, but the chief executors of the project had been Gasparri and Pacelli, his assistant as Secretary to the Commission entrusted with the task of codification. Indeed, the Code was one of Gasparri's two major achievements, the other being the Lateran Pacts of 1929 which finally resolved the Roman Question. The effect of the Code was to re-inforce the authority of the Pope, and the Roman Curia, over the Church. In particular, it centralized still further the decision-making structures of the Church, especially in relation to the appointment of bishops. Along with Infallibility, it was a pillar of modern papal primacy. And it was in Benedict's reign that Gasparri and his pupil Pacelli began their campaign to use concordats, that is treaties between the Holy See and other powers, as a means of effectively enforcing the writ of canon law inside states, the first major guinea pig of this policy being Germany.[19] Benedict's contribution to the implementation of the new Code, apart from encouraging the policy of Gasparri and Pacelli, was to set up a 'Commission for the Authentic Interpretation of the Code of Canon Law', and a school of canon law studies.[20] The application of the Code as promulgated was restricted to the Latin Church, but it was also in Benedict's reign that the first steps were taken towards creating a code of canon law for the Oriental-rite churches.

Benedict and the Eastern churches

On 1 May 1917, Benedict established a new organ of the Roman Curia, the Sacred Congregation of the Oriental Church, separating it from Propaganda Fide, of which it had been a semi-autonomous part since January 1862.[21] The new congregation was given jurisdiction over all matters affecting the Oriental Church, except those reserved to the Holy Office, the Congregation of Rites, the Congregation of Seminaries, the Secretariat of State and the Sacred Penitentiary. It is symptomatic of the importance which he attached to the new congregation that Benedict made himself its prefect or head, a fairly unusual practice, demonstrating his concern for both the Eastern churches in communion with Rome and those, the schismatic or 'Orthodox' churches, which were not. By the middle of his successor's reign, the jurisdiction of the new congregation had been confirmed as covering all 'uniate' churches, and in territorial terms, southern Albania, Bulgaria, Greece, Cyprus, the Dodecanese Islands (under Italian rule), the successor states to the Ottoman Empire, Iran, Egypt, Eritrea and Northern Ethiopia: in all of these areas, there was a complicated mix of schismatic churches, uniate churches and small communities of Latin Catholics.[22] While Benedict was ultimately concerned with the great goal of the hoped-for reunion of the schismatic churches, for which he had instituted a prayer in 1916,[23] his initial concerns were about defending the rights, and in some cases the existence, of the eastern branches of the Roman Catholic Church.

At the outset of Benedict's pontificate, the Roman Catholic Church had counted roughly three hundred million adherents world-wide: of these, the non-Latin-rite Catholics amounted to six and a half million.[24] Yet of all the Christians in communion with the Holy See, these groups had suffered worst from the vicissitudes of the First World War. We have already considered the appalling death and suffering inflicted upon the Armenians (see p. 116), but as Benedict pointed out in his consistorial allocution on the Oriental Church in 1919, Catholics, and in broader terms, all the Christians of Lebanon, Syria and Mesopotamia had suffered very badly under Ottoman rule: Churches, schools and other ecclesiastical property had been destroyed and confiscated, both clergy and laity had been persecuted, and in some cases imprisoned, and many of them had been murdered.[25] This was the result of what Andrea Riccardi describes as the breakdown of multi-religious coexistence in the Ottoman Empire during the course of the First World War; another example of the unfortunate consequences of nationalism.[26] For the Vatican in the months immediately following the end of the First World War, the future for Catholicism in the Middle East looked very bleak indeed.

Benedict's allocution of 1919, with its slightly hysterical worries about both Jewish and Protestant activities in Palestine, against a background of continuing uncertainty about the political future of that and other ex-Ottoman territories, has to be read in this context. He made strenuous efforts to help these Christian, mainly Catholic, communities both before the end of the war and after, in particular, he sent considerable financial aid.[27] His encyclical of October 1920, elevating St Ephraim the Syrian, deacon and anchorite, to the honour of Doctor of the Church, though produced in response to the request of Eastern patriarchs and bishops, was clearly intended as a means of heartening and encouraging these communities, and Eastern Catholics in general. In addition, it was a less than subtle reaffirmation of the primacy of Peter and his successors over the whole Church, as even its title *Petrus Princeps Apostolorum* (Peter, Prince of the Apostles) demonstrates. This was a moment when Rome and the Pope needed to mobilize all their resources in defence of their Eastern brothers.

During the course of the war, the Roman Church had faced other threats in the east, the most serious of which being the clear intention of Czarist Russia, once it had finally defeated the Ottoman Empire, to take over both the Straits and Constantinople itself.[28] What it thus proposed to accomplish was the definitive establishment of Constantinople as a strong centre of Orthodox, Slav

Christianity, with Santa Sophia, cleansed of its centuries of use as a mosque, restored as its symbol. In such circumstances the rivalries between Latin and Orthodox Christianity, between the 'two Romes', would be revived, and to Catholic Rome's political disadvantage once Russia had established its expected hegemony in Eastern and South Eastern Europe following the defeat of the Central Powers. Gasparri had repeatedly protested against the support of the Entente Powers for Russia's ambitions on the Bosporus (see pp. 90–1). A related worry was about the extension of Orthodox influence and control over the holy places of Palestine in the wake of an Ottoman defeat. When the Russian threat to Constantinople seemed finally to be receding in January 1917, Gasparri rejoiced that 'this would mean that there would be a great sign of the cross over Constantinople, and that Russia would be forced to sing the [famous] Neapolitan song, "Goodbye, beautiful Naples, goodbye, goodbye".'[29]

Gasparri's rejoicing must have appeared a trifle premature when a new, albeit less serious, threat appeared at the end of the war. Greece, having finally been dragged into the hostilities on the side of the victorious Allied powers, now believed that her moment had come, that the *Megali Idea* (literally, 'the great idea') of winning back Constantinople from the Turks, and much of Eastern Anatolia, the home of large Greek-speaking communities, was becoming possible as well.[30] In this way, the Byzantine Empire would be resurrected on the ruins of the Ottoman Sultanate and Caliphate which had destroyed it. Greek control of Constantinople would also have led to a resurgence of Orthodoxy, a revitalization of its resources in competition with Rome. The reconversion of St Sophia was as central to the *Megali Idea* as it was to Russian designs on Contantinople and furthermore had much support in Britain.[31] But it would also have been a slap in the face for the Vatican as this Anglican enthusiast of reconversion explained in 1919:

The traditional diplomacy of the Vatican has certainly laboured for decades under the influence of what would happen if the Oecumenical Patriarch, a dangerous witness against Roman claims, even when half-buried in the slum of Phanar and paralysed by Turkish tyranny, should emerge and be the symbol of a great and progressive Communion which functioned with glorious St Sophia's as its mother church.[32]

The Vatican on the Tiber was saved the nightmare of a rival, Orthodox 'Vatican' on the Bosporus by the objections of the British Foreign and India offices, who feared the effects of desecrating a mosque in the city of the Caliph on the Muslim populations of the British Empire, and by resurgent Turkish nationalism, with diplomatic support from Benedict and Gasparri.[33] The Treaty of Sèvres of August 1920, of which Gasparri thoroughly disapproved, gave Greece much of what it desired: the rest could be taken by force of arms. Was not the Greek king, although of Danish and German origins, himself called after the founder of the great Christian city of the East? But in 1922 the Greeks suffered a terrible defeat in Anatolia and lost Smyrna at the hands of Turkish armies led by Kemal Ataturk, and King Constantine went back into exile.[34] Once more, Rome had been spared.

In fact, even before the end of the war, Rome seemed to be about to win new victories over Orthodoxy. Benedict and Gasparri entertained high hopes that the 'schismatic' churches of both Bulgaria and Romania would turn to Rome in the wake of Russian defeats in the Balkans, and that Russia too might be converted. In September 1917, Benedict confided to Carlo Monti that 'it is not improbable that Romania and Bulgaria will unite with Rome', and again in July 1918, he told him that talks towards this end were actually in progress.[35] It is really very difficult to understand on what the Vatican had built its hopes: the only possible basis for such an unlikely change was the fact that the King of Bulgaria was a Catholic and that, as the head of a defeated state, he might now in some sense see adherence to Rome as a way of currying favour with the victorious powers. As far as Romania was concerned, the Hohenzollern dynasty, and therefore the church system, looked set to stay. And Benedict's establishment of a seminary for Romanian Roman Catholics in Santa Susanna in Rome in 1920 was a confirmation of that.[36] Not even increased Italian influence in the Balkans was likely to change the religious situation there, so all of these hopes came to nothing, but one big, bright hope remained for some years to come – the conversion of Russia.

The conversion of Orthodox Russia, like that of Protestant England, was one of the great hopes of the Roman Catholic Church. It was Pius IX who had given instructions for regular prayers for the conversion of Russia. They were more than necessary because during the course of the nineteenth century relations between Rome and St Petersburg had deteriorated, and with them the lot of Catholics in Russia.[37] The stolid hostility of the Orthodox Church was the main impediment to better relations, hence the refusal of Russia to admit a nuncio, and the Polish uprising of 1863 only made things worse. The czars became even more suspicious of their Catholic subjects and the Vatican's communication with the Catholic bishops in the Russian Empire was rendered more difficult.[38] Worse was to come: the Russian conquest of Austrian Poland – Galicia – in the early part of the First World War led to persecution of the Uniate Church there, its metropolitan being imprisoned and church buildings handed over to the Orthodox Church.[39] The fall of Czarism in the February Revolution of 1917, therefore, brought a glimmer of light: Gasparri expressed optimism to Monti about the future of the Roman Catholic Church in Russia.[40] The Kerensky government's offer to establish reciprocal relations with the Vatican strengthened these hopes.[41] Even the ascent of the Bolsheviks to power in October 1917 did not dim the optimism in the Vatican. While it meant the beginning of an official campaign of militant atheism, against all religions, the separation of Church and State decreed in January 1918 seemed to be positively advantageous to Catholicism: given the centuries-long dependence, not to say subservience, of the Orthodox Church to the Russian State, with disestablishment it seemed likely that it would wither and decline.[42] The reports of Baron Ropp, Archbishop of Vilna (Lithuania), who actually declared that 'the great masses of Russians were more and more inclined towards recognition of the Roman Pope', undoubtedly fed the Vatican's unrealistic hopes about the possibility of improving relations with the Bolsheviks.[43] This much is clear from the various articles about the religious situation in Russia, which appeared in *La Civiltà Cattolica* in 1919, yet it is surprising considering that at roughly the same time, articles were also appearing in the same journal about the persecution of the Church under the short-lived Soviet regime in Hungary.[44]

Apart from the unremitting ideological hostility of the Bolsheviks towards Catholicism, two problems stood in the way of Catholic advances in Russia. One was the fact that the bulk of the Catholics in the territories of the old Russian Empire were minority peoples – Poles, Ukrainians and Lithuanians. The Vatican's relations with the new Catholic states of Lithuania and Poland were already difficult and complicated enough, as Benedict's envoy in the Baltic successor states, Mgr Ratti, found to his cost,[45] but in the eyes of the Russians Catholicism was equated with Polishness. The Vatican was also, inevitably, seen as a dangerous 'foreign power'. Nevertheless, 1921 brought renewed hope that something could be achieved. The 'miracle on the Vistula', when the Red Army was defeated outside Warsaw and the worsening economic conditions in Russia, which resulted in both famine and the New Economic Policy, forced a softening in Lenin's attitude towards various religious groups.[46] As a result, the last months of Benedict's reign saw the 'Voronski Affair', when the Soviet trade representative in Rome negotiated a deal with Mgr Pizzardo, the Sostituto, to allow Catholic clergy into Russian territory in order to administer famine relief and 'promote moral and religious education' in return for the Vatican's *de facto* recognition of the beleaguered Soviet regime.[47] Gasparri also seems to have believed that the Bolsheviks saw the agreement as a means of isolating and weakening the Orthodox Church: 'And here one sees the hand of Providence.'[48] It is said that among the last words that Benedict uttered were these: 'Have the visas come yet from the Bolsheviks?'[49] The illusions which Benedict and Gasparri nurtured about the prospects for the 'conversion' of Russia lived on into the next pontificate: Papa Ratti (Pius XI) did not abandon all hopes of coming to terms with the Bolsheviks until 1929.

Benedict and the missions

In his first encyclical, *Ad Beatissimi*, Benedict expressed 'a loving desire for the salvation of the whole world'.[50] For other popes, this might have been only a normal, necessary, ritual acknowledgement of the evangelizing mission of the Church at the commencement of their reigns, but for Benedict it was something very much more than that. Neill speaks of 'Three great missionary popes, Benedict XV, Pius XI and Pius XII'.[51] It is strange that he does not include Leo XIII, for the last nineteenth-century Pope was also deeply committed to the missions and wrote four encyclicals on the subject: indeed, it is likely that Benedict was inspired in his efforts to promote a native clergy by Leo's encyclical *Ad Extremas*, which addressed that very subject in the restricted area of the Indian sub-continent.[52] While Benedict had inherited a flourishing missionary situation at the beginning of his reign, by the end of the war the situation was rather different. Because of the war, many missions had been abandoned by their sponsors in the war-torn European powers; in any case, the need for service chaplains and the deaths of many priests depleted the ranks of those who, in the normal course of events, would have gone out to reinforce the missions in Africa, Asia and Oceania.[53] A further problem was the fate of the missions in the former German colonies: the Belgian, British and French governments, who acquired most of these territories under the system of League of Nations 'mandates', were anxious to expel the German missionaries in order to remove their influence.[54] Benedict and Gasparri took the threat so seriously that they sent Mgr Cerretti, the Sostituto, to the Versailles Conference to lobby the 'Big Four', with success (see pp. 142–3). The problem of nationalist, colonialist interests seeking to exploit missionary work was to remain for a long time after the war. European colonialism could be beneficial to missionary activity; colonial powers tended to favour missionaries as supporters of white European cultural superiority and authority. It was for this reason that France in the early twentieth century did not pursue in its colonies the anti-clerical policies which reigned at home.[55] On the other hand, nationalism and colonialism could be, as Pius XI was to say, 'a calamity for the missions, indeed it would be no exaggeration to say it is a curse'.[56] Benedict would never have been so bluntly outspoken as his successor, but he had ample reason to share his sentiments during the course of his pontificate.

While, as we have seen, Gasparri was not averse to playing off one colonial power against another in furtherance of the Vatican's interests in the Middle East (see p. 148), the attempts by the powers to exploit missionary activity could cause difficulties and embarrassment for the Holy See. The Italian government, for instance, was anxious to assert its claim to parts of Anatolia by sending Italian missionaries, Franciscan friars and Salesian sisters there, a policy which Monti sought to persuade the Vatican to accept, though the missionary Congregation of Propaganda Fide was less than enthusiastic.[57] Indeed, it is clear that in general terms, Monti was used by the Italians to push a policy of aligning the interests of the Vatican with those of Italy in the Near and Middle East.[58] The French also vigorously pursued their colonial interests at the Vatican, even before the resumption of diplomatic relations in 1920. In late 1918 their unofficial representative pressed the case for the appointment of a French auxiliary bishop to the (Italian) Latin patriarch of Jerusalem.[59] The British also sought to safeguard their interests: in 1915 they asked that the next Bishop of Fort Victoria in the Seychelles should be an Englishman in order to consolidate their rule in the former French colony and in 1917 they asked that the heads of Catholic religious houses in Egypt (who were mostly Italian) should all be British.[60] But the most outrageous assertion of national, colonial interest over the interests of the Universal Church was the obstruction which the French, supported by other European imperial powers, placed in the path of the establishment of relations between China and the Holy See; they feared it would diminish the influence which they exerted in that country through their 'protectorate' of the missions there, and by association the status of the 'unequal treaties'.[61] The Vatican on the other hand, would have preferred to see this protectorate lapse, as the French protectorate over Christians in the Ottoman Empire had disappeared upon the latter's collapse, and to defend its missions and missionaries through the strength of its own diplomatic efforts, rather than rely upon the help of secular governments. Cerretti's success in dealing with the missionary question at Versailles in 1919 suggests that the Holy See now had the international prestige and stature to make such a policy work.

Benedict's missionary policy was not only directed towards escaping the entanglements of nationalism and colonialism. It was much more radical than that; it was designed to prepare for nothing less than the post-colonial future of the Church in Africa, Asia and Oceania. His apostolic letter on the missions, *Maximum Illud* ('On the Propagation of the Catholic Faith throughout the World') of November 1919 did indeed warn of the perils of nationalism and colonialism. In particular, he highlighted the dangers of the missionary serving the interests of his own country: 'Without a doubt, his whole work will become suspect', the native will think that 'Christianity was only the religion of a given nation . . . and that he must submit himself to that nation . . . We must never forget that the missionary is an envoy not of his own country but of God.'[62] But the main thrust of *Maximum Illud* was the call to missionary orders and institutes and to the whole Church to co-operate in the formation of a native priesthood and native episcopacy in as many countries as possible, so that they might one day assume the government of local churches: 'Once the indigenous clergy has been formed, then the Church has been well-founded and the task of the missionaries has been accomplished.'[63] And Benedict was critical of the failure of missionaries in a number of countries to form a native clergy 'despite long years of missionary activity, and the work of the seminaries in Rome'.[64] Having in mind perhaps the persecution of Chinese Christians during the Boxer Uprising in China, and nineteenth-century Ugandan martyrs whom he beatified in 1920, Benedict argued that 'if persecution comes, a native church will have a better chance of survival'.[65] Sadly, China was to prove him right on this score. Under the influence of the Belgian missionary, Fr Lebbe, who was one of the main advocates of an 'indigenization' policy, he and his vigorous new prefect of Propaganda Fide, the Dutch Cardinal Von Rossum, sent Mgr Celso Constantini to China as Apostolic Delegate with the specific task of laying the foundations of a native Chinese episcopate.[66] The resistance of the white missionaries was strong, and it was not until 1924 that Pius XI, who would brook no further prevarication in the matter, consecrated six Chinese bishops in St Peter's.[67] Unfortunately for the Roman Catholic Church in China, the process of creating a native priesthood and episcopate was not sufficiently advanced when the Communists established their People's Republic in 1949 and embarked upon their persecution of religion. The expulsion of foreign missionaries which followed left the Church seriously short of manpower.

Benedict followed his words in *Maximum Illud* with eminently practical measures. He reorganized studies at the college of Propaganda Fide to provide practical training for future missionaries, including the improvement of language teaching; he founded the Ethiopian College in 1919 for the training of clergy for that country, and he encouraged the spread of missionary 'support' societies, such as the Clergy Mission Association, throughout the Church, bringing Angelo Roncalli to Rome to organize fundraising. Roncalli was to go on to greater things, ending up being elected Pope John XXIII in 1958.[68] *Maximum Illud* was the most important Church document on the missions until the Second Vatican Council, and the most significant papal pronouncement on the subject until Paul VI's encyclical *Evangelii Nuntiandi* in 1976. Taken together with Benedict's other measures it constituted a veritable revolution in the mission field, as several historians have pointed out.[69]

Benedict and Christian unity

Like most Italian priests of his generation, Benedict was notoriously anti-Protestant. According to Carlo Falconi, it was from his tutor Franzelini that he acquired his 'strong distaste for Protestantism'.[70] The protests of the Vatican against Protestant propaganda and proselytism in Italy, and especially Rome, grew more and more vociferous as his pontificate progressed. The Jesuit organ was particularly exercised by the rise of the Protestant 'peril' in Italy. In a report of May 1919, it made the point that adherents to Protestantism in Italy before the war had doubled and after it, certain factors encouraged further growth: tourism, return migration – especially from the United States – and the well-funded activities of highly organized British and American religious groups.[71] While admitting the good material works done by Protestant organizations both during and after the war, through the opening of recreational facilities for soldiers, and schools, colleges, orphanages, nursing or convalescent homes, and student and youth hostels – the YMCA and the YWCA – *La Civiltà Cattolica* complained that the British and American organizations that funded them were only doing so in order to draw Italians away from Catholicism.[72] It does not seem to have occurred to the editors of the journal that the Pope's famine relief work in Russia might also be interpreted as an aggressive attack upon the Orthodox Church there ... or that the work of the Foreign Missions board of the US Protestant churches, which it alleged was deliberately directed at European Catholic countries like France, Belgium and Italy, could be fairly compared to the missionaries whom Benedict sent to Russia from 1917 onwards.[73] But this was still an age in which the Roman Catholic hierarchy believed that 'error has no rights'.

Given Benedict's attitudes towards both Orthodox schismatics and Protestant heretics, it is ironical that the period of his reign should have been characterized by such strong ecumenical activity in other Christian churches. During the course of the reign, the Vatican was approached by leading Protestants involved in a number of initiatives aimed at bringing about closer relations between the Christian churches, a movement to which the First World War lent an especial urgency. In the summer of 1914, the American Episcopal Church made an approach for Vatican support for its project of a World Christian conference: Gasparri's reply came too late to be of much value because the outbreak of the war banished all hopes of a meeting, but it established the pattern for all such exchanges. The Cardinal Secretary of State, on the Pope's behalf, was politely vague but ended by reasserting that Benedict

as Pope was the 'one to whom all men have been given over to be
fed, [is] the source and cause of all unity in the Church'.[74] In
March 1918 it was the turn of the Scandinavian Lutheran metro-
politans – the Bishops of Oslo and Zealand and the Archbishop of
Uppsala – to invite the Vatican to be represented at a conference
to bring about peace to be held at Uppsala. Though Archbishop
Soderblom was flattering in his letter, 'The Pope speaks in the
name of the whole Church when he champions peace', it elicited
much the same reply as previous invitations.[75] The leaders of the
American Episcopal Church returned to the fray in 1919 when
they sent another letter to Gasparri inviting the Vatican to
participate in the founding of a 'World Conference on Faith and
Order', the precursor of the World Council of Churches. Gasparri
passed on the letter to Merry Del Val in his capacity as Secretary
of the Holy Office, the guardian of the faith of the Church; not a
very propitious choice in view of Merry Del Val's hostility to
Anglican orders.[76] The answer (in Latin) was inevitably negative.
The Episcopalians did not give up: further correspondence in April
1919 elicited the reply from Gasparri that: 'You may rest assured
that the Holy Father will pray that the Holy Spirit will enlighten
the minds and acts of all those who labour today for the reunion of
Christendom – that they should acknowledge the centre of unity
and rally around the same.'[77] In the Italian drafts written in
Gasparri's own hand, and in the first English draft, the final words
are 'rally around the Throne of Peter'.[78] Even that did not deter
them, and in May the Episcopal Church sent a delegation to Rome,
led by the Bishop of Chicago. It was received in audience by the
Pope who treated the delegates with great courtesy, but the answer
was still the same: 'Everyone knows of the Catholic Church's
position, and therefore it will not be possible for Us to take part in
such a Congress or send a delegation': he added in his kindly way
that he did not want to disappoint them and prayed that they
would see the light.[79] In this episode, the Vatican's behaviour may
have been made more rigid by the suspicion that Anglicans and
Orthodox were getting closer together.[80] All of this was, of course,
entirely predictable; the Roman Pontiff, fortified by infallibility,
was not at all likely to allow the character of the 'One, True

Church' to be compromised by dealings with heretical bodies, however well-intentioned. As with the individual cases of England and Russia, all that Catholics could do was wait and pray that one day all non-Catholic Christians would be reconciled to Rome.

In the light of these episodes it is all the more extraordinary, therefore, that the 'Malines conversations' of 1922 to 1926, between Catholic representatives, led by Cardinal Mercier, and Lord Halifax and other Anglicans, should have had their origin in Benedict's reign. The answer to the puzzle lies with Cardinal Mercier, whose heroic wartime role had established him as a figure of world stature in the Allied countries. In October 1919, for example, he received a standing ovation at the General Convention of the United States Episcopal Church.[81] Though Benedict had not always seen eye to eye with Mercier on the methods he used during his four-year struggle with the German occupying authorities (see p. 95), he had immense respect and admiration for the Belgian cardinal. It was Mercier who proposed to Benedict in December 1920 that he should host discreet discussions in his see city between theologians from the Roman Catholic and Anglican Churches; in fact, he originally suggested inviting representatives of the Orthodox and other Protestant churches as well.[82] Ironically, under Mercier's influence, the Malines initiative was more readily accepted in the Vatican than it was at Lambeth. The Archbishop of Canterbury was very cautious in giving his blessing to the conversations for fear of offending the Evangelical wing of his church.[83] Inasmuch as the first exploratory discussions were held at Malines from 6 to 8 December 1921, it can be said that it was under the aegis of Benedict that the modern ecumenical movement was initiated in the Roman Catholic Church.

With the exception of his strategy for the missions, Benedict's government of the Roman Catholic Church was not marked by revolutionary initiatives. Yet he left it a stronger and more prestigious institution in the world than he had found it. He had done much to rescue and revitalize the Uniate Catholic churches of the Near East and he had laid the foundations for the Church's future success in Africa and Asia. Above all, he had succeeded in healing the divisions caused by the anti-Modernist campaign of his predecessor, and to some extent, those caused by the war. Within the Church itself, at least, he had brought back peace.

Notes and references

1. Carlen (ed.), vol. 4, pp. 143 and 145.
2. Ibid., p. 149.
3. For the text of *Providentissimus Deus*, see ibid., vol. 3, pp. 325–39.
4. Brown *et al.* (eds), *The New Jerome Biblical Commentary*, p. 167.
5. See *La CC*, 71, 3 (1920), pp. 136 and 338, and 4 (1920), p. 137.
6. Carlen (ed.), vol. 4, p. 186.
7. Ibid.
8. *La CC*, 71, 3 (1920), p. 427.
9. Morozzo Della Rocca (1996), p. 562.
10. *La CC*, 70, 2 (1919), p. 459.
11. Morozzo Della Rocca (1996), p. 562.
12. De Giorgi, p. 455.
13. Carlen (ed.), vol. 4, p. 33.
14. AAES, Stati Ecclesiastici, 1432, pp. 574–81, 'Testo Unico del Catechismo per la Chiesa Universale'.
15. Ibid., circular 27805 to papal representatives, 10 March 1917.
16. Ibid., Latin text of the letter to diocesan ordinaries, 18 March 1917.
17. Ibid., replies.
18. *New Catholic Encyclopedia*, vol. III, Can–Col, p. 973.
19. See Stehlin (1983), pp. 368–412.
20. *New Catholic Encyclopedia*, Vol. III, Can–Col, p. 974.
21. *AP*, 1948, p. 733.
22. Ibid.
23. Holmes, p. 27.
24. AAES, Stati Eccl., 602, p. 42. Statistiche delle religioni nell'Est-Europa.
25. *La CC*, 70, 2 (1919), p. 6.
26. A. Riccardi, 'Benedetto XV e la crisi della convivenza multireligiosa nell'Impero Ottomano', in G. Rumi (ed.), *Benedetto XV e la Pace, 1914–1918*.
27. Dalla Torre, p. 1298.
28. *Diario*, I, pp. 248–9, 16 July 1915 and pp. 275–6, 2 October 1915.
29. Ibid., II, p. 475, 31 May 1919.
30. Goldstein, p. 39.
31. Ibid., p. 46.
32. As quoted in ibid., p. 48.
33. Ibid.
34. Woodhouse, pp. 207–10.

35. *Diario*, II, p. 10, 11 January 1917.
36. Ibid., pp. 208–9.
37. For an account of relations between Russia and the Roman Catholic Church in the late nineteenth and early twentieth centuries, see Stehle (1981), pp. 12–14.
38. Stehle (1981), p. 15.
39. Ibid.
40. *Diario*, II, p. 151, 20 September 1917 and p. 346, 3 July 1918.
41. Ibid., 2 May 1920.
42. *Diario*, II, p. 61, 26 March 1917.
43. Stehle (1981), p. 5.
44. See for example *La CC*, 70, 2 (1919), pp. 167–8 and 72, 1 (1919), pp. 117–20 and 481–5.
45. Stehle, pp. 19–20.
46. Ibid., p. 26.
47. Ibid., pp. 27–30.
48. *Diario*, II, p. 570, 4 January 1922.
49. As quoted in Stehle (1981), p. 29.
50. Carlen (ed.), vol. 4, p. 143.
51. Neill, p. 518.
52. Carlen (ed.), vol. 3, pp. 307–9.
53. *La CC*, 70, 2 (1919), p. 10.
54. See V. De Marco, 'L'intervento della Santa Sede a Versailles in favore delle missioni tedesche', in G. Rumi (ed.), *Benedetto XV e la Pace, 1914–1918*, pp. 65–83.
55. Rhodes, p. 212.
56. As quoted in Pollard (1985), p. 89.
57. *Diario*, II, pp. 496–7, 30 October 1919.
58. Ibid., pp. 500–1, 9 November 1919.
59. Ibid., p. 374, 1 September 1918.
60. Ibid., p. 225, 15 December 1917; see also PRO, FO, 371/169966, De Salis to Curzon.
61. Leung, p. 43.
62. *La CC*, 70, 4 (1919), pp. 492–3.
63. Ibid., p. 490.
64. Ibid.
65. Ibid.
66. Leung, p. 45.
67. Neill, p. 523.
68. Hebblethwaite (1984), pp. 100–2.
69. Tramontin, p. 139 and Holmes, p. 25.
70. Falconi, p. 100.
71. *La CC*, 70, 2 (1919), pp. 231–3.

72. Ibid., and 71, 3 (1920), p. 427.
73. Ibid., p. 428.
74. As quoted in Rouse and Neill (eds), p. 413.
75. Rouse and Neill (eds.) p. 416.
76. AAES, Stati della Chiesa, 1433, pp. 582–3, Restaurazione della Cristiana Unità: Corrispondenza.
77. Ibid.
78. Ibid.
79. Ibid.
80. AAES, Stati della Chiesa, 1433, pp. 582–3, memorandum of 6 September 1920 which expressed just such fears following the visit of the Anglican Bishop of Gibraltar to Smyrna.
81. Pawley, p. 262.
82. Ibid., p. 263.
83. Ibid., p. 265.

Epilogue

Benedict died relatively young. Though not the youngest man to be elected Pope this century – John Paul II was only 58 when he was elected, whereas Benedict was two months short of 60 – he was the youngest reigning Pope at his death – 67. His death on 22 January 1922 was unexpected. Despite his delicate health in childhood, he had been of a robust constitution throughout his adult life: he told Gasparri that in all his life he had only spent one and a half lire on medicine.[1] In old age his only infirmity appears to have been rheumatics.[2] His death was caused by the catching of a chill while waiting to say Mass for the nuns of the Vatican's Santa Marta Hospice.[3] Rarely indisposed, Benedict did not take much care of the illness which he developed, which eventually went to his lungs and gave him pneumonia. Without antibiotics, there was little his doctors could do for him.

According to Jemolo, there was unprecedented public mourning in Italy for Benedict's death.[4] Hebblethwaite says that 'For the first time since 1870, flags were flown at half-mast on all government buildings'.[5] No such tribute had been paid to previous popes. This reaction may only have been only an indirect tribute to the man, that is, it reflected the extent to which Benedict's pontificate had improved the relationship between Italy and the Papacy. Though, as expected, the Catholic newspapers paid handsome tributes, the secular press was grudging. *Il Corriere della Sera*, the leading organ of the Liberal-Conservative establishment, was extremely critical of his peace efforts and the best encomium that it could offer was that he was 'Not an exceptional pontiff by reason of his wisdom or love, he was all the same, in very difficult times, a Pope worthy of his high office'.[6] Other Italian reactions were even less positive: the Socialist newspaper *L'Avanti!* described him as 'cold, mediocre and obstinate' and prophesied that 'Tomorrow history will have forgotten him'.[7] The prophesy was not far wrong. But he was mourned beyond Italy. Giuseppe Motta, the Swiss president of the League of Nations, paid him a fulsome tribute.[8] Charles Schol, the president of the American Union of Hebrew Congregations, wrote to the Apostolic Delegate in Washington, sending his condolences and calling Benedict 'a constant exponent of the finer spiritual values of life and a great standard-bearer of morality among men and of peace and concord among nations'.[9] Some Jews since then have passed a rather harsher judgement on him.

What kind of Pope was Benedict XV? His predecessor Pius X is often considered to have been a 'religious' rather than a 'political' Pope, that is one whose overwhelming interests and concerns were with the Church, rather than the secular world and its problems, in contrast to Leo XIII. Of course, Pius X also had to contend with the problems of the secular world, most notably anti-clericalism in France, and he also adopted his own policy to do with the political consequences of economic and social change in Italy during his pontificate. Nevertheless, by comparison with Pius X, Benedict could still be described as 'political', certainly the problems of war and peace, and peace, that is both between and inside nations, largely engaged his attentions and those of Gasparri. Yet he did dedicate himself to his pastoral mission, the government of the Church, as is seen in Chapter 8. Benedict was the very epitome of an ecclesiastical bureaucrat and diplomat, but he also remained a priest in the full sense of that term, a saviour of souls with a pastoral concern for those around him. One of the most moving episodes narrated by Carlo Monti in his diary concerns himself. In early 1918, Benedict discovered that Monti, a widower, was effectively 'living in sin'.[10] He might well also have been concerned about the danger of scandal were the facts to become public knowledge, but it is clear that his primary concern was for Monti's spiritual welfare and he eventually persuaded Monti to remarry, performing the ceremony himself.[11] Boselli, the Prime Minister of

212

Italy, once asked Monti whether Benedict was a pious man: Monti replied that he was a man of great but quiet piety.[12] He clearly was deeply pious, though much of his piety would nowadays perhaps be regarded even in Catholic circles as narrow and old-fashioned. Frugal and abstemious in his habits, he was also very conventional about matters of public decency: he was, for example, scandalized by the rage for the tango in the years just before the First World War.[13] On the other hand, there was nothing exceptional about his piety, no 'heroic virtues' of the sort which Merry Del Val quickly noticed in his master Pius X who was beatified in 1951 and canonized in 1954. Benedict has never been considered for beatification or canonization, unlike his successors Pius XII and John XXIII. Yet, though his human defects were very evident – irascibility was his besetting sin, offset by immediate remorse – he was also full of human virtues, the most conspicuous of which was undoubtedly his boundless charity.

Where does Benedict's reign fit in the modern history of the Papacy? On the one hand, his pontificate marked a clear break with that of his predecessor, both in terms of his abandonment of the anti-Modernist 'crusade' and of the change of direction of papal diplomacy. But Benedict changed nothing of the reforms which Pius X initiated in the field of liturgical practice, and it was in his reign that Papa Sarto's great project for the codification of Canon Law was brought to fruition. On the other hand, it could be argued that in some important respects Benedict returned to the policies of Leo XIII, and of his mentor, Rampolla. This is certainly true in regard to the diplomatic policies of Benedict and Gasparri. It is also true of the concern and commitment which Benedict showed for the Oriental Church and for the Missions, and his encyclical on biblical scholarship, *Spiritus Paraclitus*. It can also be argued that in Benedict's reign the Roman Catholic Church assumed the most characteristic features of its modern physiognomy, with the Code of Canon Law, the attempt to introduce a universal catechism, the emphasis on the autonomy and special needs of the Oriental Churches and the reinvigoration of its missionary outreach through a renewal of the underlying ideology of that endeavour in an anti-colonialist direction. In this sense, Benedict laid the foundations for the massive presence in Africa and Asia which the Roman Catholic Church enjoys today. Perhaps most important of all, Benedict, ably assisted by Gasparri, was responsible for revitalizing papal diplomacy, which had languished under his predecessor. Under Benedict XV, the Holy See assumed a high profile in international affairs, becoming a major diplomatic player in its own right, in a far better and stronger position to defend its interests. Whereas, in 1914, the Papacy seemed doomed to follow the fate of the Ottoman Caliphate, which by then was on its way out, by the end of Benedict's reign the Papacy had completely emerged from its pre-war isolation.[14]

It is perhaps the greatest evidence of the success of Benedict's policies that they were all followed by his successor, Pius XI. Ironically, Achille Ratti was not Benedict's favourite as his successor, it was Cardinal La Fontaine of Venice who filled that role, presumably because he had had considerable pastoral experience.[15] But the real battle in the 1922 conclave was not initially between La Fontaine and Ratti, but between Merry Del Val and De Lai on the one hand and Benedict's 'followers', most notably Gasparri, on the other.[16] Benedict did not make sufficient creations to reduce the strength of the *integristes* in the College of Cardinals – they could still count on 31 per cent of votes in the 1922 conclave according to Zizola.[17] There is no evidence that he consciously sought to do so, and even if he had, he reigned for too short a time to seriously affect the composition of the Sacred College. Nevertheless, Merry Del Val's attempt at a comeback was a failure: Gasparri had built up a strong following after twenty or so years as a curial cardinal. But when it became clear that Gasparri could not win, partly because of fears of his nepotistic tendencies and partly because he had no pastoral experience, he persuaded his supporters to give their votes to Ratti instead.[18] The election of Ratti still can be counted as a triumph for Benedict because he stuck to the latter's policies and indeed developed them further, particularly in the mission field, in the pursuit of concordats with states, in the continuation of the Malines conversations and in the attempt to 'convert' Russia.[19] Indeed, the British Minister at the Vatican remarked on the lack of changes in Vatican policy and personnel after the election of Benedict's successor, the most significant element of continuity being provided by the retention of Gasparri as Secretary of State, which was almost unprecedented in the history of the Papacy.[20]

The greatness of Benedict XV

Several historians have referred to the greatness of Benedict XV, most notably Scoppola and Pizzuti.[21] It might at first sight seem rather extravagant to apply such an epithet to a Pope whose reign, apart from anything else, was so short. What makes a Pope 'great' is, in any case, very hard to say. In Benedict's case, what made him great was the way in which he rose to meet the tremendous challenges posed by the state of the secular world, and especially the horrors of the First World War. Though he regarded both as the being the result of mankind having rejected the Church and followed the path of error for the previous one hundred and fifty years, he did not stand back from them in complacent self-righteousness. Instead, he responded to them in a Christian, humane and humanitarian way. Above all, his pursuit of peace in all spheres was sincere, committed and courageous. He steered the barque of St Peter through some very stormy waters, waters which Pius X and Merry Del Val would have carefully avoided, and in the process he left his enduring mark on the Roman Catholic Church.

Notes and references

1. *Diario*, II, p. 398, 20 January 1922.
2. Molinari, Benedict to Menzani, 23 June 1919.
3. Vistalli, p. 34.
4. Jemolo, p. 168.
5. Hebblethwaite (1983), p. 105.
6. *Corriere della Sera*, 23 January 1922, front page.
7. *L'Avanti!*, 24 January 1922.
8. Rope, p. 314.
9. ASV, DAUS, V, scatola 97, letter to Bonzano of 22 January 1922.

10. *Diario*, II, p. 287, 24 March 1918.

11. Ibid., pp. 312–14, 9 May 1918.

12. Ibid.

13. *Corriere della Sera*, 23 January 1922, p. 2.

14. Stehlin (1994), p. 13.

15. Falconi, p. 42.

16. Zizola, p. 198.

17. Ibid., p. 199.

18. Ibid., pp. 202–3.

19. Stehle (1981), chap. III.

20. Hachey (ed.), p. 13.

21. Pizzuti, p. 54.

Bibliography

Archival sources

AAB Archivio Arcivescovile di Bologna (Bologna Diocesan Archives)
  diary Diario delle Visite Pastorali di S.E.R. Mons. Giacomo Della Chiesa, Archivescovo
AAES Archivio degli Affari Ecclesiastici Straordinari (second section of the Vatican Secretariat of State, now Council for the Public Affairs of the Church)
ACS Archivio Centrale dello Stato (Central State Archives, Rome)
  MI, DGPS Ministero dell'Interno, Direzione Generale Pubblica Sicurezza
AFDC Archivio Famiglia Della Chiesa (Della Chiesa family papers, consisting entirely of documents relating to Benedict XV)
ASV Archivio Segreto Vaticano (Vatican Secret Archives)
  SS Segreteria di Stato
DAUS Delegazione Apostolica United States
DDI Documenti Diplomatici Italiani, 5ⁱ Serie, Rome, 1952–
PRO, FO Public Record Office, Foreign Office, London

Printed archival sources

Diario
  Scottà, A. (ed.), *La Conciliazione ufficiosa: Diario del barone Carlo Monti 'incaricato d'affari' del governo italiano presso la Santa Sede (1914–1922)* (2 vols; Vatican City, 1997).

Periodical materials

The following newspapers and journals were consulted:
Annuario Pontificio (*AP*) (Rome)
L'Avvenire d'Italia (Bologna)
Il Bollettino della Diocesi di Bologna (*Bollettino Diocesano; BD*)
    (Bologna)
La Civiltà Cattolica (*La CC*) (Rome)
L'Osservatore Romano (Rome)
The Tablet (London)
The Times (London)

Secondary sources

Adams, J., *Peace and Bread in Time of War* (New York, 1945)

Albertazzi, A., *Il cardinale Svampa e i cattolici bolognesi 1894–1907* (Brescia, 1971)

Alexander, S., *Church and State in Yugoslavia Since 1945* (Cambridge, 1979)

Alix, C., *Le Saint-Siège et les nationalismes en Europe (1870–1960)* (Paris, 1960)

Alvarez, D., 'Vatican Communications Security, 1914–1918', *Intelligence and National Security*, vol. 7, no. 4 (1992), pp. 443–53

Alvarez, D., 'A German Agent at the Vatican: the Gerlach Affair', *Intelligence and National Security*, vol. II, no. 2 (April 1996), pp. 345–56

Anonymous, 'La politique de Benoît XV', *La Revue de Paris*, XXV, 20–21 (15 October–1 November 1918), pp. 973–96, 183–214

Arbizzani, L., *Lotte Agrarie in Provincia di Bologna* (Milan, 1951)

Astori, L., 'La Santa Sede e gli stati europei dopo la prima guerra mondiale: riflessioni su alcuni libri recati', *Quaderni di diritti e politica ecclesiastica*, 2 (1993)

Auerbach, B., *L'Autriche et la Hongrie pendant la guerre* (Paris, 1925)

Barnes, J. S., 'Benedict XV: an impression', *The Dublin Review*, CLV (October 1914), pp. 373–7

Bazin, P., *Récits du temps de la guerre* (Paris, 1915)

Bedeschi, L., 'La Questione Romana in alcune lettere di Benedetto XV', *Rassegna di politica e storia* (September 1964), pp. 21–41

Bedeschi, L., *I pionieri della Democrazia cristiana, 1896–1906* (Milan, 1966)

Bedeschi, L., *Il Modernismo e Romolo Murri in Emilia-Romagna* (Parma, 1967)

Bedeschi, L., *La Curia Romana durante la crisi modernista* (Parma, 1968)

Bedeschi, L., 'Il comportamento religioso in Emilia-Romagna', *Studi Storici*, 10 (1969), no. 2, pp. 387–406

Bendiscioli, M., 'La Santa Sede e la Guerra' in G. Rossini (ed.), *Benedetto XV, i cattolici e la Prima Guerra Mondiale: Atti del convegno di studio tenuto a Spoleto nei giorni 7–8–9 settembre 1962* (Rome: Cinque Lune, 1963), pp. 25–49

Benvenuti, S., 'Lettere del vescovo Celestino Endrici al papa Benedetto XV, etc.', *Studi Trentini*, 70 (1991), pp. 162–223

Bernstein, C. and Politi, M., *His Holiness: John Paul II and the Hidden History of Our Time* (London, 1996)

Berselli, A., *Alle origini del movimento cattolico intransigente* (Livorno, 1955)

Binchy, D. A., *Church and State in Fascist Italy* (Oxford, 1970)

Bissolati, L., *La politica estera dell'Italia dal 1897 al 1920: Scritti e discorsi* (Milan, 1923), p. 369

Bonfiglio, C., *Direttive del Papa Benedetto XV per il laicato italiano* (Rome, 1987)

Boyer, J., *Political Radicalism in Late Imperial Vienna: Origins of the Christian Social Movement, 1848–1897* (Chicago, 1981)

Brennan, A., *Pope Benedict XV and the War* (London, 1917)

Brezzi, C. 'La *Rerum Novarum* e il movimento cattolico in Italia', *La Crisi di fine secolo* (Milan, 1980)

Bridge, F. R., 'The foreign policy of the monarchy 1908–1918' in M. Cornwell (ed.), *The Last Years of Austria-Hungary: Essays in Political and Military History, 1908–1918* (Exeter, 1990)

Brien, M. C., *HarperCollins Encyclopedia of Catholicism* (New York, 1995)

Brown, R. E., SS, Fitzmyer, J. A., SJ and Murphy, R. E., OCarm (eds), *The New Jerome Biblical Commentary* (London, 1990)

Bruti Liberati, L., 'Santa Sede e gli Stati Uniti negli anni della Grande Guerra', in Rumi, G. (ed.) *Benedetto XV e La Pace – 1918* (Brescia, 1990), pp. 129–51

Buehrle, M. C., *Rafael Cardinal Merry Del Val* (Milwaukee, 1957)

Bumpus, T. F., *The Cathedrals and Churches of Northern Italy* (London, 1907)

Burgess, A., *Earthly Powers* (Harmondsworth, 1980)

Calise, 'Il Cardinale Pietro Gasparri', *Nuova Antologia*, 68 (16 March 1933), pp. 225–36

Canavero, A., 'Filippo Meda e la fondazione dell'Università Cattolica', *Bollettino del Movimento Sociale Cattolico*, 25 (1990), pp. 321–42

Cappa, P., *Il Pontificato di Benedetto XV* (Rome, 1953)

Carcel Orti, V., *León XIII y los católicos españoles: Informes vaticanos sobre la Iglesia en España* (Pamplona, 1988)

Cardoza, A., *Agrarian Elites and Italian Fascism: The Province of Bologna, 1901–1926* (Princeton, 1982)

Carlen, C., IHM (ed.), *The Papal Encyclicals, 1903–1939* (Raleigh, NC, 1990)

Carr, R., *Spain, 1808–1975* (2nd edn, Oxford, 1982)

Celestino Endrici (1866–1940), vescovo di Trento. Atti del convegno (Trento 23 maggio 1991) (Trent, 1992)

Cenci, P., *Il Cardinale Merry Del Val* (Rome, 1933)

Cento Bull, A., *Capitalismo e fascismo di fronte alla crisi: Industria e società bergamasca 1923–1937* (Bergamo, 1983)

Chabod, F., *L'Italia contemporanea, 1919–1948* (4th edn, Turin, 1961)

Chadwick, O., *Britain and the Vatican During the Second World War* (Cambridge, 1986)

Chadwick, O., *A History of the Popes, 1830–1914* (Oxford, 1998)

Charles-Roux, F., *Souvenirs diplomatiques* (Paris, 1958)

Clark, M., *Modern Italy, 1871–1982* (London, 1984)

Clerici E., 'Il primo ministro cattolico in Italia', *Civitas*, 41 (1979), 5, pp. 59–71

Cobban, A., *A History of Modern France: 1871–1962* (Harmondsworth, 1965)

Cornaggia-Medici, L., *Il passato e presente della Questione Romana* (Florence, 1930)

Cornwall, M. (ed.), *The Last Years of Austria-Hungary* (Exeter, 1990)

Crispolti, F., *Corone e porpore: Ricordi personali* (Milan, 1936)

Crispolti, F., *Leone XIII, Pio X e Benedetto XV* (Milano, 1939)

Crispolti, G. B., 'Benedetto XV e i giornali della Soc. Romana', *Studium*, 85 (1990), pp. 43–75

Cross, F. L. (ed.), *Oxford Dictionary of the Christian Church* (Oxford, 1957)

d'Agnel C., *Benoît XV et le conflit européen* (2nd edn, Paris, 1916)

Dai-Gal, R. P., *Le Cardinal Merry Del Val* (Paris, 1955)

Dalla Torre, G., *Memorie* (Verona, 1965)

D'Attore, P. P. (ed.), *Bologna: città e territorio tra '800 e '900* (Milano, 1983)

D'Azeglio, M., *Gli ultimi casi della Romagna* (Florence, 1846)

De Felice, G., 'Lettere di Benedetto XV al Barone Monti', *Nuova Antologia* (1933), f. 1460, pp. 161–73

De Giorgi, F., 'Forme spirituali, forme simboliche, forme politiche: La devozione al Sacro Cuore', *Rivista di Storia della Chiesa in Italia*, vol. 48:2 (July–December 1994), pp. 365–459

Del Giudice, V., *La Questione Romana e rapporti tra Stato e Chiesa fino alla Conciliazione* (Rome, 1947)

Delzell, C. F. (ed.), *Mediterranean Fascism: 1919–1945* (New York, 1970)

De Marco, V., 'L'intervento della Santa Sedea Versailles in favore delle missioni tedesche', in G. Rumi (ed.), *Benedetto XV e la Pace: 1914–18* (Brescia, 1990)

De Rosa, G., *Storia politica dell'Azione Cattolica in Italia*, vol. II (Bari, 1954)

De Rosa, G., *Il Partito Popolare Italiano* (Bari, 1974)

De Rosa, G., *Luigi Sturzo* (Turin, 1977)

De Rosa, G., 'La corrispondenza del vescovo Celestino Endrici con il papa Benedetto XV', in *Celestino Endrici (1866–1940), vescovo di Trento. Atti del Convegno* (Trent, 1992)

De Waal, A., *Der neue Papst: Unser heilige Vater Benedikt XV* (Hamm, 1915)

Dillon, E. J., 'Italy's new birth', *The Fortnightly Review* LXXXIII (July 1915), pp. 1–15

Di Pietro, M., *Benedetto XV* (Milan, 1936)

Dizionario Biografico degli Italiani, vol. 8 (Rome, 1966)

Duffy, E., *Saints and Sinners: A History of the Popes* (New Haven and London, 1997)

Durante, A., *Benedetto XV* (Rome, 1939)

Dizionario storico del movimento cattolico in Italia (Turin, 1981–82)

Ellis, J. T., *The Life and Times of James Cardinal Gibbons, Archbishop of Baltimore, 1834–1921* (2 vols; Milwaukee, 1952)

Engel-Janosi, F., 'The Roman Question in the first years of Benedict XV', *The Catholic Historical Review*, 40 (1954), pp. 343–56

Engel-Janosi, F., *Österreich und der Vatikan, 1846–1918* (2 vols; Vienna–Graz–Cologne, 1960)

Engel-Janosi, F., 'The Church and the nationalities in the Hapsburg Monarchy', in John Rath III (ed.), *Austrian History Yearbook* (Austin, Texas, 1967), pp. 67–82

Epstein, K., *Matthias Erzberger and the Dilemma of German Democracy* (Princeton, NJ, 1959)

Euc, J. (ed.), *The Popes* (New York, 1964)

Fabrini, G., *Il conte Giovanni Aquaderni* (Rome, 1945)

Falconi, C., *The Popes in the Twentieth Century* (London, 1960)

Fattorini, E., *Germania e Santa Sede. Le nunziature tra la Grande Guerra e la Repubblica di Weimar* (Bologna, 1992)

Felice, G., *Il Cardinale Pietro Gasparri* (Milan, n.d.)

Feller, J. G., 'Notations of Cardinal Gibbons on the Conclave of 1914', *Catholic Historical Review*, 46 (1960), pp. 184–89

Fogarty, G., *The Vatican and the American Hierarchy from 1870 to 1965* (Collegeville, MN, 1982)

Foot, J. M., '"White Bolsheviks'? The Catholic Left and the Socialists in Italy, 1919–1920', *Historical Journal*, 40, 2 (1997), pp. 415–33

Forbes, F. A. M., *Rafael, Cardinal Merry Del Val: A Character Sketch* (London, 1932)

Gallet, C., *Le Pape Benoît XV et la guerre* (Paris, 1916)

Garzia, I., *La Questione Romana durante la I guerra mondiale* (Naples, 1981)

Gasparri, Pietro Cardinale, *Il Cardinale Gasparri e la Questione Romana. Con brani delle memorie inediti*, ed G. Spadolini (Florence, 1972)

Goffi, G. (ed.), 'I rapporti fra Chiesa e Stato all vigilia del fascismo negli articoli di Francesco Ruffini sul *Corriere della Sera*', *Nuova Antologia*, 574 (1995), pp. 263–318

Goldstein, E., 'Holy Wisdom and British foreign policy 1918–1922, the St Sophia Redemption', *Byzantine and Modern Greek Studies*, 15 (1991), pp. 36–65

Goyau, G., *Papauté et Chrétianité sous Benoît XV* (Paris, 1922)

Graham, R., *Vatican Diplomacy* (Princeton, NJ, 1959)

Gregory, J. D., *On the Edge of Diplomacy: Rambles and Reflections, 1902–1928* (London, n.d.)

Grenville, J. A. S., *The Major International Treaties, 1914–1945. A History and Guide with Texts* (London, 1974)

Grissell, H. de la Garde, *Sede Vacante, Being a Diary Written During the Conclave* (Oxford, 1903)

Guasco, M., 'Seminari e educazione del clero', *Einaudi Storia d'Italia*, vol. 9, La Chiesa e il Potere Politico (Turin, 1986)

Hachey, E. (ed.), *Anglo-Vatican Relations* (Boston, 1972)

Hales, E. E. Y., *The Catholic Church in the Modern World: A Survey from the French Revolution to the Present* (New York, 1958)

Hardach, H., *The First World War, 1914–1918* (London, 1977)

Hayward, F. *Un Pape méconnu: Benoît XV* (Tournai, 1955)

Hebblethwaite, P., *John XXIII: Pope of the Council* (London, 1984)

Hebblethwaite, P., *Paul VI: The First Modern Pope* (London, 1993)

Holmes, J. D., *The Papacy in the Modern World* (New York, 1981)

Howard Bell, D., *Sesto San Giovanni: Workers, Culture and Politics in an Italian Town, 1880–1922* (New Brunswick, 1986)

Horstenau, E. von Glaise, *Il crollo di un impero* (Milan, 1935)

Hudal, A., *Die österreichische Vaticansbotschaft, 1806–1918* (Munich, 1952)

Impagliazzo, M., 'Francia e Santa Sede nella Grande Guerra. "Les Papes n'ont besoin que la vérité"', *Studium*, 88 (1992), pp. 43–62

Institut Pius X, *La Papauté et les questions internationales* (Paris, n.d.)

Jedin, H. *Storia della Chiesa nel Ventesimo Secolo (1914–75)* (Milan, 1975)

Jemolo, C. A., *Church and State in Italy, 1850–1950* (Oxford, 1960)

Johnson, H., *The Papacy and the Kingdom of Italy* (London, 1926)

Johnson, H., *Vatican Diplomacy in the World War* (Oxford, 1933)

Kelley, F. C., *The Bishop Jots It Down: An Autobiographical Strain on Memories* (New York and London, 1939)

Kelly, J. N. D., *Oxford Dictionary of the Popes* (Oxford, 1986)

Kennedy, P., *The Rise and Fall of the Great Powers: Economic Change and Military Conflict from 1500 to 2000* (London, 1989)

Kent, P. C. and Pollard, J. (eds), *Papal Diplomacy in the Modern Age* (New York, 1994)

Keogh, Dermot, *The Vatican, the Bishops and Irish Politics* (Cambridge, 1986)

Kertzer, D., *Famiglia contadina e urbanizzazione. Studi di una comunità alla periferia di Bologna, 1880–1910* (Bologna, 1981)

Knock, T. J., *To End all Wars; Woodrow Wilson and the Quest for a New World Order* (Oxford, 1992)

Korecs, P., 'Les relations entre le Vatican et les organisations juives pendant la première guerre mondiale; la mission Deloncle-Perquel (1915–1916)', *Revue de Histoire Moderne et Contemporaine* 20 (1973), pp. 301–33

La Bella, F., *La Questione irlandese e il Vaticano* (Turin, 1996)

Lai, B., *Finanze e finanzieri vaticani fra '800 e '900 cento*, vol. 1 (Milan, 1979)

Lama, F. Ritter von, *Die Friedensvermittlung Papst Benedikt XV und ihre Vereitlung durch der deutschen Reichskanzler Michaelis (August–September 1917); eine historische-kritische Untersuchung* (Munich, 1932)

Larkin, M., *Church and State after the Dreyfus Affair* (London, 1974)

Larkin, M., *Religion, Politics and Preferment in France since 1890: La Belle Epoque and its Legacy* (Cambridge, 1995)

Le Ciseleur, C., *Les poèmes de la vraie guerre* (La Varenne-St. Maur, chez l'auteur, 1918)

Leflon J., 'L'Action diplomatico-religeuse de Benoît XV en faveur de la paix durant la première guerre mondiale', in G. Rossini (ed.), *Benedetto XV, i cattolici e la Prima Guerra Mondiale* (Rome, 1963), pp. 53–70

Leslie, S., *Cardinal Gasquet, a Memoir* (London, 1953)

Lemaitre, V., *SS Benoît XV et la guerre (1914–1918)* (Avignon, 1932)

Leung, B., *Sino-Vatican Relations: Problems in Conflicting Authority 1976–1986* (Cambridge, 1992)

Levillain, F. (ed.), *Dictionnaire de la papauté* (Paris, 1997)

Liebman, M., 'Journal secret d'un conclave', *La Revue Nouvelle*, 19, XXXVIII (1963), pp. 32–52

Link, A. S., 'Woodrow Wilson and the peace moves', *The Listener* (London), 75 (6 June 1966), pp. 868–71

Lo Bello, N., *L'Oro del Vaticano* (Milan, 1975)

Loiseau, C., 'Une mission diplomatique près le Saint Siège, 1914–1919', *Revue des Deux Mondes* (May 1956), pp. 54–60

Loiseau, C., 'Ma Mission auprès du Vatican (1914–1918)', *Revue d'histoire diplomatique*, 64 (1966), pp. 100–15

Luca, G. de, 'Il Cardinale Pietro Gasparri', *Nuova Antologia*, 69 (December 1934), pp. 380–85

Luca, G. de, 'Discorendo col Cardinale Pietro Gasparri', *Nuova Antologia*, 71 (16 November, 1936), pp. 195–205

MacNutt, F. A., *A Papal Chamberlain* (London, 1936)

Majo A., 'L'Azione Cattolica italiana 1919–1926. Memorie inedite di avv. Luigi Colombo', *Civitas Ambrosiana*, 3 (1986)

Manfroni, G., *Sulla Soglia del Vaticano, 1870–1901*, vol. 2 (Rome, 1921)

Marc-Bonnet, H., *La Papauté contemporaine* (Paris, 1951)

Marchese, S., *Francia e problemi dei rapporti con la Santa Sede (1914–1924)* (Naples, 1969)

Marcora, C., 'Carteggio tra il Card. Rampolla e Mons. Bonomelli (1907–1913)' in *Studi storici in memoria di Mons. Angelo Mercato* (Milan, 1956), pp. 195–243

Margiotta Broglio, F., *L'Italia e la Santa Sede dalla prima Guerra Mondiale alla Conciliazione* (Florence, 1963)

Marks, S., *The Illusion of Peace: International Relations in Europe, 1918–1933* (London and Basingstoke, 1976)

Martini, A., 'La Nota di Benedetto XV per la pace (agosto 1, 1917)', *La Civiltà Cattolica*, IV, 2696 (1962), pp. 3–29

Martini, A., *Studi sulla Questione Romana e la Conciliazione* (Rome, 1963)

Martini, A., 'La Nota di Benedetto XV alle Potenze belligeranti nell'agosto 1917' in G. Rossini (ed.), *Benedetto XV, i cattolici e la Prima Guerra Mondiale* (Rome, 1963), pp. 361–86

Martini, A., 'L'invio della missione inglese presso la Santa Sede all'inizio della prima guerra mondiale', *La Civiltà Cattolica*, IV, 2818 (1967), pp. 343–4

Martini, Ferdinando, *Diario 1914–1919*, ed. Gabriele De Rosa (Milan, 1968)

Mayer, F., *The Vatican* (New York, 1980)

Meda, F., *I cattolici e la Guerra* (Milan, 1928)

Mellinato, G., 'Benedetto XV e il PPI', *La Civiltà Cattolica*, 3 (7–21 August 1993), pp. 271–8

Merry Del Val, R., *Memories of Pope Pius X* (London, 1951)

Migliori, G., *Benedetto XV* (Milan, 1932)

Minerbi, S., *The Vatican, the Holy Land and Zionism, 1895–1925* (Oxford, 1986)

Misonne, O., *Le Pape, la Belgique et la guerre* (Paris, 1918)

Mitchell, H., *Le Cardinal R. Merry De Val, Secrétaire d'Etat de Saint Pie X* (Paris, 1956)

Mizzi, P., *L'Unione Europea nei documenti pontifici* (Malta, 1979)

Molinari, F. 'Il carteggio di Benedetto XV con Mons. Ersilio Menzani', *Rivista di storia della Chiesa Italiana*, Anno 20, no. 2 (July–December, 1966)

Molony, J. N., *The Emergence of Political Catholicism in Italy: Partito Popolare 1919–1926* (London, 1977)

Monticone, Alberto, *Nitti e la Grande Guerra, 1914–1918* (Milan, 1961)

Montoisy, J. D., *Le Vatican et le problème des Lieux Saints* (Jerusalem, 1984)

Moore, T. E., *Peter's City: An Account of the Origin, Development and Solution of the Roman Question* (New York, 1930)

Morozzo Della Rocca, R., *Problemi e interpretazioni delle storie cattoliche durante la prima guerra mondiale* (Rome, 1986)

Morozzo Della Rocca, R., *Le Nazioni non Muoiono: Russia rivoluzionaria, Polonia independente e Santa Sede* (Bologna, 1992)

Morozzo Della Rocca, R., 'Première guerre mondiale', in P. Levillain (ed.), *Dictionnaire de la papauté*, pp. 775–9

Morozzo Della Rocca, R., 'Benedetto XV e Constantinopoli: fu vera neutralità?', *Cristianesimo nella Storia*, 14 (1993), pp. 375–84

Morozzo Della Rocca, R., 'Benedetto XV e nazionalismo', *Cristianesimo nella Storia*, 17 (1996), pp. 541–66

Mosca, R., 'La mancata revisione dell'articolo 15 del Patto di Londra' in G. Rossini, (ed.), *Benedetto XV, i cattolici e la Prima Guerra Mondiale* (Rome, 1963), pp. 399–413

Moynihan, J. H., *The Life of Archbishop John Ireland* (New York, 1953)

Neill, S., *The Pelican History of the Church, vol. 6: A History of Christian Missions* (Harmondsworth, 1964)

Negro, S., *Vaticano minore* (Milano, 1936)

New Catholic Encyclopedia (New York, 1967)

Norton, R., 'Benedict XV and the Save the Children Fund', *The Month*, 28 (July 1995), pp. 281–83

O'Brien, A. C., 'L'*Osservatore Romano* and Fascism: the beginning of a new era', *Church and State* (Spring, 1971)

Occhi, L. degli, *Benedetto XV* (Milano, 1921)

O'Connell, Cardinal William, *Recollections of Seventy Years* (Boston, 1934)

O'Connell, Cardinal William, *Sermons and Addresses* (9 vols; Boston, 1930)

O'Hare-McCormick, A., *Vatican Journal: 1921–1954* (New York, 1953)

O'Neill, H. C., *A History of the War* (London and Edinburgh, 1920)

Ori, Giuseppe, 'La recente politica della Santa Sede nell'Europa nord-orientale', 3 (August 1936), pp. 623–36

Orlando, V. E., *I miei rapporti di governo con la Santa Sede* (Milano, 1944)

Osbat, L., 'Aspetti e problemi del pensiero di Benedetto XV sui temi di guerra e della pace', *Rivista di studi salernitani* (1970), pp. 213ff.

Pacelli, Eugenio, 'À propos de l'offre de paix du Saint Siège en 1917', *Revue d'Histoire de la guerre mondiale*, 4 (1926), pp. 131–40

Page, T., *Italy and the World War* (New York, 1920)

Pallenberg, C., *Vatican Finances* (Harmondsworth, 1971)

Panzera, F., 'Benedetto XV e la Svizzera negli anni della Grande Guerra', *Rivista Storica Svizzera*, 43 (1993), pp. 321–40

Paris, E., *Le Vatican contre l'Europe* (Paris, 1962)

Pasztor, 'I cattolici ungheresi e la prima guerra mondiale' in G. Rossini (ed.), *Benedetto XV, i cattolici e la Prima Guerra Mondiale* (Rome, 1963), pp. 815–32

Pawley, B. and M., *Rome and Canterbury Through Four Centuries* (London and Oxford, 1981)

Pease, N., 'Poland and the Holy See, 1918–1929', *Slav Review*, 50 (1991), pp. 521–30

Penco, G., *Storia della Chiesa in Italia*, vol. II (Milan, 1977)

Perin, R., *Rome in Canada: The Vatican and Canadian Affairs in the Late Victorian Age* (Toronto, 1980)

Pernot, M., *Le Saint-Siège, l'Eglise Catholique et la politique mondiale* (Paris, 1924)

Peters, W. H., *The Life of Benedict XV* (Milwaukee, 1959)

Pichon, F., *Benoît XV* (Paris, 1940)

Pioli, G., 'Benedict XV: the significance of his election', *The Contemporary Review*, CVI (October 1914), pp. 506–14

Pizzuti, G. M., 'La grandezza di un pontificato misconosciuto: Benedetto XV', *Humanitas*, 45 (1991), pp. 126–32

Poincaré, R., *Au Service de la France*, vol. V (Paris, 1928)

Pollard, J. F., *The Vatican and Italian Fascism, 1929–1932: A Study in Conflict* (Cambridge, 1985)

Pollard, J. F., 'Conservative Catholics and Italian Fascism: the clerico-fascists' in M. Blinkhorn (ed.), *Fascists and Conservatives: The Radical Right and the Establishment in Twentieth-century Europe* (London, 1990)

Pollard, J. F., 'Italy' in T. Buchanan and M. Conway (eds), *Political Catholicism in Europe* (Oxford, 1996)

Pollard, J. F., 'Religion and the formation of the Italian working class' in R. Halpern and J. Morris (eds), *American Exceptionalism: US Working Class Formation in an International Context* (London, 1997)

Pollard, J. F., *The Experience of Italian Fascism* (London, 1998)

Povlat, E. *Catholicisme, Démocratie et Socialisme* (Paris, 1977)

Premoli, O., *Storia Ecclesiastica Contemporanea (1900–1925)* (Turin and Rome, 1925)

Procacci, O., *Soldati e prigionieri italiani nella grande guerra* (Rome, 1993)

Quadrotta, G., *La Chiesa Cattolica nella crisi universale* (Rome, 1924)

Quadrotta, G., *Il colloquio di un secolo fra cattolici e socialisti 1865–1963* (Rome, 1964)

Ragazzi, F., *Alfonso Rubbiani fra cattolicesimo intransigente e cattolici liberali* (Bologna, 1982)

Ragionieri, Ernesto, *Il Movimento Socialista in Italia (1850–1922), cronologia del mov. operaio italiano di Franco Pedone* (Milan, 1976)

Randall, A., *Vatican Assignment* (London, 1956)

Ravaglia, G., *Guida del catechista cattolico* (Rome, 1913)

Renouvin, P., *La Crise européene de la grande guerre, 1914–1918* (Paris, 1934)

Rhodes, A., *The Power of Rome in the Twentieth Century: The Vatican in the Age of the Liberal Democracies* (London, 1983)

Rhodes, A., 'The Pope of the First World War, Benedict XV (1914–1922)', *The Month*, 250 (1989), pp. 248–52

Riccardi, A., *Alleati non amici. Rapporti fra l'Italia e l'Intesa durante la prima guerra mondiale* (Brescia, 1992)

Ricci, G., *Bologna: Le città nella storia d'Italia* (Rome–Bari, 1980)

Roncalli, A. G. (John XXIII), *My Bishop* (London, 1969)

Rope, H. E. G., *Benedict XV: The Pope of Peace* (London, 1940)

Rossini, G. (ed.), *Benedetto XV, i cattolici e la Prima Guerra Mondiale: Atti del convegno di studio tenuto a Spoleto nei giorni 7–8–9 settembre 1962* (Rome, 1963)

Rouse, R. and Neill, S. C. (eds), *A History of the Ecumenical Movement* (London, 1954)

Ruffini, F., 'Il potere temporale negli scopi di guerra degli ex-Imperi Centrali', *Nuova Antologia* (16 April 1921), pp. 289–300

Rumi, G. (ed.), *Benedetto XV e la Pace, 1914–1918* (Brescia, 1990)

Rumi, G., 'Un epistolario inedito', *Civitas* (1991), pp. 3–83

Salandra, A., *Souvenirs de 1914–1915. La Neutralité italienne e l'intervention* (Paris, 1932)

Salata, F., *La Questione Romana e la Triplice Alleanza, secondo nuovi documenti austro-germanici* (Rome, 1923)

Salter, J. A., *Allied Shipping Control. An Experiment in International Administration* (Oxford, 1921)

Salvatorelli, L., *La Politica della Santa Sede dopo la guerra* (Milan: Istituto per la storia e politica internazionale, 1937)

Sauro Onofri, N., *La Grande Guerra nella città rossa; socialismo e reazione a Bologna dal 1914 al 1918* (Milan, 1966)

Scattigno, A., 'Il Cardinale Mistrangelo (1899–1930)' in F. Margiotta Broglio (ed.), *La Chiesa del Concordato: Anatomia di una Diocesi, Firenze, 1919–1943*, vol. I (Bologna, 1977), pp. 197–263

Scheinman, M. M., *Il Vaticano tra le due guerre* (Rome, 1951)

Schmidlin, J., *Papstgeschichte der neuesten Zeit*, vol. III (Munich, 1953)

Scoppola, P., *La Chiesa e il fascismo: Documenti e interpretazioni* (Bari, 1971)

Scottà, A., *I vescovi veneti e la Santa Sede nella guerra 1915–1918* (3 vols; Rome, 1991)

Scottà, A. (ed.), *La Santa Sede, i vescovi veneti e l'autonomia politica dei cattolici, 1918–1922* (Padua, 1994)

Seldes, G., *The Vatican: Yesterday–Today–Tomorrow* (New York, 1934)

Serra, E., 'La tragedia di Mayerling nei rapporti di Constantino Nigra', *Nuovo Antologia*, vol. 1 (1995), p. 574

Seton-Watson, C., *Italy from Liberalism to Fascism* (London, 1967)

Sforza, C., *Contemporary Italy* (New York, 1944)

Sladen, D., *The Secrets of the Vatican* (London, 1907)

Sladen, D., *How to See the Vatican* (New York, 1914)

Snell, J. L., 'Benedict XV, Wilson, Michaelis and German Socialism', *Catholic Historical Review*, 37 (July 1951), pp. 151–78

Sonnino, Sidney, *Diario, 1866–1922*, eds Ben F. Brown and Pietro Pastorelli (3 vols; Bari, 1972)

Spadolini, G., *Giolitti e i cattolici* (Florence, 1977)

Speranza, G., *The Diary of Gino Speranza: Italy, 1915–1919*, ed. Florence C. Speranza (New York, 1941)

Steglich, W. (ed.), *Der Friedensappel Papst Benedikts XV* (Wiesbaden, 1970)

Stehle, H-J., *The Eastern Politics of the Vatican* (Athens, OH, 1981)

Stehle, H-J., *Geheimediplomatie im Vatikan. Die Päpste und die Kommunisten* (Zurich, 1993)

Stehlin, S. A., 'Germany and the proposed Vatican State', *Catholic Historical Review*, 60 (1974), pp. 402–6

Stehlin, S. A., *Weimar and the Vatican, 1919–1933: German–Vatican Diplomatic Relations in the Interwar Years* (Princeton, 1983)

Stehlin, S. A., 'The emergence of a new Vatican diplomacy during the Great War and its aftermath' in P. C. Kent and J. Pollard (eds), *Papal Diplomacy in the Modern Age* (New York, 1994)

Stevenson, D., 'The failure of peace by negotiation in 1917', *Historical Journal* 34 (1991) pp. 65–88

Storia della Chiesa, vol. xxii/i: *La Chiesa e la società industriale (1878–1922)*, eds E. Guerriero and A. Zambarbieri (Milan, 1990), ch. III, 'Il pontificato di Benedetto XV'

Sturzo, L., *Church and State* (Longman, 1939)

Taliani, F. de, *Vita del Cardinale Gasparri. Segretario di Stato e povero prete* (Milan, 1938)

Taylor, A. J. P., *From Sarajevo to Potsdam* (London, 1966)

Toma, A., *Benedetto XV e l'inutile strage* (Rome, 1993)

Tramontin, S., *Un Secolo di Storia della Chiesa. Da Leone XIII al Concilio Vatican II*, vol. 1 (Rome, 1980)

Trinchese, S., *La Repubblica di Weimar e la S.S. tra Benedetto XV e Pio XI (1919–1922)* (Naples, 1994)

Valente, G., *Aspetti e momenti del movimento cattolico in Italia (1892–1926)* (Rome, 1968)

Valiani, L., 'Nuovi documenti sui trattativi di pace nel 1917', *Rivista Storica Italiana* 75 (1963), pp. 559–87

Van Den Hewel, J., *The Statesmanship of Benedict XV*, trans. S. C. Burns (London, 1923a)

Van Den Hewel, J., *Benedetto XV* (Rome, 1923b)

Van Der Kiste, J., *Kings of the Hellenes: The Greek Kings, 1863–1974* (London, 1994)

Van Der Veldt, E., *Exploring the Vatican* (London, 1947)

Vanier, G., *Gli ultimi governi liberali e la Questione Romana* (Milan, 1976)

Veneruso, D., 'I rapporti fra stato e chiesa durante la guerra nel giudizio dei maggiori organi della stampa italiana' in G. Rossini (ed.), *Benedetto XV, i cattolici e la Prima Guerra Mondiale* (Rome, 1963), pp. 679–738

Veneruso, D., 'Ricerche e problemi relativi ai rapporti tra cattolici e socialisti durante la Prima Guerra mondiale', *Critica Sociale* 4 (31 March 1965), pp. 129–56

Veneruso, D., 'Benedetto XV' in F. Traniello and G. Campanini (eds), *Dizionario Storico del Movimento Cattolico in Italia, II, I Protagonisti*, pp. 32–5 (Casale Monferrato, 1982)

Venturi, G., *Episcopato, cattolici e Comune a Bologna (1870–1904)* (Bologna, 1976)

Vercesi, E. *Il Vaticano, l'Italia e la guerra* (Rome, 1925)

Vistalli, F., *Benedetto XV* (Rome, 1929)

Walsh, M., *An Illustrated History of the Popes: Saint Peter to John Paul II* (London, 1980)

Webster, R. A., *Christian Democracy and Fascism in Italy: 1860–1960* (London, 1961)

White, T., *The Last Kaiser: A Biography of William II, German Emperor and King of Prussia* (London, 1977)

Woodhouse, C. M., *Modern Greece: A Short History* (London and Boston, 1986)

Zanetti, F., *Nella Città del Vaticano: Cinque Papi attraverso gli annedoti, da Pio IX a Pio XI* (Rome, 1929)

Zangheri, R., *Storia delle città: Bologna* (Bari, 1986)

Zivojinovic, D. R., 'Robert Lansing's comments on the Pontifical Peace Note of August 1917', *Journal of American History*, 56 (1969a), pp. 556–71

Zivojinovic, D. R., 'The Vatican, Woodrow Wilson and the dissolution of the Hapsburg monarchy 1914–1918', *East European Quarterly*, 3 (1969b), pp. 31–70

Zivojinovic, D. R., *The United States and the Vatican Policies, 1914–1918* (Boulder, CO, 1978)

Zizola, G., *Il Conclave: Storia e segreto* (Rome, 1993)

Index

233

INDEX